Contents

Part 6   Aftergrowth (1867–1985)

Foreword

Ron Roberts' book is enjoyable reading and provides an important piece of the mosaic made up of the people of Iowa. For me, the book has a special meaning.

My father, born in 1886, worked for more than twenty years in the coal mines—from about 1906 until the 1920s. He worked in mines near Melrose and Lucas, and was a great admirer of John L. Lewis.

My father married late in life and was well into his fifties by the time I was born. It was during my years in high school that my father used to tell us stories about working in the mines when they tried to organize a union. They had to meet in farm houses so that the Sheriff and the "Pinkertons", as my father always referred to them, would not find them. If they had been caught trying to organize they would lose their jobs and perhaps even get beaten up. I can also remember his story about when he and the other miners were down in the shafts, and the bosses cut off the fans or the air in order to teach the miners a lesson about organizing and union activities.

The ethnic and racial diversity amongst the coal miners in Iowa was enormous. My mother and her first husband were both immigrants from Yugoslavia, coming over about the time of World War I to work in Iowa's coal mines. He died working in the mines and my father married the widow who by this time already had three children. My father was Irish, so marrying a Slav who could barely speak English made for an interesting mix.

There was an operating mine about a mile from the small town of Cumming where I was born and raised. Besides Irish and Slavs, there were Welsh, Italian, Mexican and Black American miners.

It must have been during World War II when I was younger than five, that I recall some men coming to our house to meet with my father. They had worked in the mines previously with him and some of the visitors were black— this is my first recollection of ever seeing a black man. The memory is vivid in my mind.

As I have travelled around the country and the world since becoming a member of Congress, I continue to come across people, especially in the East Coast of the United States, who think of Iowa as this "conservative, WASPish State" with little diversity. Nothing could be further from the truth. Ron Roberts' book gives us insight into why Iowa is not that way. And, I believe this is a piece of the history of Iowa that has not been written about enough. The miners, like my father and his friends, have left a rich heritage of cultural and religious diversity which has given Iowans a much more tolerant view than we are given credit for.

Ron Roberts' book is imaginative, funny, sad, historical and above all just plain fun to read.

Tom Harkin
United States Senator

PART 1

Strange Roots in Southern Iowa

My Own Dung Heap

"Sure you're interested in Lucas, Ronnie. Everyone's interested in their own dung heap."
——Gerald Baker, 1984
President, Farmers and Miners Bank of Lucas, Iowa

Driving south along Highway 14, moving toward what some writer called "the gently rolling hills of Southern Iowa." It is almost evening as the rutted, bumping highway curves up and around those rolling hills. It is November, 1984, and I am in Lucas County. The area farmers have put one hundred white crosses in the ground to symbolize their desperation. Many are losing everything and going out of business. Only about sixty people come to watch the crosses being planted in the ground and to hear the speeches. There is too much agony concentrated here and most people want to avoid it. The next day a man puts the white wood slats in his garage. He wants to use them for tomato stakes in the spring.

I'm thinking about this as I drive to my Lucas County ghost town. It is called Lucas. It may not be a ghost town in the strictest sense. A few people still live there. There are some real ghost towns in the county—Zero, Ragtown, Time, and Last Chance. They are dissolved absolutely out of sight. But if a ghost town can be defined by its ghosts and memories and decay, Lucas is surely a ghost town.

Also I'm thinking, why is it "my" ghost town? It's true I grew up here and it's true my family came from here. But did I feel at home here? Maybe not. Do I feel at home anywhere? Maybe not. It's my town because I know the ghosts and memories, and because I want to know them even better. So I spend my weekends talking to the storytellers around the place, as I have been doing these past four years. The old folks still know how to tell stories. I tape record them and I tape my own stories, too. I do some delicate wrestling with nineteenth-century newspapers of the town, and every time I open them the acid paper loses more words to dust. I take pictures of the yellowed photographs of the town. I read letters written to aunts and lovers and children from last century's warm-blooded writers. I look at tombstones and try to find where the Welsh, the Blacks, and the Swedes were buried a century ago. I take photographs of the buildings falling in on themselves slowly from inner decay and Iowa weathering. Sometimes I try to imagine the images and sounds and smells

1

of the miners who dug for coal long ago. I don't hear anything. I don't see much and I mostly smell the grass and dust and decay of Lucas. The town is going to grass.

Sometimes, sometimes, driving to my ghost town, I get a feeling of some sort of joy and it has a distinct physical location. It is just below my throat. I have felt it in the late summer dusk when the wicked heat of the day dissipates in the blue-grey haze over the lower parts of the town and gives it a coloration of a vague and gentle richness. It is a reward for the hard times and tragedies of the place. It is nature's temporary forgiving for the things we have done to each other and a consolation for what she has taken away from us. Anyway, that is the joy I feel in my throat. I feel it, also, when someone tells me a new, delicious story about the townsfolk.

Lucas only produced one person of note in its history, John L. Lewis. He shook the world some for a time. He was on the cover of *Time* Magazine a half-dozen times because he had become the most powerful labor leader America ever produced. He would come back to the town when he could, to talk to people about little things, insignificant things. He would escape into the smallness of the town for rest and to become reacquainted with the lives of people who made no difference to the world. People like my family. They, for the most part, lived and died without making a ripple on the world's shape.

The town had it's moments, nevertheless. It was a boom town in 1875, when coal was discovered there. It was one accentuated mix of hope and joy and terror and exploitation. For the next twenty years it was larger than life. The Miners Union in Iowa was formed in the town, the Populist Party thrived, and the Woman's Suffrage Movement grew there. Immigrants from Wales, Scotland, England, Ireland, Poland and Sweden mixed with the new black arrivals from the South. It was a time of excitement and despair, and no small amount of violence. Most people endured all that.

By the turn of the century Lucas was still working its mines but more slowly, and people were moving on more rapidly. The town was beginning a decline. Oh, the mines went on until 1926, but the boom was over and houses began to be deserted. Some people stayed out of habit as much as anything and because they wanted not to break the web of friendships and families Lucas provided.

When I was born there, the mines were all closed and the Opera House had been destroyed. There really weren't a hell-of-a-lot of ways people could make money to live in the town. On the other hand, it didn't take much. When I was a baby, my family moved to a city in Illinois. We would have a better life there than in a half-dead ghost town. My dad didn't like the industrial world. To be more specific, he didn't like the grinding boredom and the grating roar of the assembly lines. Still he worked on those lines for eight years. Then it was time to come home to Lucas. And he did. We lived there in the pleas-antness, poverty, silliness and tragedy of a town held together by the residue of people who, by and large, would never share the American Dream.

2

I left for college when I got the chance. The idea was to get the hell out of Lucas. Maybe I did get out and maybe I didn't. It's hard to say. I liked college so much that I stayed around for a Ph.D. When I came back to Lucas a few years later, my generation had deserted the place. They joined the Navy or worked in Des Moines. They were gone, in any case. My family was there from my dad's side, and they began to die in a flood of days of grief I had dreaded and denied in my childhood. My grandparents, uncles, cousins, aunts, my father—all seemed to be dragged into eternity by some startling chain which was to pull them under the ground in the cemetery south of town.

Everything fit so well the dying town—my dying family, the near-dying union movement put into place by John L. and others during the '30's. And in the 1980's people spoke about the dying of Iowa itself, as tens of thousands left us for work and survival. I thought of the dying of all these things and the demise of the people in my life and I thought this dying tendency was not so complete and perfect as I had imagined. Life still grows around the edges. Besides, growing up in Lucas I have become distrustful of all sorts of perfection promised here or in the next world.

When I was eleven years old, I lay on a tin-roofed building on my father's place, watching cumulus clouds moving in some strange pattern across the sky. As I looked I became nearly convinced, and then really convinced, that Jesus was coming down to save us from our messes and our impending doom. I was slightly unhappy that the cloud formations looked like Jesus because I thought I might have gotten all raptured up to heaven without experiencing sex. When the clouds got less spiritual looking, I climbed down and figured not to let myself be tricked by myself again.

What I had, in my primitive and dramatic way, was hope. The people who have left Lucas and the people who stay have some hopes. That is why writing about a ghost town is not despairing. Sometimes the hopes of Lucas folk have been grandiose and radical, as when the Knights of Labor fought for social justice in the town in 1882. Sometimes people's dreams were as dopey as my eleven-year-old, near-miss ascension to heaven. Mostly, the Lucas folk hoped for small things—things they could control. When I was twenty-one my grandfather was ninety-four. I was working in the Forest Service in Idaho and Oregon and he was worried. He worried about the old car my best friend, John, and I drove out there. He sat in his bedroom window and worried about me that summer. I came home safely and he told me how much he had worried about me and how good it was to see me. Within a month he died. He had placed his hope in a little thing—my homecoming.

Hopes are smaller in the small towns of Southern Iowa, but people still have them. Yes, and more than once, the engines of economic well-being have shut down in Lucas County. Some get bitter, some leave, and some scale down their hopes for smaller victories. Some laugh at themselves but, as they say, "not so's you'd notice."

3

The laughter and the leaving and the hoping and the dying and the making-do in a ghost town. That is what this book is about. And it is a book about little people who are not nobodies. And it is a book about a strange part of Southern Iowa, which is a strange part of America.

The fact is, I tried to write this book six other ways and I failed. I tried to stay out of the story—if not out of it at least not in it too much. I didn't want to be connected with the egotism of yet another autobiographer of young and formulative years. I wanted to pretend that it was the autobiography of the town. I wanted to pretend that the town could speak. I wanted to pretend that this was a story without a storyteller or that this book was Lucas, Iowa's self-consciousness in some way. It is only a played-out, old coal mining town in Southern Iowa. I thought if it could talk it would say these things to passersby.

"Walk real careful over my grown-over slag heaps if you can find them. They are graves. Men once like you are fossils underneath my coal beds."

"Smell my decaying wood. It was once new hope-painted lumber. It was the structure of dreams like yours."

"People have left me and will never return. People will leave you, too."

"Do not ridicule me unless you have no intent of becoming old and barren, as I am."

"I am now without power and, therefore, harmless. You who have power now—you had better watch yourselves."

"My streets have returned to their mud-nature. I do not mind. You should not mind your return, either."

"Leave me alone. I am resting from the exhaustion of my possibilities."

That, I figured, was what the town could say if it would talk, but I can't confuse myself with the town. I just grew up there. So I couldn't write the entire book from the town's point of view. Now what? Anyway, I'd better write this hundred-years, slapdash saga before some new video disks replace both books and the storytellers.

I'm telling stories about Lucas. They are as true as I can stand them to be. I'm a little cowardly about hurting people's feelings. I'm a little sentimental and lean toward irony. When I tell stories about Lucas, its life seems to be more in color when the town's life touches mine. That's because I know the colors best when I have seen them.

One strange thing has been happening as I write this book. I have been dreaming about it a lot. In the last year I have spent a good deal of time in Los Angeles, Managua, Nicaragua, Montreal, and East Africa. But what do I dream about? Lucas, Iowa. It must be something I ate thirty years ago.

I'll just give you one example. Two nights ago I dreamed about my grandfather, who has been dead twenty-four years. He was very old when he died, 94 and quiet and he didn't talk much. As a stupid kid, I didn't ask him about his work in the mines, his hard drinking, and what Lucas was like in the boom days. I didn't care. Now I do. So there he was in my dream, with his long, high-cheekboned face and his soft, white hair and lank body. And I said,

4

"Grandpa, I never asked you all the important things. Can you tell me stories?" "Sure," he said in his quiet voice. "I reckon." In my dream I wanted to ask him about how he pulled the heavy slate rock off Uncle Bill Angove in the mine, and if he was hungry as a kid, and what he thought of seeing Lucas boom and build and bust and decay. I tried to push the "Record" button on that tape recorder in my dream, and it was stuck. I fixed it and had to tape the broken cord of the machine with black tape. Then I woke up. It was as frustrating as my sex dreams when I was sixteen.

Someone once told me that dreams are about unfinished business. I think that may be true. It is also true that certain books are about unfinished dreams.

Listen to my voice as a child in the town and as an adult connected to it. Listen to the voices of the townsfolk. Imagine their days and times. Imagine that Lucas, Iowa has importance and imagine that the stories I tell you are true. Welcome to the ghosts we call memory.

A Mystique for Southern Iowa

"Lucas, in Iowa, a South by East County, area about 430 square miles; Rivers, Whitebreast and Chariton, besides many smaller streams; Surface undulating; Soil fertile; Capitol Chariton; Population in 1870, 10,388."
Zolls Popular Encyclopedia, *1876*

"Population of Lucas County, Iowa, 10,313"
U.S. Census, *1980*

Well why the hell not? Other places and peoples have had mystiques named after them. There have been feminine mystiques, California mystiques, Chic mystiques, and lots more where those came from.

Now a mystique is a half-understood complex of murky ideals with romantic connections and nuances to who laid it. Mostly and naturally, the very rich and famous have created mystiques about themselves.

Lots of mystiques have to do with ancient passions and mysteries. The culture of ancient Iberia, the mysteries of the creators of Stonehenge, the glory that was Rome—they all cry out mystery, tragedy and romance.

Why can not a humble (with good reason) part of the world, develop a mystique all its own? My candidate for "mystiqizion" is Southern Iowa. I long for the day when the meek shall inherit the mystique. And the word pictures we can draw from this humble mystique are full of the summer mists in the heated, fog-rimmed morns around the gently rolling hills of our Southern Iowa dream. It is a poor and ordinary place and it deserves a place in some history.

We Southern I's insist upon our status as a mystical and magical land. We love the strangely average nature of our clay hills and fertile bottoms. We will not abuse our mystique to mystify the traveler through Ottumwa, Flagler, or Woodburn. We only want to tell the outside world a secret or two about our living and dead, and our forests. We still have many, and Iowa as a whole, has gone from 18 percent to only 4 percent forest. Nobody wants to plow up our land from ditch to fence post. We have clay. We could start playdough factories with half a mind.

All in all, Southern Iowa is like every other place on the globe, peopling its landscapes with the standard number of fatbrained saps, dabblers, enlightened folk, cranks, and saints. Mostly though, folks from Southern Iowa are just regular folks who know enough to come in out of the rain. They have experienced pain and confusion and hearts hurting with unrealized dreams.

It is true that Southern Iowa people are like some other people in that waves of prosperity and economic slumps hit the place. If it seems that Southern Iowa is a little ragged-eared or mildewed, it is only because it is part of the rust belt of our country, and that just means that the big monied boys aren't investing here very much. That isn't our fault.

And yes, yes, yes, we have heard the joke about how you raise the average IQ of Iowa ten points. (Give the two southern tiers of Iowa counties to Missouri!) And how you raise the state of Missouri's average IQ ten points. (Give the two Southern tiers of Iowa counties to Missouri!) We are not sure we like that joke about us and we are damned sure Missourians don't care for it.

Still, the fact remains that Southern Iowa seems like a strange place to people—even people from the more civilized sections of Northern Iowa. It goes beyond the fact that we talk different down there. People do talk differently in Southern Iowa. In the Northern half of the state people wash their clothers with a "w-ah-sh" sound. In the Southern part of the state folks "warsh" their clothing. In Lucas, where I come from, the folks that did so would "w-oy-sh", which must relate to some yet-undiscovered Jewish influence on us Southern Iowa Wasps. Once in a while in my home town, people will say "din't" instead of "didn't." These are not the kinds of differences people go to war over but they are differences.

It's just not the fact that some of us talk like Northern Missourians, either. Southern Iowa has always been slightly out of the mainstream, whatever way it was headed. Way back in 1859 when the Iowa State Agricultural Society published their Sixth Annual Report on the works of the hardworking pioneer farmers, the folks from Lucas County turned in their report to the state. Most of the county reports were full of the successful experiments of hardworking local farmers. Did Lucas County report the successes of its farm folk? Not so's you'd notice.

"Our farmers are poor agriculturalists with few exceptions," the reporter wrote in '59. "They are not reading men and are generally disposed to plow as shallow as they can. Many fields of wheat are sown upon corn grown without plowing, and much that is raised is suffered to go to waste. Cattle are often

6

wintered without shelter and allowed to tread much more of their feed into thé mud than they eat. Hogs run at large during the summer and are fattened without shelter and fed in deep mud, so that what they eat is used up in keeping the temperature of the system and much that is given them is wasted in the mud. Usually, where corn is gathered, the large cracks in the wagon bed permit the corn that shells to be wasted; and when corn is carried to market, a thick trail is left from the house of the producer to the residence of the purchaser." The writer goes on and on, but you get the idea.

Lucas County farmers were not dumb and not all of them were born tired, either. They made their mistakes. The next year in 1860, they showed their political wisdom by giving Honest Abe Lincoln 586 votes and only 482 to Mr. Breckenridge in the Presidential contest.

It is probably true that Lucas County farmers are a bit smarter than their forebearers of the nineteenth century, but in 1986 they were still losing the land to the folks who had corporate backing and lots of credit. Still it was true in the nineteenth century, and it is true today that all is not lost when people hang on and grit their teeth—and hold on to each other while they are gritting.

By 1871, Chariton, the seat of Lucas County and one of the centers for Southern Iowa culture, had decided that to become a real city, it should punish folks who let their estates become seedy and weedy. They proceeded apace to purge the town of botanical trash and they did it with a vengeance. (Not many things are done in Southern Iowa with a vengeance.) That is, they did it until they came in conflict with City Councilman Copeland's burdock stalk.

Lucas County, as the center of Southern Iowa, has much in the way of beautiful plant life, almost sacred oak groves, giant and scrub cedars, shag-bark hickory—enough to make one give a sigh for the beauty of it all. Now, no plant in Southern Iowa loves mankind more than the burdock. Any young boy or girl tramping through the fields and forests of the area brings back shaggy burrs from the flowering part of the weed. They are called cockleburrs in Lucas County. Whatever else they are called, they stick to denim or wool like money to a miser. That didn't make any difference to Mr. Copeland.

"By motion in order, Mr. Stackhouse is instructed to cut down every damned burdock on the town plot regardless of the tears or threats of the inhabitants."

Councilman Copeland, having two burdock and mullen stalk growing handsomely near each other, asked that they might be spared the sweeping order, promising to build a neat iron fence around them, and the city fathers should have the choice of names: Council Grove, Bonny Clabber Park, etc., or some name this council would ever cherish, but he pleaded in vain. Alderman Gibbon, with folded hands and sympathetic voice, said his heart went out to Brother Copeland. Jealousy had no lodgement in his heart but no other councilman had a grove, and why should Copeland's stand.

The fiat went forth!
Stockman cut em down!

7

Hastily the council adjourned and that cheerful idiot, Copeland, went and sold out his business, shook the dust of the city from his feet and his fist at the city fathers, saying: "Go up thou fools? Not a bit of it, but down to hell and say I sent thee. And I will to the west for fur and skin and be cru-el-y mur-der-ed by a bloody in-ge-in—where in peace I can have my burdock and mullens." (*Chariton Patriot,* July 10, 1871). Being a damned fool has always had a certain charm for Southern Iowans if it is done in a charming way.

Of course, things were not as tame in Southern Iowa in the last century as they are today. People just expected the unexpected and didn't think too terrible much about it. Wild deer roamed in the forests along the banks of the Whitebreast Creek, wolves would moan and whoop up their howls at night, and all manner of game abounded in the raw prairie.

And naturally, there were ghosts and spirits to keep farmers and settlers of that era entertained before the advent of movies and video recorders. The *Iowa State Register* of January 7, 1883 cheerfully reported that the town of Mount Pleasant "has a haunted mill. The ghost converses with visitors, says that it is that of a stranger who came to the place 20 years ago, was murdered and robbed of $7,500 and that his body remains unburied in the northeast corner of the mill. The noise made by the spook has been heard in the day time as well as in the night and runs from one room to another as it is pursued."

Now other parts of the country may have had their ghosts, but only a Southern Iowa ghost would be so informative about itself and only Southern Iowans would be so discourteous as to chase the poor spirit from one room to another.

Well, if that isn't enough to convince the reader that there is an historical basis for the Southern Iowa Mystique, what would be? We could talk about Ottumwa's gold mine, started in 1882. They got a lot of digging done over there for a year or two. The folks who did it were damned fools with a good deal of style, needless to say. What about the fact that they built a palace (a real one) 230 feet long and 130 feet wide in the same town. They built it in 1890 out of coal from the local mines. In it were given operettas like "The Mikado" and the local elites attended. It was described as a black mixture of the Gothic, the Byzantine, and the Southern Iowa Rococo.

They put in it a mosaic portrait of Chief Wapello, who had lived in Southern Iowa years before the white folks came. They did the mosaic in corn. Then they confected a statue of Miss Monroe (named after a Southern Iowa county). She was composed of graham flour, mustard seed, pulverized coal, and beet juice. Her hair was constructed out of marijuana (called hemp at the time), her eyes were constructed out of buckeyes. Grains of corn formed her teeth.

In a lapse of bad taste, they tore down the coal palace a year after it was built but it does go to show what Southern Iowans can do when they put their minds and souls into their work.

Things just seemed to happen in that neck of the woods—things people might find strange. Like the summer day in the late 1920's when some tramp walked along the dirt on the side of the Illinois Central Railroad tracks in Lucas County. He spent the better part of a day playing in the mud with a handtool he had, but when he had finished people were shocked at what he had created. It was a finely-sculpted Madonna, a Mary and Baby Jesus formed out of the mud. She seemed to be laying in the ditch, and so finely were she and the Christ child perfected by the tramp that her face and garments seemed to be born in the minds of the Italian masters. People took pictures of the Mud Madonna. The tramp charged a quarter to see his work. Within a few days the rain came and wiped the artist's work into the natural chaos of mud. No one ever saw him after that. The mystique at work again.

Strange things happen in Southern Iowa, in Lucas County and in the little town of Lucas in the county. Just how strange it is depends on what a person wants to make of it. Lucas County came into the twentieth century rural and friendly and poorer than other places. It appears that it will end the century in the same way. Maybe that makes it strange, too, in America where everything is supposed to get bigger and better and glittering and new. Lucas County should have a mystique if only because it is splendidly commonplace and because, when you look at the commonplace with a telescope or a microscope, it is full of surprises.

The best thing to do with Southern Iowa is to look at the ordinary as what it is and as what it might be connected to. In the town of Lucas, which is a little runt of a place thrown onto a couple of hills in Lucas County, things look poor, decayed, and ordinary. How far can you stand to look into the hearts and souls and stories of the people who live there and who used to live there? How important is anything which happens to us ordinary people from Southern Iowa? What meaning do you want to give to us?

In the late 1950's two cars from Lucas smashed into each other at high speed. It was a dangerous stretch of Highway 34 and two people were killed. Two other people were injured really badly. Tragedies bring the people of the town together in a way that breaks through the easy courtesies and time-passing people do with each other. People meditate on the chanciness of life. They talk in little groups in still voices. That is what happened the evening and day after the wreck.

The next week after things had normalized, someone told the folks hanging around one of the gas stations that it sure was something because when the Highway Patrolman looked through the wreckage of the two cars, they found empty beer cans in one and a Bible in the other. Most of the folks at the gas station just shook their heads and thought or maybe said, "Isn't that just the way it is?"

What did they mean by that? Was it that those cars crunching together represented some clash of good and evil? Maybe. The problem was no one ever figured out exactly what it meant that there was a Bible in one car and empty beer cans in the other. Nobody really figured out who was really at fault in the wreck. (It was on a foggy, raining night.) Could the fellow with the Bible in his car have been musing on scriptural truths to the neglect of his driving? Could the fellow with empty beer cans in his car have been carrying them around empty for a month of Sundays?

You can think what you will of what happened. The only thing we know happened for sure is that people died that night in a violent, untimely way. The rest of it we use the ghosts in our heads to explain. Anything we cannot explain, we try to connect to something—good, bad, foolish or brilliant, according to our dispositions. That is what we must do to Southern Iowa, and that is what I do.

When I think of my ramshackle Southern Iowa town, Lucas, I look and listen. I see the streets closing up, going back to nature. I hear frogs letting the crickets get the jump on them in the late-night, cackling breezes by the town pond. Then I imagine sounds of 19th century beginnings with carpenters' saws, men yelling sometimes and dreaming aloud where to put windows in new houses for future sunrises. I think a neighbor must have called to someone over the soft, still air in the town, one hundred years ago in the dusk. I think about the preaching and cussing and loving that happened through those years, and how they didn't leave echoes. I think of the work men and women did to shape and control their lives and how many were cheated out of their dreams.

That is what I think about. What I see is what everyone else sees—a ramshackle town in a rundown part of the state. So whether there is a Southern Iowa Mystique depends on what you think of ordinary people. All but one person who came from Lucas is ordinary by the standards of, let us say, *Time Magazine*. If you take the time to languish in your thoughts about ordinary places like Southern Iowa, and make connections with the people and their lives, you can be dazzled and dazed with partial understanding. Then you understand that it is not coal palaces, ghosts, or Mud Madonnas which create the Southern Iowa Mystique. It is the wink of some ordinary person telling you a story. It is the tattered fabric of sons and daughters of working people connecting to their children with dreams. It is the complaint of people denied power to walk in pride. It is the deep recognition of our human silliness as well. It is a place where the tragic and the absurd spring out of the same human heart.

In other words, Southern Iowa is no different than any place else at all.

PART 2

Coal, Blood and Dirt (1850-1926)

Farmers and Miners Put Down Roots:
Old Joe McKinney and Other Stories

The pioneers trekked into Lucas County shortly after Iowa joined the Union of States. They came from the East—Ohio, Indiana and Pennsylvania. They were native stock at first, with at least one generation of roots in the United States. They were people like J. C. Baker, who had been given a land grant in the county by President Franklin Pierce. J. C. had come into the area to open up the new land in Southern Iowa. There was the rich black soil— bottom land which often was flooded by the Chariton River on the White- breast Creek. Then there was the hilly ground, less fertile, long on clay and short on top soil. Lucas County is in the South Central part of Iowa on the natural borderline of the eastern hardwood forests and the hills of the great plains to the west. The lay of the countryside gave the immigrants a good deal of variety. So, too, did the weather. Summer heat could become mighty un- comfortable and winter cold could kill a person. Lucas County's winters were not kind to those unlucky settlers who were unprepared for it.

Some of the settlers, like J. C., thrived in the new countryside. The fact is J. C. Baker thrived to the point of weighing over three hundred pounds in his later years, to say nothing of founding a general store and a bank.

Most people in the 1850's were glad merely to survive the harsh, new life they had chosen. These were the times when the silence of winter's night was broken by the occasional sound of wolves, and when the coal-oil lamp and fireplace seemed weak barriers from the outside and uncaring nature. So the folks in the area invented reasons to gather together. Schools and churches sprang up every two miles or so, as ways of drawing the settlers together. Lucas County folks had a wry sense of just how places should be named, and they gave humble names to their schools and churches, names like Last Chance, Ragtown, and Zero.

The people were rugged, tough, half-puritan and part-ruffian. Of course, they had to work to survive. Many of them worked hard and didn't survive. They were living close to nature and close to the edge. It was a "root, hog, or die" time for them. The old tintype photographs of the county people show serious faces, tightly drawn mouths, eyes disposed to a flinty kind of stare. The older faces seemed to say, "there is work and survival and that is what life is all about." There was the excitement of the Iowa frontier as well, but excitement is quickly dulled by the tedium and exhaustion of the farm settlers' lives.

Now it is true that not all the Lucas County settlers were dour-faced puritans, even in those early days. There were many tales to be told when the menfolk came together and many stories were shared by the women. If daily life and toil were tedious, the men would embellish it with near-truths and half-lies.

Some of the settlers around Lucas town claimed that they had witnessed hoop snakes in the summer grass of those Southern Iowa hills. When a boy would come across a hoop snake, that old snake would just naturally put its tail in its mouth and roll down the hill like a unicycle. It would roll right into the Whitebreast Creek, unfold itself, relax, and float down the stream just as pretty as you please.

The early farmers talked about other kinds of snakes, such as rattlers, which still abide in the county today. Those with the most acute eyesight (or imagination, as some would have it) did not discuss blue racers, rattlers, puff adders, or even hoop snakes. Their fascination was naturally enough with the joint snake. The Southern Iowa joint snake would get addle-pated upon seeing some Lucas settler and immediately fall to pieces in a literal sense. Each joint would wiggle around, a law unto itself, wondering what in the Sam Hill was going on. Naturally, when the danger was passed, the snake would reconnect itself, get its parts all readjusted and go on about its snakey business. Some skeptics didn't hold with joint snakes but skeptics were not so great a source of entertainment as believers, and so the stories flourished right up until the 1980's.

Of course the early Lucasites told each other stories about spooks and horrors, and how so and so had been buried and the person wasn't quite dead yet and woke up in the coffin. Or tales were told of the brothers swimming in the Whitebreast Creek—how one brother drowned trying to save the other and eventually how they found both their bodies twined together. Strong stuff.

The early farmers, or at least those with a sinful turn of mind, told off-color jokes as well. Their jokes were side splitters and gut busters in the 1860's, but people today would likely not even understand them because the jokes were tied into the nineteenth century way of life. One example: "Name the three parts of a stove." Answer: "Lifter, leg, and poker." That simply doesn't sound "dirty" to those with central heating.

The boys in the new villages of Lucas County had surplus energy, even after their daily work. Often the old folks thought that the young folks were up to no good, and they were right. One of the most unhappy diversions of the frontier boys was to take two full-grown tom-cats, tie their tails together and throw them over a fence or clothesline, where they would scratch and bite each other to death. That noxious tradition was not often practiced, but sometimes boy barbarians in Lucas in the 1950's were still following the tricks of the bad boys of one hundred years earlier.

The houses and cabins in Lucas County would have smelled odd to the modern nose, with odors of horse liniment, human sweat, and fried mutton fat permeating the air. The modern sensitive nose might have been put out of joint by such an epiphany of odors. Yet in that time it meant home.

Early on, the settlers built schools—one about every two miles. Sometimes the older boys would try to whip the school master, and some they were able to terrorize. Still book-learning had its place, even though the more unlearned settlers liked to quote the Bible the fact that "the wisdom of the wise shall perish." The more cynical folks of the time would add to that "the bullheadedness of the ignorant will live forever." Both sides were probably wrong. Debating clubs and oratoric groups practiced their learning. Church denominations in the county would debate each other with much heat and occasional light.

Circuit riders would come into the communities and save the souls of the drunkards, hysterical people, and those who just didn't feel right about themselves.

Joe McKinney had moved into Lucas County just shortly after the State of Iowa had been taken away from the Sac and Fox Indians. In 1851 he had left Kentucky with his new wife, Melissy for that homestead out in the land of Ioway. The problem was, he landed in Lucas County dead in the middle of winter. His wife was the daughter of a Methodist preacher and used to hard times but when she and Joe came into a Southern Ioway blizzard she remarked to Joe that the snow was "amazin' deep in them flabergasted snowbanks." Joe seemed not to pay attention to her because that was his way— but when they had come close to their new homestead their team of horses got the wagon stuck so they were unable to stir at all. "Now this is a perdickerment" Melissy said half wanting to cry and half just curious about how her new husband would deal with the crisis.

The stars were a vision that cold March evening as Joe and Melissy sat under their cowhide blankets. Melissy expected Joe to curse and shake his fist at the heavens as her father would have done. He did say "consarn it" but almost like he didn't mean that. The fact is he got lost in the stars for some moments and he was quiet and pensive for nearly twenty minutes. Melissy was holding him for the warmth and wondering if he would ever move. "Do you suppose any of the stars would have snowdrifts on them, Melissy?"

"Joe," she said, "I don't know whether I will just die a laughing at you or freeze to death." "Don't be scornful to me", Joe said. Melissy said she didn't mean any such a thing but as her man walked over the hill she was hoping that she had not married a dreamer instead of a farmer. He had the build of a long bony farmer she reckoned, and the shoulders. She would wait to see if he had the stomach for it as he had claimed back in Kentucky.

Some folks living near the Chariton River gave them a hand out of their fix and within a few days they had moved into a cabin in Ottercreek Township. A family had built the cabin in 1847 but it had remained empty after the whole bunch had died off of cholera morphus. Joe wasn't superstitious about that at all. And Melissy needn't have worried about Joe's ability to farm or hunt and trap for that matter. With the money they had brought from Kentucky and with the selling of honey, sorghum and some runt pigs, the McKenneys were settled into Lucas. They would sometimes see a neighbor at the M. E. Church or at the store in Chariton.

Melissy worked in the fields beside Joe and she kept a good garden. She kept her work board busy as well. She made sweet cakes when they had sugar. In the long winter evenings she would want to talk with Joe, just to see what kind of idea was passing through his head. He spoke so little. Her curiosity about him was dulled by fatigue and she would sometimes fall asleep in the middle of her knitting. Joe would be seeing something in the fire until his eyes would glaze over and then he would turn down the bed and snore the night away.

When Melissy got big with child in 1853 she was not so spry as she had been before and one night she had so much pain that she couldn't finish pearin' the apples. She was hard pressed not to cry and she didn't. The doctor up at Chariton came to see her and told Joe that she had some female troubles and there wasn't alot he could do. And he was right; Melissy got weaker and had to stay abed. She had it figured out that she wouldn't be alive to see her 28th birthday which was the next month. Joe worked harder during the day and he sat beside Melissy's bedside at night and tried to think of things he could make sense out of to talk with her. Mostly the words didn't come.

One evening Melissy was having a rest from her pain and Joe was looking at the patterns on the quilt his mother had given them. "Joe", Melissy said with a loud and forceful voice. He turned and looked at her all startled. "Joe", she said, "we're all poor critters, ain't we?" She said it and laughed, getting some satisfaction Joe didn't understand. She paused a minute and laughed again. It was a warm, pleasant laugh but Joe didn't understand where it came from or what it meant.

He was thinking about it on the day they buried Melissy over at the Fry Hill Cemetary. She had twins shortly before she died.

There comes a time in the life of a man or woman when folks see them in a different light than they used to. Joe lived alone with his children in that cabin where he and Melissy had spent their three years together. He came into town less than he had before. Took to drinking corn whiskey out at his place. People in the county felt sorry for him but then again, they reckoned a man had a right to live the way he chose to.

When a young boy told some of the farmers that they had seen Joe drinking and carrying on out at his place with three Indian beggars, folks began to call him Ol' Joe McKinney and their lips would curl up in a half grin when they saw him. He had just gotten too plumb peculiar for anyone to take serious. And of course he kept to himself, except for the raisin' of his young ones.

That is why folks were surprised to see Ol' Joe at the United Brethren Church's revival in the spring of 1869. The revival was going strong after 8 days of miraculous conversions, healings, speaking in tongues, and a general

14

spiritual tension you could cut with a corn knife. It was a bouncing, joyful group of the saints, alternately sharing the sweet love of Jesus and the message of the horrors of eternal damnation. Women who had found it unusual to smile in their daily lives were caught up in the warm sensual spirit of eternal love and words of love came from their throats that staggered their menfolk. It was the love of God that the U. B. preacher was showing the flock and it had let loose a flood of pent up emotions.

Even the feuding of the United Brethrens and the Methodists as to who got to keep the new radiating Christians didn't dampen the excitement. Toward the end of the revival, it seemed that folks were singing and shouting morning, afternoon and late into the night.

It was a Thursday afternoon that Ol' Joe walked into the church and for the next three days and nights there was a powerful prayer sent up that Ol' Joe would recognize his sins then and there. Most folks more or less believed Joe was too far gone for redeeming anyhow. He would sit in the back pew, tall, boney, white haired with sunken eyes and cheeks not saying a word—but coming back, meeting after meeting.

It was just after Aunt Sally Fuller sat down after giving her heart to the Lord again, when the unexpected thing happened. The preacher was calling for another volunteer for the Army of the Lord, when all at once he threw up his hands like a boy ready to dive off a log. "Look at there, brethren and sisters!" Everybody looked and sure enough, Ol' Joe was going up to the front, a section at a time, until he finally towered up like a sycamore in a hay field.

"Oh, brethren and sisters", went on the preacher. "Old Uncle Joe McKinney has risen for your prayers; bless the Lord." And amen was heard from every corner of the house. "He is going to drop his old life; he is going to quit his drinking and his lying and his swearing and his . . ."

Joe grabbed the preacher by the back of his collar and raised him off his feet. "Hold on, Mr. Preacher, thats all right but there aint a bit of use of your making a godurn fool of yourself about it." Joe walked out of the church and the singing that followed couldn't get the crowd back to the spiritual place they had enjoyed a few minutes before.

Joe had had a wetnurse for his boy-twins in their first couple of years but as they got older he trained them in his idea about what a man should be. "A feller should never lie if he's not drunk and a feller should never steal off his neighbors unless his family is going hungry." Since Joe made a good enough living and usually drank alone, stealing and lying were not problems for him at all. That was why he put down his buttered biscuit and coffee the morning one of his boys told him that Mr. Danner in Lucas was accusing him of stealing some pork curing in Danner's smoke house.

Well, when he came over to see Danner about stealing that meat, there was a good chance for trouble, and those who were looking for it were not disappointed, either.

Old Joe commenced by asking Danner what he meant. Danner replied that he meant what he said. This is usually a forerunner of trouble. Old Joe straightened up and said: "Mr. Danner, you live in a white house, and you have shutters to your windows, and you are a taxpayer; you go to church, and the preacher takes dinner with you, and stays all night. Now, there never was a preacher in my house that I know of, and there ain't no invitations out. I live in a log house, and the only winder in it has a rag stuffed in whar the glass used to be. I'll admit that I would rather fish than cut corn; I swear a good deal and my children use some bad words, but it seems to me as they allus did it in fun, and it never sounded very bad to me, but I never stole anything yet, and I aint goin' to commence with your pork. Now, Mr. Danner, I heard that you said I went into your smoke house and stole some meat. Am I right?"

"You are," replied Danner.

"Then all I've got to say is you must either take that back or Old Joe himself couldn't save you for gettin a lickin'. Now you can either take it with yer coat on or off."

Danner was from Indiana, and it wasn't the first time he was ever invited to take his coat off to accomodate a neighbor. He squared himself, took off his coat and laid it down by the side of the road. Where this happened was right at the cross roads, and the room was ample. It is a matter of history that it was the best fight that ever took place in Otter Creek township. Here is how the blacksmith described it:

> There wasn't any rounds about it. It was just one glorious entertainment from start to finish; and they fought like gentlemen. Everything was fair, and you couldn't tell which one was going to whip any more than you could tell how a hoss race was coming out when they all bunched.
>
> Old Joe was the tallest and had the longest reach, but then he was the oldest. Abe was the heaviest and youngest, but he hadn't the wind. Joe lammed away first and when that old arm of his'n shot out it was enough to make a man on the outside holler 'nuff. If he'd hit Abe square the fight would have been over with, but Abe was on the lookout, and dodged to one side, so that Joe's knuckle just grazed his temple and peeled off a little strip of skin, and three or four drops of blood trickled down the side of his face. But this was just simply tuning up. The next I knew, Joe shot backwards about ten feet and landed square agin me, and I went like a freight car kicked into a siding. That lick would have laid out any other man in Otter Creek Township. I never saw where it struck him, and you couldn't tell after the fight was over with, for both of them looked like they had tried to stop a stampede of steers and had failed. I heard Joe's teeth come together, and it sounded a good deal like a gopher trap shutting up. Then the fighting was awful. No pulling hair nor scratching and kicking, but just good, manly blows that made you feel sorry that there wasn't a bigger audience. I have read about prize fights, where one feller kept jabbing the other in the face, and it disgusts me. There was no jabbing here; it was the whole-arm movement from beginning to end, and whenever one of them licks landed it made you bat your eyes. No mortal being could stand that pace long. Finally Abe's wind began to play out, and you could hear him breathe across a forty. Joe with what little sight he had left, saw that Abe was about finished, so he made a rush and got him by the

16

throat with his left hand then he drew back and said: 'Abe Danner, are you going to holler 'nuff?' I heard a 'No' kind of rattle in Abe's throat, but he was helpless. Old Joe looked at him about a minute, it seemed to me like then he gave Abe a kind of push and started down the road, and he never looked back as far as I could see him. Abe just dropped and laid there panting like a lizard for the better part of an hour. They were two of the grittiest men that I ever saw.

It was sometime after this when the diphtheria got into Danner's family, and Old Joe came to 'nuss' the children. When he came up to the house blinds were down and everything was still. He knocked at the door; there was no one there except Abe and his wife and the sick little ones, and there were three of them. Abe came to the door looking pale and worn out, and when he saw it was Joe he didn't say a word, but just looked at him as if he was in some doubt about how to proceed. Joe was the first to speak. He said "Mr. Danner, you and I have had some trouble. You gave me the gamest fight I ever had; and since I come to think it over, maybe you wasn't so far wrong about the piece of pork you missed; but I have heard that your children are sick, and that the neighbors are scared about coming here. I have always been able to nuss my children through all the sickness they ever had, and I believe I can nuss yours if you will let me try." Well, sir; Abe just broke down, and he kind of sobbed out: "Joe, I knew there was lots of good in you when you didn't hit me that last time. I belong to church, but I don't know if I would come to help take care of your children if they had been sick like mine."

After this the people thought a good deal more of Old Joe, and when they had a Christmas tree that winter they had the hardest time in the world to get Old Joe and his family to come out and finally Danner had to go to him and make him promise that he would come and bring his family. It was a great Christmas tree—about the first in the neighborhood. The boys had gone down in the woods and cut a young Haw tree (there was no evergreens in the neighborhood), and when it was all trimmed up it was the most beautiful sight a person ever saw. Folks have seen costlier trees and richer presents since then but for a lasting impression, there is nothing to compare with that first Christmas tree. How the old church was crowded! Everybody was there it seemed, and the sleds hitched up and down the fence reached from the church down almost to the schoolhouse. John Pedigo was Santa Claus. He kept the audience laughing all the time, and when all the presents were distributed the people stayed until after 12 o'clock, and talked and laughed and carried on until it really looked like a genuine case of "peace on earth, and good will to all men." One of the neighbors put a butcher knife on the tree for his wife and when Santa Claus took it down and presented it everyone yelled. Old Joe was there with his family, but they seemed to feel out of place. They fidgeted around a good deal and acted like they would rather have stayed at home. But it wasn't long before the name of "Joe McKinney" was called out. Immediately it was still, for nearly everyone was "on" except Joe and his family. It was a big bundle of something. Joe rose up and it was amusing to see him. Afterwards he said he was never so scared in his life. He was pale and his knees shook until you could feel the floor of the church vibrate. There must have been half of the audience that called out: "Open it, undo it!" Old Joe hesitated a moment, and then commenced to untie the package. When he had finished he held up a suit of clothes, suspenders and all. Then he sat down, and everybody clapped their hands. After awhile Dan McKinney's name was called. He got a cap and a pair of skates. The children were all well taken care of. Then Dan threw back his head and howled. The other children followed suit, and for five minutes it looked like there would have to be a recess taken. Then came candy and nuts for everyone; children and everything quieted down.

Well, that Christmas was the turning point in Joe's life. A company opened up a coal mine in that township and Danner hired Joe to cut 5,000 wood props.

It was steady work and paid well enough to raise Joe's two children. That is what he did and when he became white haired and toothless he would call up some early times in his mind and he would laugh to himself about something Melissy had said 35 years before. He wished she could answer him back when he would talk to her. He thought he had been too damn flinty and maybe confused to talk to her while she was his wife. One time he wished he could go back and tell her what was on his mind. Then he realized that he still wouldn't be any different if she stood there before him. He was smiling a rare smile thinking of this. "We are poor critters sure enough," he was thinking as his ancient eyes closed for sleep.

Maybe Joe wasn't a typical "pioneer" as we would call him today. Yet he did see in his lifetime the changes that shaped the early town of Lucas. Like most of us today he was too busy trying to survive to philosophize much. He saw the railways cut through the county and he saw the coal mines take their shape in the new town. He worked and survived in the new country. He saw the changes that were coming.

The railroads, for one thing, were coming, pushing west toward free land and optimism. The Chicago & Southern Railroad pushed into Lucas County, and by 1867 it came out to the Tallahoma Station. Tallahoma was named after an Indian Chief who had lived far away from Southern Iowa. The settlers would take the land away from the Indians and then name the places in honor of them. The Indians did not appear to be grateful for the white man's courtesies.

In May of 1868, Mr. Russell plotted out the town of Lucas just a couple of miles south of the Old Tallahoma Station. He laid out streets and lots for about one square mile, which seemed big enough for a town created for no particular reason. They named the town after Iowa's first governor and set about getting a post office and a few businesses for the settlers.

The town sat on a flat piece of bottom land, extending north up several hills. The westbound trains would come lickity-split past the new Lucas depot in the next several years. They would come down the half-mile grade onto the flatland and speed on west, occasionally running down a deer or some careless farmer's prize cow.

Lucas was on the main line of what became the C. B. & Q. Railway, and it was in a curiously convenient place, for underneath its earth was the precise fuel needed to keep the steam whistle of the Iron Horse happy. It was coal.

Even the earliest settlers had seen chunks of coal lying randomly about the beds of the Whitebreast Creek. They tended not to burn it much in their fireplaces and stoves because if they did, their window ledges would pick up a constant layer of black dust. Even the water jug would develop a dark scum in it. The coal burned hot all right, but there was plenty of forest in Lucas County and the land needed clearing anyway. They would burn wood while they could.

This new railroad line was developing an appetite for coal and the farmers, newly prospered by the Civil War, were needing the railroads more all the time. People got interested in those lumps of coal along the Whitebreast. They began to dig for it.

It had been placed there more than a quarter of a billion years before, when all of Iowa, indeed almost all of America, was a swamp. It was a swamp containing a soup of bacteria with ferns, scale trees, and bamboo-like plants growing out of it to a height of one hundred feet or more. There were insects and reptiles of all manner here, and they thrived on the plants and each other in the warm, steamy swamp that was Iowa.

When the trees of this enormous jungle grew together in a tangled web, they also fell into the swamp to be jammed and mashed up, turning the decay into peat. Eventually the peat was buried and covered with clay, silt, and rock. The peat began to lose carbon dioxide, carbon monoxide, methane and water, and over a period of more than ten thousand years compressed into the shining, sharp cleaved carbon rock called coal.

Coal was spread all over Southern and Central Iowa. However, it was not easy to get to because it was spread out in odd-sized, discontinuous seams and pockets cut through by rivers and creeks like the Whitebreast, which also runs through Lucas.

Some of the old folks around Lucas claim it was a ground hog burrowing in a creek which found the coal around the town. Less romantic people claim it was found by the Iowa Geological Survey. Some of the more adventuresome folk from Burlington took a lease on the land next to the small village in 1874 and they hired workers to dig black diamonds out of the oak colored clay.

Laborers, with pickaxes and spades, came hurrying to the spot and began to dig a circular hole of some seven feet in diameter. Then other men came with a great, wooden roller on a stand with a well rope wound around it. They let it down and filled it with dirt and stones. As the shaft deepened, the carpenters came with tools and lumber and they cut posts and frames for the inside of the shaft. After days of work, the men were in the depths of the earth, unable to be seen.

Someone gave a cry down below that there was water flowing into the shaft. They hoisted the men up, clinging to the basket attached to the rope. They leaped and scrambled out of the way and the rope was lowered again to bring up other men. This was the first danger in setting down a shaft—drowning under the earth.

Meanwhile they were bringing the steam pumps out to the Whitebreast Mine to rig up the works. Soon the water was pouring out, mud-colored, clay-colored, gray and chalky. Finally the water was gone and the men and boys went down to dig again.

Up came the clay and sand and gravel and stones for days more as they worked into the worst of the winter. Those turning the ropes on top were freezing and the men down below were no warmer. Finally there was a shout from 238 feet below, and the next basket brought up limestone, grit, red sandstone, and chunks of coal.

Buildings were put together at the top of the mine, and a 30-horsepower engine was attached to a rope that passed over a large drum or broad wheel. The rope was extended to the shaft and a small iron wheel was placed underneath the rope at the mine's entrance. The men went down on this rope and the coal came up.

After a time, wood work and iron work went down the shaft, with sledges and trucks with little wheels. Finally, broad belts were put around mules and ponies, and they were lowered, kicking wildly in the air and staring with horrified eyeballs, into the black abyss with every limb trembling. Although they made it safely to the floor of the shaft, many of them would never see the sunlight again. They would die in harness. That was true also of many of the miners.

Another shaft was sunk into Lucas' first mine. That was for ventilation. The Lucas men would go down the shaft in an iron box called a cage. They would hook chains, loop them to the rope, straddle their legs and go down the shaft at a speed just short of falling.

The Lucas men would be naked from the waist up, and black with coal dust. They lit the way with candle lamps or kerosene lamps attached to their head gear. They would slap some clay into the sidewall where they were working, stick an iron "miner's needle" into it and light a candle to see, however, vaguely, the "room" in which they were working.

In the winter of 1876, the town of Lucas may have been "too wet to plow, too cold to cut butter", but in the mines on the east edge of town the miners were using pickaxes, sledge hammers, scoop shovels, and blasting powder to get at that rich, two-hundred-million-year-old swamp muck turned to black stone.

In those early days, each Lucas miner would buy his black powder and carry it in an old stocking, wrapped around his waist to keep it dry. They would go to the face of the coal vein, strap on a metal breastplate and press their chests to an auger drill. They would drill into coal for a foot or more, then put black powder into the hole, tamp it with old papers or clay. They would light the squib, or fuse, and get as far away from the blast as they could in the next minute. The coal would blast away, and they would scoop it into the cars pulled by the unfortunate mules or ponies.

The Lucas miners took canaries into the mine to warn them of poisonous gases. The canaries would warn them by dropping dead. They took extra food for the rats in the mine. The rats had come down with the grain for the mules. The rats were good warning devices, too, and some of the miners called them four-legged canaries.

The early Lucas miners dressed for the cold and the damp. They wore boots but always got wet, anyhow. The miners worked the "streets" of the underground town. The Whitebreast Mine was taking on a shape like the town of Lucas, itself. Usually, though, it was more quiet than the town itself. It was a wonderful quiet, some of the men thought, broken only by some occasional hissing of gas or the faraway noise of a blast in another part of the mine.

The miners would come up at the end of a shift cold, dirty and stiff from crawling through the tunnels. They were proud and they were strong. In Lucas' first mine, the rich risked their capital and the miners risked their lives. That was the way life worked in the coal town that was Lucas.

Only one generation had passed since the white settlers came to the county with great expectations about their fortunes in the new land. Now a generation of miners would come from halfway across the world with great expectations about their fortunes in the Lucas mines. Life would be hard and dangerous, but it would treat the families fairly, the miners hoped. If we are treated fairly, the early miners and farmers thought, our hard work will carry us through and we may have an adventure to boot.

The Welsh Connection: Roedd yr Eisteddfod yn Lucas*

"But now all these are gone, like dreams in the morning."
　　—A. G. Prys-Jones

It was in the thirteenth century, they say, that King John of England forced all the people of Wales to take the name of Jones (son of John) to show their allegiance to him. They were, it seemed, in constant battle against the English and they wished to be left alone. They were an ancient people and spoke in an ancient tongue far stranger to the English ear than French or German.

Although they were surrounded on three sides by the sea, they were a farming and hunting people, for the most part. Some of the land was gentle in its hills and gentle streams and some of it was rock and small mountain. There were ancient stones in the green, mist-covered land which reminded the Welsh of the ancient people and the old ways of druidical magic.

*There was a festival in Lucas.

It was said that the ancient forest in the Rhonnda Valley was so thick with trees that a squirrel could hop from one to the another for twenty-five miles without touching the ground back in the eighteenth century. That all changed, you see. It changed when Mr. Anthony Bacon leased the coal and iron rights around Merthyr Tydfil, in 1765, right in the heart of South Wales. When Mr. James Watt invented the steam engine eighteen years later, it was the beginning of the modern world—the Industrial Revolution.

From 1803 to 1806, steamship production accelerated and the railroads came for the first time to England. Well, it was just then that South Wales began to light up with fires under the smelts at night and open deep into her hills for the coal-to-fire industry. In Trevithick, Wales, in 1804, the first locomotive was built. It was the iron furnaces of Wales that produced the iron rails and the trains for them to run on. The mines were taking hundreds of men with their candle lamps or carbide lamps down into the earth. The anthracite coal came up to the surface with a rich, four-feet-wide vein in some places in the South of Wales, and scarcely a mile or two across country it would loop and dive into the earth at 2,000 feet below the surface. Over the years, depending on the markets for the black, shiny rock, the men would go deeper and deeper beneath the sun and farther from the pure air above.

Then the families left the farms in the north of the country, or were thrown off by their English-speaking landlords, and the men found work or the promise of work in the mines or ironworks. Glamorgan, in the South and East of Wales, nearly doubled in population from 1801 to 1831. Workers were coming to the old druidical land from other places for work and a chance at survival. Tin miners arrived from Cornwall and skilled miners from the North of England came. Irishmen came to work in the mines, and they were used to break strikes and lower the wages of the Welshmen.

Hunger was always hovering over the old country with the coming in of industry and international markets. There were the hunger riots at Carmarthen in 1818. There was the remembrance of Ap Vychan, who that very year saw an overseer remove a feather bed from beneath his father, who was dying of fever and starvation. There were the excessive tolls paid by the farmers for carrying their grain or animals on the mud roads. And there was the terror of unemployment forcing one into the inhuman misery of the workhouse. This happened again and again when famine, the "corn laws" (which pushed wheat prices out of control), or economic downturns hit the countryside.

The Welsh could sing and tell stories, but in the nineteenth century they could also rise up against oppression. And they often did. When land was "enclosed", (meaning taken control of by the local gentry), it destroyed small farms and villages in one blow. It was in the beginning of that century that "incendiaries" would come out at night and torch the houses of the land grabbers. This was vexing to the landowners and made them give consideration to their actions.

In 1842 groups of Welshmen dressed as women came out at night, rioting and destroying the tollgates of their roads. They were the Secret Society of Rebecca, and they burned the hayfields of unpopular magistrates. A year later rioters attacked a toll gate at Pontardulais (the home of John L. Lewis' grandparents), and the rioting spread until the leaders were captured.

Then the Chartist Movement from England spilled over into the Welsh countryside. It demanded a "charter" for working people, the right to vote for laborers, and economic justice for the have-nots in Britain. Chartism grew fast on Welsh soil and it had great appeal to the rebellious, romantic Welsh militants. For the most part, the Chartists were content to educate and agitate the "higher orders" of the society to advance the lot of working folk. Some of the Welsh Chartists, however, began to believe that direct violent action was the answer. Among these were the secret "Scotch Cattle". They burned the houses of employers who lowered the miners' wages, and they sometimes "scotched" those individuals who broke ranks to work for less pay.

The Chartists promoted a large demonstration at Newport, on the South Wales Coast, in 1839. Three contingents of armed miners and textile workers came to town, angry and looking for justice. Troops stationed outside the main hotel in town fired on the men, killing many. The leaders of the Chartist movement—John Frost, Zep Williams and William Jones—were all arrested, and the Chartists were never again to have much power in the country except as a reminder, from time to time, that men and women pushed too far will put on the bloody cloak of rebellion whatever the odds for success may be.

If the political rebellion of the Welsh was put down, the economic struggles were just beginning. Time and time again the miners and other workers went on strike, and it was never to promote raises in pay but to defend against cuts in the living wage. Union clubs were formed in the 1840's and 50's to promote working-class cooperation against pay cuts. A cooperative store was opened in Aberdare in 1860, run by the miners, themselves. The miners were often paid in private script, which was only good for high-priced necessities at the company-owned store.

Still the coal came out of the massive, artificial caves under the ground. Men were forced to crawl on hands and knees for sometimes a mile to get to their work. Children of no more than five years worked in the mines all day, opening and closing the air traps to control the ventilation of the deep shafts. Poverty and hunger were always one accident away. The accident could occur in the mine, itself, or it could be an accident in the world of commerce, leading to falling coal prices.

And there was death. In July of 1856, an explosion at the Cymer Colliery killed one hundred and fourteen miners instantly and injured scores of others. There were many other mining catastrophies in the latter part of the century, including an unspeakable disaster at Abercarn, when two hundred and sixty-eight miners were killed in an explosion in 1878.

The 1870's saw a reduction in miners' wages in South Wales and an increase in the misery of the working families. By 1875 the miners went on strike to protest wage cuts but they had not the resources to continue for more than a few months. They were broken and went back to work for less money. The miners union was broken. It was many years later that effective unions were able to fight for the miners.

The Welsh were not only workers and radicals in politics; they were also deeply religious folk. Their religion of choice was a kind of puritanism, an antiestablishment nonconformity based on the teachings of the Bible, a strict moral code and occasional fiery revivals. Notwithstanding their sometimes tendencies to the violence of desperation, the Welsh were law-abiding folk. Preachers would rant on to the people about the torments and flames of hell and this moved the people deeply. The iron workers and miners needed very little imagination to understand hell.

The Puritan vision of the Welsh insisted on hard work and thrift, integrity of character, moderation and temperance of spirit (alcoholic spirits as well), and an insistence on the equality of all people within the sight of God. In the latter sense, the nonconformist principles of nineteenth-century Welsh religion fit the radical political beliefs of the people. One could say that Welsh religion gave a person great inner strength and integrity, or one could say that it made the Cambrian folk pigheaded and stiffnecked. Both ideas may be correct.

Unlike many other people deeply influenced by puritanism, the Welsh always maintained a romantic streak and the need to give form to romantic ideas in song and story, myth and rhyme. The obvious centerpiece for all this poetic and musical excursion was the *Eisteddfod,* a celebration of Welsh culture and history given in song, poetry, and public speech. The idea of the *Eisteddfod* goes back some six hundred years in the history of the country. It was gradually forgotten and then revived in 1789 in a burst of nationalistic fervor and optimism generated, in part, by the two great revolutions of the day, the French and the American. The *Eisteddfod* was a collective tribute to the bards and musicians of the country, and contests were held to reward the best of the lot. Poets were crowned; a ceremonial procession of bards in splendid robes moved through the town, and the Welsh observers would break into song at the least provocation.

The poetry at the contests was set to a difficult and intricate structure and the Welsh love of the sound of language was framed in it. Myths were generated and revived at the *Eisteddfod*. The universal rights of man and other radical ideas blended with stories such as that of the Welsh Prince Madoc, who had discovered America it was said some three hundred years before Columbus.

At the *Eisteddfod* in 1791, William Jones announced that the Welsh descendants of Prince Madoc were living in America as free Indians, and that they would welcome their brothers and sisters to the new country, the Promised Land. Some believed that to stay in Wales would be to learn to live with tyrants and slaves only. Several expeditions by the Welsh did come to America, the "Beulah Land". John Evans led a group to America in 1797. Morgan John brought another group and Morgan John Rhees still another.

The Welsh formed a Utopian settlement called Beulah in Western Pennsylvania. In 1801, George Roberts wrote back to Wales that the last ship bringing immigrants from the Old Country had lost fifty-three out of one hundred and two passengers. Then there was the problem that America did not turn out to be as conducive to Utopia as the Welsh had thought.

A half century later land-hungry Welsh farmers bought 100,000 acres of land in Eastern Tennessee, but the land was poor and the Welsh, opposed to slavery, were not welcome in that state during the Civil War. The community eventually disbanded. Still, for many of the Welsh, America was the Promised Land. When Mormon missionaries came to the countryside in the 1850's, two by two, they promised the Kingdom of Heaven on Earth in the land of Zion, which happened to be America. On some occasions, whole villages in Wales were converted to the new religion with its fullsome promises.

When coal was discovered in Lucas, a few Welshmen and their families were in the area. A small village south of town was called Cambria, which is another name for Wales. The word moved fast and advertisements for skilled miners found their way across the Atlantic, as well as to the other mining camps in Pennsylvania and Tennessee, where the Welsh had congregated. Just as the mines in Lucas were beginning to boom in 1879, a harsh depression took hold in the Old Country, wages were slashed, and jobs were lost.

Thus, the Welsh found their way to the rolling prairie hills and forests of Southern Iowa. They were ready to work. Ready to make new lives and homes. Many came directly from Pontypool, the Rhonnda, or Cardiff. For others, the way to Lucas was not so direct. Tom Lewis, John L.'s father, left Pontardulais in 1870 at the age of sixteen and sailed for Australia after a stint of mining in his native country. After a short time, Tom caught a ship for San Francisco. He worked a claim in the short-lived gold rush in the Black Hills of South Dakota before coming to work in the Lucas mines in 1876.

John L.'s maternal grandpa, John Watkins, left Carmarthen in 1869 with his family. He was forty-six years old at the time and worked his way through various mining camps until he reached Lucas in 1876. There he met his young son-in-law-to-be, Tom Lewis.

John L. Roberts was born in Wales in 1833. He came to the United States to mine in Cass County, Illinois, for a time. Soon he was in Lucas County, Iowa. He enlisted in the Civil War in 1861. He left his wife, Sarah, with her children for only a bit more than a year, when he was wounded in action with an Iowa Regiment. He came back to Lucas and produced another set of sons after the war. He died just before the mines came to life in Lucas. His sons would survive him and work the pits from the very first in 1876.

So many Evanses, Robertses, Thomases, and Williamses came to Lucas in the few years that followed the coal discovery. Many wanted to get out of the satanic pits altogether. That was not always possible. The Welsh's skills in mining were considerable, and the mine owners in Lucas and in other coal camps sought them out and encouraged them to write to friends to immigrate as well.

When the Welsh came in they were tired but hopeful. Hopeful for a scratch of land and full lunch bucket. Hopeful to the point of allowing themselves to believe that Lucas, in the New World, would provide an end to the wanting and insecurity and struggle that was a Welshman's lot in the Old Country. The landscape of Southern Iowa was less forbidding than in the Old Country, and the sun poked through the clouds more often than at home. Besides, a man could make something of himself here where the class lines hadn't hardened and the earth was yet unscarred.

To be sure, it was a rowdy place they had come to, and the native American working-man didn't have the thirst for knowledge that the Welsh miners sought. Still, all in all, the move from Wales was half desperation and half adventure. Many people came from the same Welsh towns and knew each other. They shared herb gardens and concern for the young ones. And yes, the diseases from the Old Country followed them to Lucas—cholera morphus, typhoid and measles. On the other hand, traditions they held firm to in that first generation were comforting. The boys would follow "da" into the mines and work closely with their fathers. The girls learned the cooking with mother, just as they would have done back home. So there were grand times and uncertain times, but they knew it would be an adventure crossing the seas and the endless pastures and prairies. They were young men and women and their lives in Lucas had a newness to it. Still, it would be hard work and not reflection that would give them the chance here.

They talked about work and gossip and politics in the lilting, sing-songing voices, and their English came with time and a Welsh twist, "You'll be settling down here in the town, isn't it?" They ended their thoughts with questions, didn't they?

They came to Lucas and they made their mark. They would work hard, stand up, by God, for their rights, and raise their children with strictness. They would carry their pasties (meat and potato pies) to the Cleveland No. 1 Mine. They would sing on their way to work. They would speak the language of the Old Country at work.

They would get hurt and die and they would rage at the operators and their unconcern. Years later they would read about all the trials and tribulations Mr. Haven and Mr. Osgood had raising the money to sink that first Lucas mine in 1875. Mr. Haven wrote a history of the mine, told everyone about his discouragement, the lack of financial backing, and so on. He just happened to mention that the miners worked for more than two months without pay on the chance of getting work. Mr. Haven praised the bankers who had faith in him but forgot to mention the names of the miners, Welsh and otherwise, who did the real work. The Welsh miners knew how valued they were by the bosses. They took note of it.

After they got their company houses built and moved into and kept up, the Welsh commenced to build a church. It was strict Congregational and Welsh-speaking. It wasn't long, only four years after they came to Lucas, that they began to have the *Eisteddfod* in Lucas in springtime. They sang the old songs, gave awards and applause for the orations, and praised or despaired of the poetry by the miners, their wives, and the children. It was healthy and it was the transplanting of the old ways onto the new land. Some of the Welsh boys could sing and recite so powerfully it would make the rocks cry. At least that's what folks said.

"Quite a number of Lucas young people went out seranading Saturday evening."—*Chariton Patriot,* July 15, 1891.

Indeed there was a great lot of singing in the town. Some of it was in Knott's Opera House, the only real-fine, brick building in the town. But some of it was in the yards and streets in the late twilight of summer, when the miners were fed and washed. The old Welsh hymns and country songs would float up the Lucas hills. Folks were there singing in their front yards. Then on lazy, Sunday afternoons, the bandstand would ring out with vocal harmonies or amateur efforts of the town band. You could humanize the life of work and insecurity by singing about it. That was what the Welsh folk believed.

They kept some ties to the Old Country by letter. They even had an occasional visitor. William D. Davies, a reporter for the *Y Drych* in the Old Country, visited his people in 1886 and then again five years later, "I went to Cleveland and Lucas and found the Welsh there are similar to the Welsh in other locations. But the three Welshmen who were the most open-hearted and kind to me were George Williams, the agent for *Y Drych,* the Welsh-language newspaper, Mr. Owen C. Roberts ("Pererin", his poetical name), and Mr. Ellis Nichols, the policeman at Cleveland, who willingly went with me to see the Welsh of the City." (December, 1886).

When William Davies came back to Lucas to report on his findings half a decade later, Lucas had been through the trials of strikes and strikebreakers, and the whole of the United States was in an economic slump. The demand for coal was down and the Cleveland No. 1 Mine had just closed.

"In my most recent visit at Lucas and Cleveland, Iowa," he wrote to his readers in Wales, "I noted a cold and feeble look surrounding the two towns. The coal mining has ended, about half the houses were empty, many of the Welsh had moved and the Welsh churches have died. But there were some Welsh remaining there." (December, 1891)

Yes, some did remain and the mines would start up again, though not so vigorous as before. In 1890 the county mines produced 351,000 tons of coal, the next year only 800 tons. Some of the Welsh could hang on and do it all in a way not always grim and sober-like. They had an easy laugh given the slight chance of a lucky break for making money to survive. Lots of the Welsh moved to the mines at What Cheer or Hiteman or Des Moines. For those who could survive in Lucas, life went on, not as folks had planned, but it went on.

The few people in Lucas who can remember the Welshfolk like to do it with a certain softness. One tells a story of these two Welshmen driving their buggies through the muddy Lucas Main Street at the turn of the century. One of them was What Cheer Joe Knotts, so-named because he worked the mines over there for a while. Another fellow, Albert Baker, asked him if he might want to swap horses. They were both on the suspicious side because they had both been stung in earlier swaps. They finally decided to trade. When they got their animals home, they were both dissatisfied. Each thought the other had stung him. They tried to trade back but they just couldn't trust the other fellow enough to do that, either.

Most Americans about that time and place would have pulled out a six-shooter to settle matters, or at least flown into the other person with a face-cracking fist. The Welsh were a little different, sometimes. They didn't do that. The only thing that happened was that Albert named his horse after Joe's wife, Mamie. There was nothing for Albert to do but to drive his horse along the Lucas mud streets, calling "giddup Lydia." Lydia was the wife of What Cheer Joe. So the Welshmen both got satisfaction of a teasing, harmless sort. What the wives thought about the matter was never recorded.

The Welsh left a legacy in the town, and it was a progressive and thoughtful tradition. It was more than just keeping the liquor out of the Cleveland neighborhood in Lucas. It was more than being morally upright. It had to do with equality and justice.

By the turn of the new century, some of the Welsh who had left Lucas for other mining camps began to come back. The town started growing again with the opening of the Cleveland No. 4 Mine. During that time, the women of the town were organizing to fight for the right of women to vote and to be treated as equals to the menfolk. The Welsh women were in the forefront of the Ladies Suffrage Society. Their motto was "The Greatest Good for the Greatest Number", and about thirty-five of the local women would attend the meetings to agitate for equality.

The men of the town need not have worried that the womenfolk were becoming too radical in their demands or that they were becoming embittered by their struggles. This quote from the *Chariton Herald* (Sept. 22, 1898) should have given the local men a sigh of relief. "The executive committee of the Women's Suffrage Society met at the home of Mrs. Reese Monday night to complete arrangements for the supper to be given for the band boys." Even sexual militancy had its limits in Lucas.

Yet the generation of Welsh miners and their families believed that life could be better and they believed in a life of the mind. They were hungry for the lectures and plays and music and oratories. They worked with their hands and they wished to grow in the things of the mind.

"The Lucas Literary Society Debate was held Friday evening. Topic: Resolved that the negro [sic] has more right to complain of the usages of the whites than the Indian. Affirmative: Dave Morgan, John Morgan, J. C. Baker, George Croston. Negatives: Will Skidmore, Dave Daniels, Fred Knotts, John Dolphin." (*Lucas Review,* March 22, 1894)

That was the fermentation of minds hungry for expression, hungry for justice. Lest we leave the reader with too much serious thought about the Welsh, a story is in order.

Gomer Evans, son of one of Lucas' several John Evanses, was a Welsh miner who handled other jobs as well. One of those was to take tickets and keep order at the Knotts Opera House. It was a two-story, brick building which had windows on the second floor. These could be used by the penniless boys of the town to get a free peek at the traveling shows and other entertainments passing through town. Several of the town boys were perched up on the second story, including Gomer's son, Bernal. It seems the top banana of the Vaudeville Company stopped his act when he saw the boys peering in on the show. "What's the matter, little fellers? Haven't got the coins to come and see me work? You know, that's just all right. You just come down here anyways and watch our show," he said. "I just love little boys and there's no reason for you to miss the laughs. Come right down here in front." The boys did. After they had assembled quietly in front of him, he yelled out, "Now, you little nasty bastards, you've seen me and the show for nearly a minute and I want your cheap little asses out of the building now!"

The kids ran as hard as they could, jumping over seats and suchlike. Bernal was toward the back of the pack and he felt a sudden, sharp pain in his behind. His pa, Gomer, had kicked him precisely and swiftly in the seat of the pants. Later he would recall, "Yep, I guess I was raised by my pa's pointed shoes."

Gomer later worked for John L. Lewis, organizing in the steel mills of Gary, Indiana, and spying on radicals in the mines of the west. He was like many other Welsh kids growing up around the town and he knew when Lucas put a mark on you, you would never forget it.

There were about ten thousand of the Welshies (as folks called them) in Iowa at the turn of the century. When most of them left Lucas they left twenty-five years of graves in the town's cemeteries. They left a smattering of their language and stories. They left some families behind, such as the Williamses, Evanses, Watkinses, Robertses, and Joneses. They left behind the company houses. And they left behind a husky, redheaded, ornery boy, the son of Tom Lewis. They named him John, from the Bible, and Llewellyn, for an old Welsh hero. He would become Lucas' most famous mover of heaven and hell in the labor movement of his day. He would be seen as the full measure of a Welshman in his struggles for power and justice for the little people, the forgotten men in the mines. Strangely enough, his fate would entangle him in a conflict with another Lucas Welshboy, Thomas Moses. But that would be in another time in a faraway place.

One Hell of a Time: Lucas in the 1880's

The first man to die in the Lucas mines was Bill Jukes, the Englishman. He died July 22, 1880. He was killed by falling slate. About three months later a Welsh miner, Shadrack Fry, met his fate in the same way in the Whitebreast Mines. The next month, Richard Davies, from South Wales, was killed. If they could extricate the bodies from the pits, they were brought up and put on a special wagon and hauled into town for the funeral at the Welsh Congregational, the Presbyterian Church, the Latter Day Saints Church, or the African Methodist Episcopal, depending on the miner's background.

The mines were going great guns, and despite the routine deaths and injuries there was a feeling that wealth and good times were around the corner. The Chicago, Burlington and Quincy Railroad was taking all the coal the miners could produce and then some. Several winters they refused to sell coal to the locals in the area, and during one extremely cold winter unprepared folk were known to burn furniture to stay alive. But wasn't that better than some of the mines, where the miners would have only three or four months of work and would do odd jobs or hunt and fish to keep their families alive? Not only were the Cleveland No. 1 and two other mines going most of the year; the newly-opened Lucas School was open six months of the year. That was something folks were proud of.

And wasn't it true that Lucas' own Whitebreast Mining Company had the first electric light in the *entire state* of Iowa in 1881? The mine owners had bought it in person from Mr. Edison and brought it back to hang on the tipple of the mine shaft. The fact that they took it back and got their money returned a few months hence wasn't important. It was progress.

Not only that, but didn't the Oskaloosa papers say that they had discovered gold forty miles away at Ottumwa? By July of 1882, that Brisco gold find was digging up and crushing fifty tons of ore a day. Even if the gold didn't really pan out in the end, it seemed to many people that *anything* was possible in that eighth decade of the nineteenth century. Patrick Gary, a Lucas man, "went up to Dakota this spring on a land exploring trip," the *Iowa State Register* said. He was looking for gold up there. "Word came that his feet are so badly frozen that they had to be amputated" (April 7, 1883). Even if everyone wasn't so lucky, it was the idea of wealth that was let loose, and who could blame anyone for trying anything to get it. Of course, not everything was rosy—especially for the miners.

"Several accidents are reported from the coal mines at Lucas and Whitebreast. Names of the victims: Lewis, whose injuries proved fatal (left a wife and baby, the latter being christened on the father's coffin), Debard, Lloyd, Riggs, and McGowen (*Register,* April 14, 1883)."

Even if things were, let us admit it, grim for the miners, there was work to be done. It seemed as though the place would become important and thriving.

The Chicago, Burlington and Quincy was running eight passenger trains per day, four each way. "My, don't this country grow!" people said. It did. And it grew on coal.

Lucas did grow and as for the deaths, one mine operator was rumored to have said, "If a miner dies that is surely too bad but I can get lots of miners. If a mule dies, I'm out at least one hundred dollars." That was the price of progress and the price of profit.

There were lots of ways to keep one's mind off death, especially if one read the newspapers in 1882 and '83. The news was full of baseball scores, lynchings in the South (that may not have been as good in forgetting about death), Lily Langtry's new matched team of white horses, Oscar Wilde's silver cup (he refused to drink out of any other during his American tour), labor violence in Pittsburg (skim over that quickly to preserve your optimistic mood), the arrest of Buffalo Bill on charges of public drunkenness, the temperance movement to dry out America, labor violence in Pittsburgh (another article to quickly pass by), the weekly humor columns of George Peck and his "Bad Boy", and the big doings on Jay Gould's new yacht.

Meanwhile back in the boomtown, Lucas miners were organizing the Loyal Order of Forrestors, a friendly society for mutual cooperation and burial benefits, and giving a ball to choose the "Queen of Iowa".

The riproaring town acquired many saloons and there was occasional violence. Not all of it was inflicted by the miners. *The Chariton Democrat Leader,* January 11, 1883, reports the story of an area woman who took the law into her own trigger finger on the Ioway frontier.

31

"An Iowa mother shot her daughter last night, seriously wounding her. The mother's name is Cross (we don't doubt it) and she and her two daughters, one evening last week went to a party at the residence of Mrs. Fay Ross. . . . The mother took with her a revolver and when she reached the residence . . . she handed the shooting iron to Mrs. Ross. . . . When the time came she called for the shooting iron herself as her daughters were ready to go home. A young man named Blackridge asked to take one of the girls home. The mother told him that as he did not come with the girls, he would not go home with the daughter. He said he would and started to go with the girl. They had gone a few steps when—snap went the revolver, the ball taking effect in the girl's shoulder. She raised a scream and the young Blackridge took to his heels fearing his turn would come next, leaving the mother and daughter to go home together. The wound is not serious. Blackridge claims the shot was aimed at him. The mother says the pistol went off by accident."

The bubbling, fermenting brew of life went on in Southern Iowa as the miners dug deeper into the earth, and people came to the boomtown with hopes and appetites and loves and a bit of luck for good or ill. If some folks didn't have bad luck they would have had no luck at all. "During the funeral of Mrs. Mary Stebbens of West Lucas on Sunday, Prof. Fellows of the State University, who was driving ahead of the cortege, caught his foot in the laprobe and fell out upon his head. He sustained several cuts upon his cranium and a serious shock to his system. He is seriously ill" (*Iowa State Register,* August 1, 1883).

It wasn't only Prof. Fellows who had a serious shock to his system in 1883 in Lucas, for that was the year that the Big Screen Strike really took hold of the roaring mining town. The strike had started the year before in 1882. The miners were not paid by the hour or day but rather by the coal tonnage they extracted from the mine. The mine operators, Mr. G. C. Osgood, of New York, and Mr. William Haven, of Ottumwa, felt that they had found a way to reduce the miners' wages and increase their profits at a single stroke.

The miners were paid only by the amount of coal which had been "screened". Only the large chunks of coal, which would not pass through a series of screens at the bottom of the wooden tipples, were counted in the miners' tonnage. It was assumed that the larger coal was more convenient for the railroad to handle than the smaller pea coal. When Mr. Osgood and Mr. Havens decided to enlarge the screen openings from the standard one-inch holes to one- and one-half inch screens the miners saw much of their daily wage evaporate. Will Haven later commented on the miners who had helped execute the mine in 1875 that, "I want to make it clear how much we owed to that little group of miners who worked for more than a month with no certainty of pay." Mr. Haven must have calculated in 1882 that he owed the miners more than he wished to pay. Haven had made at least one tactical error in his running of the Whitebreast Coal Company; he hired Tom Lewis.

32

Tom Lewis had no love for the operators to begin with, and together with Dan Jones he helped found the Knights of Labor Local Assembly No. 850. It became the largest affiliate of the Union in Iowa.

Gomer's Revenge

Almost no one has written about the miners' struggle at that time. One exception was Gomer T. Davies, who later became editor of the *Concordia Kansan.* Gomer had an exceptionally difficult early life. He came from Wales in 1863 at the age of eight. At ten he was working in the mines of Pennsylvania. At thirteen he ran away from home, and one year later was working in the mines in Des Moines (where the Capitol Building sits today.) He had lost a leg in a mining accident in Wapello County at twenty, and two years later, in 1877, he was working in the Cleveland Mine of Lucas, hobbling about on his peg leg.

In 1937, when he was an old man, Gomer recalled his relationship with John L. Lewis' father, Tom. "We all lived on adjoining town lots [in 1878] in Lucas. Yet we lacked much of intimate friendship. Really we didn't get along."

"Tom's views as to the relation twixt employee and employer were extremely radical in disfavor of the employer. He belonged to the Knights of Labor. So did I. I didn't like that either. . . . We were engaged in a strike (in 1882). Frequent mass meetings of all the employees were held. Only a small number of all the employees were members of the Knights of Labor but its members knew of its existence. Its leaders held that if this secret order voted, by even a majority of one to pursue its radicalism in the open mass meeting, that every one of its members should advocate and vote such a radical procedure. . . . No doubt I was the only one in possession of Cushing's Manual of Parliamentary Law, bought in 1880. I flatly refused such action of the secret order, thus incurring the wrath and enmity of a dangerous element. . . ."

Gomer must have, in fact, feared Lucas' dangerous element for later in the same year he quit the mines for good and came to Kansas, where he became rather famous for his tirades against organized labor and Lucas' most notable champion of labor, John L. Lewis.

Souls of Black Folks at the Whitebreast

Gomer, of course, was not the only Lucasite to dislike Tom Lewis and his boy, John L. The fact is Gomer left town before things really got hot in Lucas. By March of 1882 the Big Screen Strike had taken a course that was usual in labor conflicts of the day. Blacks were brought in to break the Knights of Labor Strike. They came by the dozens in freight cars at first and later by the hundreds. They would work with the larger screens and the fewer dollars, and they would do it because the work of the mine and the wrath of the white workers was less an evil than the poverty they had come out of. By May of 1882, the first black miner had died in the Lucas mines, and black folk had been baptized in the sometimes-hellish life and death of the mine worker.

33

There were constant rumors of violence between the black strike breakers and the Welsh, English, Scot and Irish on the other side. In October of 1882, *The Democrat Leader* reported on the situation in Lucas. "It seems to be the war of the races . . . the determination seems to be that the negroes [sic] must go. We have talked with a number of white miners and they tell us that the conduct of the colored men is such that it is impossible for the two races to live there in peace and safety. . . . It would not be surprising to hear of a deadly encounter, and if it comes, it will no doubt be a bloody one."

At some point the white workers did go back to the mines for a time, but by the following year they were out on strike again. There was indeed anger and there was violence but it was not of the mob variety, black vs. white. The anger came out in other ways. On Valentine's Day in 1883, a mysterious and destructive fire broke out at four in the morning in the main business area of Lucas. It started between the American Hotel and Garfinkle's Clothing Store. As the Chariton Fire Department sent a streamer and hose car to the coal town, the hotel, drug store, Dr. DeWitt's office, a restaurant, ice house—all in all sixteen frame buildings—went up in flames. Only some goods and property were salvaged from the flames, which blew from the West, licking and consuming the heart of the town. The local newspaper reported that "Employees who have investigated seem to believe that it was incendiarism."

Lucas was to have other fires, and no one knows if or by whom the fire was set. Was it revenge and did it have to do with the strike? What about the incidents reported by the *Iowa State Register* on July 6th of 1883. The first article offers that "the colored men went to work in the Whitebreast Mines yesterday. There was no violence offered, nor even threats uttered by the white strikers." That is reasonable and cool-headed. In the same paper, we find a note on personal turmoil which turns or nearly-turns to violence.

Margaret Waddell's husband, the English miner, had left her for another woman sometime before 1880, and he had left her with three sons and a daughter to raise. They had come from England to Lucas by way of West Virginia, and since John Waddell had left his family he was not respected in the town. He married again, with disastrous results.

"The old man Waddell, at the Cleveland Mines, who was charged with the awful crime of rape upon his step-daughter appears to have been the victim of a faithless and scheming wife. The preliminary examination revealed a plot on the part of the wife to get rid of her husband, she preferring the companionship of another husband from whom it is said she was not divorced when she married Waddell. She publicly charged him with an attempt to violate the person of her 13-year-old daughter, hoping in this way to frighten him away from her, and aroused such a feeling in the community against him that the miners assembled with a view of lynching him. On the trial it was shown that there was not a shadow of truth in the terrible charge. What a dreadful thing it would have been if the mob had succeeded in hanging an innocent man."

Poor old man Waddell, a close call for the hapless man. The miners proved that they were ready to form a mob and ready to do violence. Again they stopped. Still the generalized anger must have remained. The operators seemed to have the upper hand but the stike continued with Tom Lewis leading the way. The strike had gone off and on for more than a year. In April of 1883 it was off; in May the miners were out again. Some of the striking miners hired out to farmers when they could. Fishing and hunting were no longer exursions into the countryside for a lark; they were a way of keeping the family fed. Gardens were set out near the company houses or on friends' plots of ground. The miners alternated between hunger and the desire for justice.

Iowa State Register, July 17, 1883: "Three more cars of Virginia Negroes arrived at the Whitebreast mines last Saturday. Last night a couple of the black fellows had a quarrel about a woman, and during the melee one was killed. The murderer was brought to this city (Chariton) and lodged in jail. There seems to be no prospect of settling the strike—the white man must go."

We see at this point two facets to the nature of race relations in the strife-ridden mining town. First and most importantly, a black man (unidentified) was killed by another (unidentified) over a woman. There were perhaps three black men in the camp per woman, and that was clearly the source of great tension. Why were not the victim and his killer important enough to be named? The answer may be all too obvious because they were black and because of the self-conscious racism of the time and place. Yet the reporter, unlike his counterpart of the year before, argues that "the white man must go." Again it is all too clear that the economic interests of the operators overrides the endemic racism of the period.

In fact, in the strange world of the struggling Knights of Labor and Mr. Haven and Mr. Osgood, even racial tolerance becomes suspect when it coincides so nicely with the exploitation of labor. Two days after the *Register's* report on July 17, a strangely tolerant and strangely-worded statement appeared in a neighboring town's newspaper—a suspect tolerance indeed. It was the *Oskaloosa Weekly Herald,* a Republican newspaper with an anti-labor bent.

"Give the Nigger a Chance" is the byline. "It is evident from the howl of the pretended monopolist of friendship for labor, that so far as this section is concerned a 'Virginny nigger' has no rights a white man need respect. These colored men from Virginia have no right to endeavor to work out a substantial betterment for themselves. It's an awful crime against the white man the moment he comes west to find labor that will recompense him, and allow him to supply his family with the ordinary comforts of life," the paper begins sarcastically. "Now we take it that unless the Declaration of Independence is a lie that there colored men have a certain God given right to go where they please, and as long as matters are satisfactory to them, as to work and wages, and they behave themselves, it is nobody else's business. . . . We have sympathy for laboring men, but it does not savor of a different flavor for one class as against another. We have long since got over that beastly prejudice that marks the wallowing place of nearly all of these latter day so called defenders of labor. . . . We have faith that the colored man will successfully work out his own salvation. His enterprise in getting out of those valleys of Virginia, where labor was illy paid, where school advantages were next to nothing, his great industry here are all hopeful signs. . . . The question of wages is for him to settle: he can either work or leave it alone, exercising the same sweet privilege that other people do. . . ."

The miners, both black and white, must have been amazed at their dilemma of working for less monies for more hours of work, or striking, with the old devil, hunger, hovering round the door as "a sweet privilege." The privilege in 1883 in the Lucas mines belonged, obviously, to Mr. Haven and Mr. Osgood, who had the power to replace a truculent workforce with one more to their account book's liking.

It was good crop weather in the summer of 1883 in Lucas, and that was expecially important for the miners on strike. Since large families were the order of the day, large gardens were necessary but not really sufficient for the needs of the strikers. Many went hungry. *The New York Times* took note of the strikes on July 26, 1883. They reported on a meeting between the operators and representatives of the miners. "John Bulger (a representative of the miners) said the main trouble between the operators and the miners was the size of the screen apparatus, which had been getting larger. Miners should be paid for the coal they dig and the owners should screen it afterward to suit themselves." The owners referred the miners' demand to a committee, which would report back in late August. Many of the miners were beginning to leave Lucas out of disgust or hunger.

The next month the *Register* reported that "The Colored men in the Whitebreast mines are worked at considerable daily loss to the operators. There are over 200 at work and the highest number of cars turned out so far in one day is thirteen. The output of an equal number of experienced men would be sixty to eighty cars. The importation of these negroes [sic] will no doubt be a costly experiment for the Whitebreast Company because as soon as they become experienced they will demand just as much as the white workers (August 7, 1883)."

After the Strike: A Normal Mining Town

Perhaps the lower productivity of the black strike breakers had an effect on the owners. The strike seemed to end ambiguously. Most white workers went back to work. Tom Lewis was fired for his part in the strike. G. C. Osgood vowed that Tom would never work in the mines of Iowa again. He made good his pledge to blacklist the Welshman by sending letters to coal operators all over the state. Tom packed up his few belongings, and with his wife, Louisa, and his two-year-old child, John L., moved to Colfax. There he worked in the mines only a short time before Osgood's letter put him out of a job. He was to move several more times before returning to Lucas some fifteen years later.

Some of the miners moved to the mining camps at Fort Dodge or the Angus Coal Camp near Perry. The Lucas boys who moved to Angus were looking for peace and a decent living wage in the mines. It was not to be in Angus for in September of 1884 a strike was called by the Knights of Labor in the town. Naturally, strike breakers were brought in and, unlike the Lucas strike, mass violence did follow. The State Militia was called out in late 1884 to quell the violence, but in the first week of January of '85 about 30 "blackleg" workers were surrounded by several hundred, angry miners and attacked with rocks and clubs. The violence was ugly, and it was the sure result of men and women struggling for existence. Several of the strikebreakers retreated to a shack, where they exchanged gunfire with the union miners. One strikebreaker was killed. By the time the sheriff and the militia had arrived, the miners had attacked a boarding house, killing one strikebreaker and wounding several others. The mines closed down immediately and some miners straggled back to Lucas.

Wild Times in the Coal Camp

What was Lucas like in 1884? Good and evil and absurd in large part but unquestionably alive with the energies of her immigrant peoples. The screening question hadn't really been settled and the miners were trying to get a state law to standardize the screen. They failed. The Whitebreast Company was sinking the shaft for the Number 3 Mine. A. M. Reid was the chief organizer for the Wilkins Assembly No. 850 of the Knights of Labor. He was also running for the state legislature as a populist Greenbacker. The Greenback party was popular among the miners, for it was the political expression of their resentment toward the monied classes. There was plentiful reason for that in Lucas.

Mostly, however, political issues of the day took a back seat to personal concerns. Several folk had contracted typhoid fever or the deadly cholera morphus. A few others had the measles in the winter of the year. Then, too, older folk were prone to be struck down with a bout of bilious fever. At least once a week the ambulance wagon rattled into town, carrying a miner with some part of his body crushed and bleeding.

Nevertheless, more was happening in the town than suffering, disease and troubles. The miners were a joining lot and they joined the Good Shepherd Lodge, or the Wapello Tribe of the O.R.M., or the Odd Fellows, or the Grand Army of the Republic, or the Court Queen of Iowa No. 6970 Ancient Order of Foresters—where holidays were celebrated and friends greeted again. People got together at the Knights of Pythias or the Druid's Hall and had really good times.

The Welsh congregated at the Druid Hall on Friday of each week for meetings of Lucas Lodge No. 21 of the I.O.G.T. (The Independent Order of Good Templars), which was organized with the purpose of "saving the young and pure from ever falling into the snares of the tempter." Since Lucas had more than a dozen saloons the Good Templars had their work cut out for them.

As Spring came to the coal camp, there was a feeling akin to exhilaration that some folks felt. On March 1st of 1884, J. Y. Stier, the editor of the *Lucas Ledger,* was fairly bursting with enthusiasm:

"Lucas had woke up from her slumbers and shaken the dust and rust of inactivity from her garments and with pockets of scrip, silver and gold, she now cuts a shine. The sidewalks and streets are now filled with people, places of amusement are well patronized, the peddler is seen upon his beat and the vender of notions is heard bellowing from his stand on the street corner all day long. Occasionally some poor fellow who has taken too much brown stout is taken up the hill and cast into prison. The pop of a pistol is now and then heard and the sound of the banjo and the violin and the noise of the merry dancers wake up the silence of the night. The click of the cue and the chuck of the balls is heard upon the gaming tables, and the loud laugh of him who wins all around. You might as well try to dam up the waters of the Whitebreast with cornshucks, as to try to stop the mirth and jollity of her people or to check her progress in wealth and enterprise. Yes, my kind reader, old times have come and come in advance of the joyful birds of Spring."

A rollicking, brawling rounder of a town Lucas was in the Spring of 1884. As to old times coming back to the place, it was only eighteen years old— barely an adolescent. To be sure, it was a wild adolescent and a mixed breed, full of the vitality of many kinds of people, young and vigorous and often drunk when not in the workplace dungeons a mile below the surface of the Southern

Iowa hills. Further, the town was invigorated and constantly challenged by its rapidly growing ethnic mix. Bill Campbell, the Scotsman, ran one of the hotels in town. T. T. Jones, the Welshman, cooked up a fine oyster stew at his restaurant. J. C. Baker, from Indiana, would sell you glassware, groceries or dried fruits. J. C. Christensen sold everything from cigars to organs at the Swede Store. One could get "doctored" and drugs from the English M.D., C. H. De Witt, and his drugstore. Jacob Lovchinskey, the Jewish merchant, claimed to sell clothing "lower than ever known in the history of this country". Bill Patterson, a black miner living in the Cleveland neighborhood, sold bootleg spirits to many Lucasites.

Then, of course, there was Herber Heller, the Polish peddler, who boarded with seventeen Swedes and one German in the home of the Irishman, James Welsh!

Later in the year, the Cleveland No. One and Two mines were bringing up black diamonds at a record pace from a mile under the earth. One day before Christmas, they brought up 560 tons of coal from the No. One shaft and 1,467 tons from the second mine. That was not a tonnage that would be maintained but it was a spectacular feat for a day's work. One day in the same year, Baker's Store took in more than $1,000 cash. The town was coming into its own. It was hearing the rhythm of success.

Success in a mining town is not like success in more gentryfied or bucolic places. It carries with it an exuberance which sometimes goes to extremes— especially with the aid of what the Temperance leaders called "the demonic democratic brew"—alcohol in all its forms. Since many of the miners were in the midst of good times, they had the money to spend on liquor, and their grinding, dirty and dangerous toil encouraged the sipping, swigging or swallowing of brain-numbing libations. That, of course, led to all the excitement the folks could handle. "A colored gentleman of East Cleveland is for a few days languishing in the County Jail on account of thumping his wife," the *Lucas Recorder* reported. The use of alcohol was suspected as the cause of the "thumping."

In fact, shootups and knockdowns were almost daily occurrences. While it is true that black and white miners did get along rather well as a group, it is also a fact that individual miners of different ethnicity were wont to seek trouble with each other.

Here is the sum of one day's reportage of the rough doing in Lucas in the Spring of '84, as given by the *Lucas Ledger*. Homer Thorn and David Litz were arrested for fighting and fined $5.00 each. Green and Spinner were arrested for fighting, with the same result. Bill Johnson and Caeyer Johnson were arrested for disorderly conduct. John Jackson was arrested for whipping his wife and was fined $5.00. Phil Jones charged John Jackson with assault on his person and John danced again to the sum of $5.00. Paul Jones, a brother to Phil Jones, had his head "somewhat impaired at the 'Colored Ball' and Dr. Wilson applied the balm of relief to the gent's cranium."

A man named Sparks was pulled off the Lucas streets for using unbecoming and perhaps creative language and fined $5.00. After being released, Sparks decided to take revenge on the arresting officer, Mr. Lane, pulling his whiskers and beard out "in such a lively manner", for which he was arrested by Marshal McCracken (who, one hopes, was beardless).

Then there was the case of Joseph James. Joe was a black man who came with other miners to have a drink or two at one of the Lucas saloons. The Cleveland neighborhood was dry and forbade any sort of liquor served in public places. On the last Sunday of February, "Quite a few white and colored people were loaded up with more poor whiskey than they could comfortably carry, which caused several fights. . . . The Marshall attempted to pull Joseph James; Joe thought he would not rather languish in the Lucas jail, deliberately drew a couple of revolvers, commonly called *POPS,* and informed the officer not to advance too close to him. Joseph retired in good order to his place of abode in Cleveland."

Mr. James may have acted hastily in pulling his revolvers on the Lucas Marshall. Then again he was, in all probability, aware of the racist nature of justice in Nineteenth Century American mining camps. For on the same day it is reported that: "A white man (Henry Turpin) and (John Jackson) a negro [sic] man went out south of town for the purpose of settling a little difficulty between them." They had been gambling and had a falling out over the results of their game. "After getting out of the city the white man commenced shooting at the negro, fired five shots, the negro was arrested but the white man was not taken. Dr. Wilson was called in to see the colored man, and relieved him of some of the cold lead that was shot into him." We note that the black man was arrested on the spot for the crime of being shot, while his white attacker was not. In all fairness to Lucas justice, Henry Turpin was later arrested and charged with the crime.

No Race War in Town

What is amazing about the relationship between the black and white miners is not their occasional violence, which seems random and sporatic, but the real lack of organized conflict between the two groups. The old folks around town used to say that Blacks and Whites got along pretty well and the evidence that exists suggests they were right. It became a common practice to use black strikebreakers in later years. This almost inevitably led to violence in the mines of Pennsylvania, the meat packing industry in East St. Louis, the metal trades of Detroit, the steel mills of Pittsburgh, or the Illinois Central strike of Waterloo, Iowa, in 1911. The violence in those labor clashes was bitter and riotous. Many men were killed. Again, why not in Lucas? The answer may be that the miners of the town really never thought of themselves as white people. Americans were and are still very quick to slice the social world into black and white. Yet the large majority of the miners in Lucas were immigrants, themselves. They thought of themselves as Welsh, Scot, Swedish, or Irish, not as American white folk. While the miners must certainly have held antagonism toward the Black from Virginia, it was not due to an elaborate myth of racial superiority, which held sway in America at that time. It was all the more likely that they resented the individual who was taking their job away. While it may be true that "When the troughs are empty, the horses bite each other," the mainly Welsh miners may well have understood that it was not the black men who were their enemies.

Only one year before the Lucas strike, a strike took place at Coalville, a few miles away. Hubert Olin describes the white-black situation there as interesting in an important way. The operator of the Coalville Mine brought in seventy-five blacks from Tennessee and paid them $.75 per ton, as opposed to the $1.50 the white miner received. The white miners, mostly immigrants, met with the black strikebreakers and promised them that if the blacks would refuse to work, the white miners would furnish them with the food and shelter they would need to live on. The black miners agreed with this and no violence ensued. Finally both Blacks and Whites moved to Fort Dodge to the mines to work together there.

Many of the Welsh miners in Lucas may have shared the view of a recent immigrant from the old country, John R. Williams. In 1895 Williams wrote back to friends in Aberdare about his experiences in the mines of Pennsylvania and West Virginia. Williams complained that the Welsh were in disfavor with the coal operators because of their radicalism and willingness to go on strike to protest wage cuts and bad working conditions. About two-thirds of the workers in Williams' mine were black. "I am extremely fond of them," Williams writes, "and have not the slightest trouble with them since I have been here. . . . I trust them very respectfully and show them that I respect their race and they appreciate that more than words can tell, for most white people treat them otherwise, which is the greatest mistake. The poor niggar [sic] has been shamefully abused and ill-treated by white men, more the shame to them. Even the niggar children when you meet them on the road are different to white children, the former are polite and thoroughly well behaved, with no coarse language, the white children, quite the reverse, a filthy low set."

Williams goes on to say that: "The white man of this state is about the most contemptible person on the face of God's earth. . . . These detestable cranks seem to think that the poor niggar was made to receive their insults and brutality. . . ."

The nineteenth-century Welsh working people were oppressed by English capitalists, and they had developed a fierce partisanship for the underdog. No doubt they brought this attitude to Lucas, and no doubt this influenced their attitudes toward the blacks in the Lucas mines.

By 1890 the boomtown wasn't booming anymore and most of the Welsh and Scots and blacks had left town for other mining camps. Life was just as hard there as in Lucas. In fact, they loaded up several of Lucas' two-room company houses and sent them to What Cheer or Buxton or Hiteman.

41

Some of the miners believed the Lucas mines would open yet again. They were tired of traipsing around from one company town to the next. Some decided they would stay in Lucas. The town might boom again and if it didn't, they would make do somehow.

And Lucas Begat John L. Lewis

"To his beloved coal miners, who revered him and loved him as the Jews loved Moses leading them out of the wilderness—he was the great hope."
(*United Mine Workers Journal,* June 15, 1969.)

The few old folks in Lucas who remain to tell the stories of young John L. Lewis are well-practiced at their tales. People still want to know if he was a power-seeking devil or a savior of the working people of America. He was more to the point when he would say of himself, "I am something of a man." He was bragging and telling the truth at the same time. No one else in town was ever likely to be on the cover of *Time* Magazine. No one else would have articles about their doings in *Newsweek, The Nation, Colliers, The Atlantic,* etc., etc.

Johnny Lewis left Lucas to change the face of America. He didn't exactly intend that. All he knew was that he would make a mark on the world. He knew that working folks were not given a fair shake, especially those who did the dirtiest and most dangerous work. He also knew it was risky to work for justice. His dad's life taught him that much.

John was only two years old when the big strike hit the Lucas mines. His dad was the ringleader of the Knights of Labor. He meant to lead the miners to a confrontation with Mr. Osgood and Whitebreast Coal. He was angry at the wage slavery the miners worked under, the way their wages could be cut at the whim of the operators. It was damnable business. Strike breakers were brought in and after months of struggle, the miners, half-starved, caved in to the operators. When the other miners were called back to work, Tom Lewis wasn't. Mr. Osgood saw to that.

Tom Lewis was a marked man. He would never work in an Iowa mine again because of his union activities. Mr. Osgood sent out letters to all the mine operators in the state, telling them to blackball the Welsh radical, Mr. Lewis. It was to be hard times for the Lewis family.

John L.'s mother, Ann Louisa, was a generous and affectionate woman— red-haired, attractive, and pious. She would often take baby John to visit her mother, Sarah Watkins. Grandpa John Watkins was a Welsh miner, and he and his wife and three children at home took in boarders. Grandma Sarah would take care of the injured Welsh miners and three of them boarded with her.

Ann Louisa was close to her mother and they both became members of the Reorganized Saints Church. She would carry baby John to church two or three times a week. The Saints were talking of the Kingdom of Heaven and how one day perfect justice would obtain down here on earth. The lamb would lay down with the lion and both would get up alive later.

John L. was to become the mirror image of his dad. Thomas Lewis was a large man, broad of shoulders, heavy set, with bushy eyebrows and a bright look to his eyes. He told John L. the lessons he had learned in the mines and in the Knights of Labor. He told him to be a fighter. He told him about the Lucas miners' fear of helping him when the blacklist came. Times were always hard for the Lewises but never quite desperate. Tom moved his family out of Lucas in 1882. He brought not only John but also his new baby brother, Tom, Jr. He sought work up at the mines near Colfax, Iowa, but was fired when his employers got word of the blacklist. Again the family pulled up stakes, which now included the new baby, George.

If Tom Lewis was constantly looking for work, Ann Louisa was never without it. She gave birth to six children, and her routine of feeding, washing, and clothing the children was done usually in a clapboard and tarpaper house without indoor plumbing or electricity. Early on, little Johnny Lewis would help his ma as much as he could.

When John L. became famous, he told people that his family had never lived in a real shack. There was always food on the table but things were tight and the Lewises just got by. Tom did police work in Des Moines in the early 1890's. The moves of the Lewis family were like those of countless other Welsh, Scotts, or English miners in Southern Iowa at the time. They adapted, but leaving home behind, even a home like Lucas, is to dismantle the center of the world. Home is a place to hang one's hat. But it is more than that. It is a place of refuge against the chaos in the world. Tom Lewis and his family needed to come home to Lucas.

In 1897, he did just that, came back to Lucas. He moved next door to his wife's parents. The Cleveland No. 1 Mine had just closed and The Big Hill Mine was hiring. Tom was taken off the blacklist. He could work again in the dark, earthen tunnels under Lucas. Fathers and sons often worked together in one of the rooms of the mine. It was a matter of trust, for one thing.

Tom Lewis bought a farm south of Lucas. He must have saved some money in his fifteen-year, forced exodus from Lucas, and he put it to good use. By the 1890's work in the Lucas mines, as well as in most others in the state, was seasonal. There was not much work in the Spring of the year and that was the time for plowing and planting. The Welsh were never far from their agrarian connections and skills even as they spent their years in the coal mines.

The people who knew John L. in his younger years have largely died off in Lucas today, but fragments, moments, and stories of John L.'s Lucas days still appear from time to time.

Sadie Page was ninety-five years old in 1965 and she lived up the street from Doc Bell's old office. She remembered Lucas' most famous son as a child. John L. Lewis was seven years old when Sadie came to town as a seventeen-year-old bride. Her pa was a carpenter who mainly worked on coffins. He had plenty of work in Lucas in 1887. Johnny had so many freckles you couldn't get a pin between them and a mop of reddish-brown hair that flopped when he ran. "There were three mines operating here then," she would reminisce to the reporter from the Des Moines Register. "There were two schools: Children of the Negro miners had their own with Negro teachers. Two years after we came here my husband, Abe, went to work in the mines as a timber man. At that time Johnny Lewis was a trapper boy—the boy who opens the doors to let the little coal cars through a passage." Sadie's memories of seventy years before were hazy but she remembered the important things about the Lucas boy who made good.

Others remembered John L. as never drinking or smoking, as a good boy raised in the Saints Church would avoid those sins. Older men remembered John L. as a fighter. He was big and strong, and he carried himself well. One story says he would go up to the Jericho Hill in Lucas and fight young fellows his age, not out of anger, just to show that he could "whup 'em."

Another story nearly all his biographers tell is that when John L. was working in the Lucas mine he was kicked by a mule named Spanish Pete. The mules and horses who worked in the mines were among the few of God's creatures who had a tougher life than the miners themselves. They would be blindfolded and hoisted down the mine when they were three years old. They would never see daylight again until they were sixteen or more years old if even then. So when Spanish Pete kicked John L. and trapped him in one of the mine rooms well over three hundred feet beneath the earth, he had his mulish reasons.

It is said that John L. hit the mule solid in the head with his huge, hamhock fist. He stunned him. Then John L. picked up a sprang, the wooden "tongue" from the coal car and brained the creature. Afterwards he put clay in the wounds and told the bosses the mule just dropped dead, probably of a heart attack.

When the owner of the Farmers and Miners Bank in Lucas, Gerald Baker, asked John L. if he had actually done that thing, John L. said, "I'm not saying yes, and I'm not saying no, but don't it make a hell of a story."

Irene Evans, who lived in Lucas all her years, recalled that she didn't like John L. When he came over to visit friends where she was visiting as a young girl, he would always say, "Irene, you'd better get home. Your mamma's calling you." "No," she'd say, "she's not. I can't hear her at all." "She sure is, Irene, and you're in big trouble," John L. would say with a great, silly grin. He was always one to tease and laugh. He would laugh whenever he got a chance. Irene liked John L.'s brother, Tom, better. He was more serious and thoughtful. When Irene got older she realized that John L. was teasing and flirting a little bit, and she began to have a fondness for him.

John did more than tease and work the mines. He dabbled in various businesses in Lucas. At the turn of the century he was managing the Lucas Opera House and playing roles as well—everything from Shakespeare to Uncle Tom's Cabin. Cecil Carnes said of him. "His jaw became the most prominent landmark in Lucas . . . Sampson must have looked like him. His bushy eyebrows, black as the coal he mined, his great bulk, powerful voice, even his uncontrollable hair fitted the description. . . . He became by some sort of mutual consent, a Justice of the Peace. But he never tried any cases. Most Lucas litigation wore off in fist fights."

In the early days in Lucas John L. was an odd mixture of enthusiast and fatalist, and these two sides of the man never left him after he moved from Lucas. That was because he still believed in some way that he could become somebody more than he was. His anger over the plight of the miners who risked their lives for $1.60 per day in Lucas was coupled with the idea that something could be done about it. On the other hand, there is a deep fatalism in many miners, and it comes from breathing dirty air in accident-prone, near-total blackness of the mine shafts. In John L.'s time, the miners in Lucas would often be heard to say, "Guess I'll take my chances—my time hasn't come yet." Deep shaft miners take chances every day which would paralyze the average person. That was how they lived their lives.

By 1901 Lucas had seen better and more prosperous days, and even though his mother, Ann Louisa, bore another child that year, John was not needed in the family's household. For the next few years he wandered about the Western United States, using his mining skills to gain work. In 1903, he was said to be at the mine disaster in Hanna, Wyoming. Saul Alinsky says that John L. worked on a rescue team, carrying out the charred bodies of two hundred and thirty-four miners. The descent into the mine that had become a charnel house was for Lewis a descent into hell, but what ripped his emotions to shreds was the sight of the numb, mute faces of the wives—now suddenly widows of the men they loved. It was at Hanna, Wyoming, that John L. Lewis was baptized in his own tears.

John came back to Lucas in 1905, or thereabouts, with little money and much to think about.

While in Lucas he joined the Good Shepherd Lodge of the Masons and was made the Junior Warden of the group. His friends from the mines made up most of the membership, and his future father-in-law, Doc Bell, headed the group.

John also started a feed and grain store in Lucas with his friend John Brown. This made him no more money than his work with the Opera House. Many of his creditors simply didn't pay up and John was hard-up for cash.

Gradually John became romantically involved with a young woman of high social standing in Lucas. This was Myrta Bell, the daughter of the town's leading doctor, John C. Bell. The Bells were far better off than the Lewis family although they were not rich. The Lucas social news was often filled with the doings of Myrta and her sister, Florence Bell. Myrta was even sent to Drake University for enough summer sessions to become a teacher. She taught a number of years in Lucas. Her examination of the State of Iowa showed her best subjects to be Physiology and Hygiene (remember, her pa was a doctor), Writing, Grammar, and History. These latter subjects would all be helpful to her future husband.

In a sense Myrta Bell was everything John L. was not—quiet, demure, and, as they would say at that time, cultivated. John L. was outgoing, well-traveled, likeable, and full of the Welsh charm. John L. said that they had known each other for fifteen years before they wed. Both were twenty-seven when they were married in 1907. John was not attending the Saints Church at the time, which grieved his mother sorely. So they went to a town west of Lucas to be married. A local paper described the ceremonies.

> Mrs. J. D. Beaman entertained the O.C.B.C. Club Monday night who had a linen shower for Miss Myrta Bell who is to be married soon. The dining room was tastefully decorated in white and yellow crepe paper. Strands of this paper being suspended from the chandelier to corners of the room and also to the table. The room was lighted with thirty candles. A two course lunch was served, the bride-elect pouring out coffee and Mrs. N. F. Baker presiding at the chafing dish. The evening was spent in various amusements and the guests departed at a late hour, wishing Myrta much happiness in her married life.

> Myrta, daughter of Dr. and Mrs. J. C. Bell, and Mr. John Lewis went to Osceola yesterday where they were united in marriage. The Rev. Wickard, Pastor of the M.E. Church, officiating. When they returned to Lucas a wedding breakfast was served, relatives and intimate friends being present. The bride, who has been a teacher in public schools for a number of years, is a popular young lady well liked by her friends and all. The groom is a highly respected young man and is worthy of the bride he has won (*Chariton Herald,* June 6, 1907).

Some people say that Myrta became the brains behind John L., but that was not quite true. She did coach him in grammar, diction, and elocution and effective speaking, generally. Yet we must not forget that John L. had those capacities and interests earlier in life when he was working in Knotts Opera House in Lucas. Myrta Bell had become the most important person in his life, but she had only given John L. a push in the direction he was persuing at the time. She expanded his knowledge and reading habits, but John L. was moving toward something neither she nor he could surmise at the time of their marriage.

At the time of their marriage John L. was having only slight success in Lucas.

> Lucas, Iowa, 12-7-1906. United Mine Worker's Local Union 779 met in regular session, Parley Batten in chair, roll call and minutes were read. Tom Harkin's defense bill was $22.00. Correspondence was read. Vote that we send $15.00 to Mrs. Larson of Des Moines. Resolve that we send a delegate

to National Convention. Carried. First vote: W. A. Johns 11, J. L. Lewis 8, Tom Hopkins 4, Parley Batten 6. Second vote: W. A. Johns 17, J. L. Lewis 8. W. A. Johns elected delegate to convention. W. A. Johns, treasurer.

Worse than that John ran for mayor of Lucas the next year and was defeated. Folks said that Doc Bell, his father-in-law, went around town convincing Lucas folk to vote against John L. because Doc was convinced John's future was too big for Lucas to contain. No one was more prophetic than J. C. Bell.

Finally John L.'s feed and grain business was doing badly. These were hard times. John decided to move to Illinois in 1908. They had just set a new mine shaft in the little town of Panama. He took his dad, mother, and several sisters and brothers with him. Over the next year he would come back often to Lucas to pick up belongings and talk to friends.

No one at that time knew that he was to become one of the most powerful men in America, or that he would shape the history of work and workers in the country for decades, or, for that matter, that he would feud with, or be praised by, several presidents of the United States. He was just a Welsh boy from Lucas, Iowa, looking for a break. With a head full of ideas and ideals, he left the quiet town. He would come back almost every year of his life and he would come back to Lucas as a giant.

The lessons Lucas taught him were hard ones about defeat, poverty, injustice, and the frailties of human nature. John L. was to teach America some lessons of his own in later life. They were not always the ones he had intended but they were made with such power that the people of his time listened. The people of Lucas listened as well, with the special pride and interest of folks seeing one of their own make good. John L. would come back to Lucas with stories about the world and Lucas would listen.

PART 3

Going to Grass: Ghost Town Visits (1907–1967)

A Long Forgetting

In 1926 the last big mine had closed down in Lucas for the last time. The Welsh had scattered, the Swedes were gone and only two black families remained. Even before the Great Depression, the Twenties saw a goodly number of poor folks in the town. They were out-of-work miners and those who did day labor for farmers, the old, and those unable or unwilling to leave the place.

Still, the people of Lucas were not so poor as to leave nothing behind. No one is that poor. What people leave is memories, and those memories become stories, and stories become the bonding of one generation to another. Of course, there must be heirs to inherit the memories and stories, and they must be ready to accept the gifts of the story-tellers.

Gradually the stories in Lucas changed. They were not told in Welsh or Swedish anymore for one thing. It may have been that the miners and their families wanted to forget the hard times in the Old Country, to start anew with new American success stories. There weren't many of those in Lucas. The ways of the Old Country were diluted and changed, and the languages of the Swedish Lutheran or Welsh Congregational Churches were forgotten when the buildings closed.

People didn't care much one way or another that the Lucas miners were the first to try to organize the whole state of Iowa into a miners union. It didn't matter to people forty years later. It didn't seem important to most folks that the clashes between capital and labor were intense and unremitting for years and years. Some people, like young John Lewis, had remembered but he left the town nearly twenty years before.

There were a couple of black families in town in 1926, the Osleys and the Rays. Not many folks talked about the hundreds of black miners living in town years earlier. They had moved on to Buxton or Des Moines long ago, and it didn't seem to matter anymore.

Nobody talked much about the Ladies Suffrage League in Lucas and the agitation for women's rights twenty years earlier.

In fact, there was a great forgetting in the town and a great gap arising between those who had worked in the mines when foreign-speaking miners argued the rights of labor, progressive politics and women's emancipation, and those who came into town later when the grass was covering the mines and threatening to cover the roads.

There were some keepers of the flame of memory about the town in its optimistic and progressive days. There weren't many. It didn't help anyone earn a nickel to remember that stuff.

Some people say that the schools are America's great keepers of tradition. Yet the Lucas schools were the primary participants in the town's collective amnesia. The school didn't talk about the cultures which had come into the town or the populist-labor politics or woman's suffrage. The schools taught Iowa History. Everyone took it and learned that the first governor of Iowa was named Lucas, and nothing much else. The Civil War happened someplace else. The wagon trains always passed through Iowa, going to some exciting place. Then there was the "Honey Bee War" between Iowans and Missourians over some stolen bee hives. Nothing to write home about.

Iowa History was perky and positive, not poetical and political. Iowa History books in the 1920's didn't talk about strikes and strike-breakers and race. It didn't seem polite. It was controversial. The less controversy in school the better. So—no chapters on unions and suffrage movements and Blacks and the Greenbackers. The Lucas students read the Iowa History texts when they had to. As they did and as people moved out and died off, the conflictual, controversial, political memories faded. Lucas hadn't started out like most towns but it seemed that it could end like the small towns all over the midwest, dying in its sleep.

There were a few who would remember the old days. For most Lucas folk, the twenties just continued the fall into the town's collective amnesia. Of course, the Lewis boy, John L., was running around the country then, stirring up the working people. He was trying to keep people remembering the miners and their still-same struggles in other places. That sort of memory had to be reinvented just about every generation.

Sometimes the miners would come back to the ghost town, to Homecoming Days at Lucas or the Miners Reunion at Hiteman. Some would drive big, fancy cars. They would pound folks on the back and laugh. And someone might say, "I knew that feller when he worked in the mines. That family was so poor they didn't have a pot to pee in. But look at them now." They had come back from Illinois or Minneapolis and they had done well for themselves. Still, people knew them "back when" and people remembered. No one begrudged those who had left their wealth or good fortune, and it was easy to talk about the old times. However, for the folks who remained in town there was a kind of gap between themselves and those returning. It had to do with the future more than the past, and it pretty much appeared the future was past in Lucas.

Those who left the mining days for jobs in the factories were doing real well in the forties, especially during the war. People from Lucas were living in suburbs—places where people were moving in and building. Lot of nice people back in Lucas, they would think, but I wouldn't like the life. Hard times, they would say. I wouldn't want to go through them again. I've had my fill of 'em. And they would be happy to drive back to their new, indebted houses with the new-wood smell. Of course, when the family had all died off in the old town, they would seldom go back.

When time and money and people pass through abandoned towns, the places never quite go back to nature themselves. The soil, disturbed by the daily lives of men and women grows up with plant life, reflecting the lives and times of earlier gardeners. Thus, vacant lots full of pigweed, crabgrass, and thistles may also hide once domesticated lilies, roses, spearmint and other herbs and perennials. The sounds of the lawnmowers are the sounds of men and women in the village, attempting to forestall the re-emergence of nature which seems to undo the works of their antecedents in the town. Graves, too, are kept with the near-dedication of the pious Japanese. Comment is passed among the older generation about whose grave is "kept up" and whose is not.

Partly this is done to assure that one will be "cared for" in a physical way after death, and partly it is "respect" for the memory of those gone on. In the end, the habitats of the dead are much better kept than those of the living in the near-ghost towns of Southern Iowa. And among the old there, as in other places and times, death is in the matter-of-fact conversation of the elderly.

By the 1950's, vacant lots outnumbered well-groomed lawns in Lucas. Some orchards were chopped down, some were left untended. Those who could care for their trees and lawns fought back the cycle of growth and decay which nature brought in to cover the works of humankind at Lucas. Grass grew in the cracks of the sidewalks and in the middle of less-used roads. It grew tall and shaggy in the vacant lots.

The European aristocrats fought against the rights of the masses through the revolutions of 1789 and 1848. "After us," they said, "the deluge." They knew they were a dying class.

51

In Lucas, the vegetation was gradually undoing the work of the townsfolk. "After us," the townspeople thought, "the grass."

Come Back to Us, John L. Lewis

"He was singular and menacing like a thundercloud rising on the horizon at the end of a perfect day."
—Raoul de Sales

"He loved life, loved the laughter and the joy and the danger of it . . . I saw him weep at the plight of others."
—Saul Alinsky

To describe the next forty years of John L. Lewis' life after he left Lucas is to envision a huge river growing in strength and power, flooding and ebbing, cutting through rock, doubling back upon itself, unstoppable and unpredictable. The power of this human river is the bond between the crusty Welshman from Lucas and the miners, who saw him as "something of a god."

John shook the coal dust of Lucas off himself in Illinois in 1909. With the help of his five brothers, he was appointed to be a one-man grievance committee and head of his local in the Miners Union in Panama, Illinois. By the next year, the union had appointed him to work with the Illinois legislature. That same year a mine explosion and fire had killed one hundred and sixty miners. Lewis raged in the Illinois legislative session and won concession after concession for his miners. He was gaining a reputation.

In 1911, he met Samuel Gompers, the president of the American Federation of Labor. Gompers offered him a job as field organizer. He sent a telegram to Gompers on October 23, 1911. "Message received. Accept position. Leave today for Santa Fe." John was on the road for the union.

In the next few years things moved fast for John. He went back to work in the Miners Union, and by 1918 he was vice-president. Moreover, the president of the union Frank Hays, was often ill or drunk, and it was John L. who ran the day-to-day business of the union. As the great war ended in Europe, the miners saw their standard of living slipping. Miners went on strike all over the eastern half of the country in 1919, and coal supplies were getting low in the homes and industries. After a prolonged struggle, President Wilson called the Lucas boy into his office on December 7. John L. appeared from the White House, saying that "the strike has been settled and the miners were yielding to the greatest government on earth." In later years John L. would yield to no one.

He Brings Home the Bacon

John argued that the mine operators had made fantastic profits during the war years, the greatest in history. While the settlement of the strike increased miners' wages, it was not enough. John Lewis believed that only a 30-hour, five-day week would spread employment and wages to the working people in the mining towns. Later he would propose a six-hour working day, and he would be called unamerican for doing it.

By 1920, Lewis was officially elected president of the Mine Workers Union. These were the times when industrial war was seriously breaking out in America. Miners were living in squalor and poverty when times were "good". When times were "bad", as in the early twenties, they were forced from their houses to wander the countryside. This was not a war of nerves or strategies, but a killing war. In Williamson County, Illinois, in 1922, strikebreakers were armed with machine guns, but they were surrounded by miners and thirty to forty of them were killed. Mine operators were hiring private police officers, who were in fact "hired guns." In Pennsylvania and West Virginia, many striking miners were killed by the operators' private police.

John L. was blamed for much of this and he, in turn, blamed the greed and stupidity of the mine owners and "radicals" or "reds" in his own union for the violence. For all his labor militancy, John L. Lewis was still a Republican. He was attacked by the business interests, who hated unionism, and he was attacked by the miners from Kansas, Illinois and Nova Scotia, who saw him as too cozy with the rich and powerful. Nevertheless, the increasingly famous, jowly John L. Lewis battered his opponents with a voice and manner full of surprising ridicule or sweeping force. John L. kept his opponents off balance.

At one of the conventions of the United Mine Workers, a delegate named Pat Ansbury violently opposed some of John L.'s proposals. John L. replied. "All I can say is that I mined coal in Illinois when delegate Ansbury was herding sheep in Bulgaria," and he looked down at Pat with great, derisive eyes. Pat jumped up and demanded an apology, said everyone knew he was an Irishman. "The president of the United Mine Workers of America does owe an apology," Lewis shouted in his bass voice. "The apology is not to Pat Ansbury, but to the Committee of the Twelve Bulgarians who came to me at noon and protested this insinuation against their group. I hereby apologize to the twelve Bulgarians for even suggesting that Pat Ansbury was associated with them."

John L. did not run the union like a democracy and he did not tolerate dissent. He had led several major strikes for the miners, but the depression was to hurt workers in a massive way. In spite of this America was continuing to industrialize, although more than one-fourth of its workers were without jobs. It was clear to John that those born to wealth did not understand his endless agitation for the workers. When, in the 1930's, a congressman from Texas told John L. that miners were making seventy-five percent more than they had in 1913, John responded that his miners were gifted with many talents but that eating percentages was not one of them.

John was increasingly dissatisfied with the conservative policies of the American Federation of Labor, who only wished to organize skilled trades. Within the group, he and several others formed the Committee for Industrial Organization to unionize the unorganized working people in steel, automobiles, and other forms of mass production. The discussions about the C.I.O. became heated in the extreme at the American Federation Convention of 1935. The miners union delegates sat next to those of the carpenters union, and John L. went over to confer with William Hutcheson, president of the carpenters. He had referred to one of Hutcheson's points as "small potatoes". Hutcheson rose up on his 300-lb. body and glared at Lewis, shouting that he was raised on small potatoes; that was why he was so small. John L. spoke softly to Hutcheson. Hutcheson responded by calling Lewis a "bastard" and the next thing anyone knew John L. had smashed Hutcheson in the face, knocking him over backwards. That was literally John L.'s first blow to organize the unorganized. John L. would claim later that he received a telegraph from a member of the Carpenters Union, saying "Sock him again, John," and he never regretted that he had done it.

John L. Lewis' fight was beginning, and before he would finish he and his C.I.O. (now the Congress of Industrial Organizations) would organize more working people into unions than had ever happened in the history of the United

States. He had begun to profoundly shock the American economic system. A decent wage and safe working conditions were not accidents; they were the rights of Americans. Thus John L. with his eyebrows flaring, his hair now turning grey, and his bull-dog jowls set in determination, was either a bogey man or a savior to the Americans of his time.

He continued to come back to Lucas for rests. His oldest daughter, Margaret Mary, died of pneumonia in the town. Her death was another tragedy for the Lewis family, and his family was about the only thing fiery John L. would trust. John lived in Springfield, Illinois, and he brought as many of his folks from Lucas to Springfield as he could. Myrta's parents, the Bells, left Lucas in their old age, but they would naturally come back to see their lifelong friends. When Doc Bell came back to Lucas, he always brought a cold tonic to young Gerald Baker, who worked at his father's bank in Lucas. Gerald told Doc Bell that the old town would miss him but the old man just shrugged and told him he didn't have the modern tools of medicine to heal the broken people of Lucas. He could ease their pain some—that was about it.

His son-in-law, John L., was trying to ease the pain of the workers in depression-wracked America. Some describe his efforts as dictatorial, mean, and stubborn. That is true. The other side of the man comes out in this letter he wrote his children during the thirties.

AT   HOME

DEAR SON AND DAUGHTER:

        I HAVE READ WITH INTERIST YOUR CORRESPONDENCE ON THE SUBJECT OF DOGS :   needless to SAY iwould PREFERa discussion   on ANOTHER subject,? i suggest THE

        subject of DOG food ha$\frac{1}{4}$ HA.. I mean the RELATIVE cost of feeding A dOg as compared with the cost OF keeping a MILCH cow. HA. HA: in addition COWS do not have to be pu t out -- they are always OUT; HA; HA. do not my observations have the RING OF truth??.

        They DO.

        father.

That was John L., teasing, funning and carrying on. He was still the same fellow who had teased Irene Evans in Lucas. He could still use his fists like he did in Lucas. One thing about John L. was different. He was bigger than when he lived in the town. He was fighting for his vision of justice in America. The entire country was beginning to focus on him and his struggles for the working people.

By 1937, the C.I.O. was attempting to organize the biggest prize of all, the auto industry. General Motors would not recognize the union. Lewis tried every trick he knew to get the big-time industrialists to sit down with him. They would not. Lewis's men got ahead of him. In Flint, Michigan, they sat down on the job and they occupied the Chevrolet plants. Governor Murphy gave orders to mobilize the National Guard. They would be used to attack the sit-down strikers and drive them out of the plants. Mass violence was in the wings.

On the night of February 9, 1937, Governor Murphy came to visit John L. and told him that, as governor, he must obey the law. John L. reminded him of his father and grandfather who were arrested by the British as members of the Irish Republican Army. Murphy's grandfather had in fact been hanged by the British for refusing to obey what he felt were their unjust laws. "You did not say uphold the law in those cases," John L. fumed. John L. then told the governor that each man must do as he must. John L. then said that the next day he would tell his men to disregard the governor's orders to leave the plant and that he, John L., would enter Chevrolet Plant No. 4, remove his shirt and bare his chest. "Then," he said, "when you give the order to fire, mine will be the first chest those bullets strike. . . . As my body falls from the window, you listen to your grandfather as he whispers in your ear, 'Frank, are you doing the right thing?' " According to John L., the governor left the room, shaking. The order to attack never was given, and two days later the United Auto Workers were recognized as the bargaining agent for General Motors. It was without a doubt John's finest hour.

The year before, the C.I.O. had contributed nearly a half-million dollars to the re-election of Franklin Roosevelt, who had shown himself to be a friend of labor. By 1937, however, the labor wars were getting more and more violent, as killings became a way of labor negotiation. On Memorial Day of 1937, about one thousand strikers walked up to the gates of the Republic Steel Mill, in Chicago. Suddenly the police appeared and shot wildly into the unarmed crowd. Thirty people were shot down. In Youngstown, Ohio, a sheriff's deputy shot into a crowd of strikers and killed many of them.

Lewis took his deep, funeral voice to the radio to protest the violence. He did not mention the president but he ridiculed "those who chant their praises of democracy but who lost no chance to drive their knives into labor's defenseless back. It ill behooves one who has supped at labor's table . . . to curse with equal fervor and fine impartiality both labor and its adversaries when they become locked in deadly embrace." Roosevelt spoke his opinion quite clearly. He supported neither labor nor capital in these circumstances—"A plague on both your houses."

John L. Lewis was outraged and threw his support to Wendell Wilkie, Roosevelt's Republican opponent. He bet his future on the outcome of the election. If Roosevelt was re-elected, Lewis would retire as president of the C.I.O. That is exactly what happened. Saul Alinsky sat with John L., Myrta, and his daughter, Katherine in October of 1941. They came together in a hotel in Atlantic City. Big John L. Lewis was in a sad and reminiscent mood. It was in this same hotel that he and others had organized the C.I.O. in 1935. Tears began to run down John's cheeks, according to Alinsky, when he stood up, pushed a table aside, and said, "Here I conceived and built the C.I.O. and here it is that I leave it."

John L. Lewis went back to head the United Mine Workers but not, as it happened, to an uneventful life. He was demanding that all men working in an union-organized mine pay dues for the services the union was doing for them. War was fast approaching in 1941, and John L. believed that labor would only be hurt during the coming conflict since patriotism would be used to stop the only weapon working people have—the strike. Lewis met with Roosevelt several times in October of 1941. Roosevelt said Lewis could not strike on this issue, that it would damage national security. Lewis said he could, and that it was a conflict not about national security but between himself and the multimillionaire, J. P. Morgan. On November 15, Lewis called his miners out on strike in direct opposition to the President of the United States. The threat to send troops to open the mines did not bother him. Coal could not be dug with bayonets, he said.

Two days later President Roosevelt surrendered by appointing a pro-Lewis arbitration board. According to the press, John L. was losing the battle for public opinion. The *Des Moines Register* sent a reporter to Lucas to do a "Now What Do You Think of Him?" story. It came out only six days before the United States became embroiled in World War II.

What Home Town Thinks of Lewis Now*

Lucas, Ia. "Dogs yawn in the streets, an occasional train roars past the red square station and Whitebreast Creek flows west over the coal beds that once were here.

They have been worked out and Lucas, which in the eighties and nineties hummed with 2,000 miners—and 27 saloons on the main street alone—today counts but 534 inhabitants with not a tavern in the village. [This had been remedied by 1985.] The last mine here, the Iowa-Nebraska Co. shaft, shut down in 1923. Since then most of the younger generation born here scattered to other parts of the state. A few have remained around Lucas as farmers.

But at least a fifth of the people are old miners, tired from years of toil in the earth. There is little business here, but N. F. Baker, owner and operator of the Lucas Bank and Grocery Store, continues to serve his patrons as he has for 55 years.

There is a harness shop and a restaurant, too, for those who remain.

But if circumstances have robbed Lucas of its former mining activity, these same circumstances have given townfolk here plenty to talk about.

When a fortnight ago President Roosevelt was forced to address three appeals to the head of the United Mine Workers Union, many people believed 'John L.' had gone too far.

Veteran white haired miners—like Dan Ferry and D. H. Evans and Robert Wilkinson—all saw in his uncompromising attitude the same belligerent nature John L. displayed in the mines at sixteen.

Evans, now 86, who wielded a pick beside Lewis' father and grandfather and who saw John L. Lewis start off at the mines at the age of 12, shook his head. 'I always thought highly of him until this last trouble came along. I think John has gone way too far in being the way he has been to the president. . . .'

When the (Lewis) family returned to Lucas in about 1900, John L. and his father went to work for the Big Hill Coal and Mining Co. and in Lucas today, there lives all alone in a 2-room frame shack the miner under whom John L. Lewis worked.

Robert Wilkinson, 72, a native of Northumberland, England, and a resident of Lucas since 1879, remembers well the bushy haired youth who was destined to head the world's largest trade union. 'Lewis drove mules— pulled coal for me at the Big Hill. He was a good worker. He was a good man. . . .' Wilkinson recalls also the working conditions in the mines those days. They aren't pleasant for him. 'The air was pretty thin. We came home more than one day because there wasn't any air in the mines.'

Wilkinson implied he'd be 100 percent behind Lewis were it not for the national emergency. 'But because of this the miners have got to go easy so as to help those boys going to war.' Then reflecting on Lewis' success in organizing the Congress of Industrial Organization, Wilkinson asserted vigorously, 'Sure Lewis got things done. But that was because we also had a president who did more for labor than any other president. I mean Roosevelt.'

One old settler remembers Lewis only as a kind of pugilistic fellow. This is Dan Ferry, 82, a native of Scotland and coal miner from the age of 12 until he was 32. Remarking on the many battles Lewis has had in the last decade with various tycoons of industry, Ferry spoke slowly. As he spoke he looked from the porch of his cottage far over the hills toward Lucas.

'Well Lewis has not been any harder on the corporations than they were on his father and grandfather. And I'll stand by that.' "

The *Register* reporter, George Coleman, had picked up on the complex feelings of anger, pride, and respect the old Lucas folk held toward John L. Lewis. They, for the most part, loved President Roosevelt. They respected the local hero made good, and the two were in combat. Even heroes need to be spanked once in a while. "Getting the big head" was not an approved mode of thought in Lucas. Beyond this reality, Dan Ferry pointed out a key to understanding John L.'s view of the world, and that was what the corporations did to John's dad, Tom Lewis.

It was J. C. Osgood who had fired Tom Lewis in the great strike of 1882. It was Osgood who had blacklisted John L.'s dad. After he left Lucas, Osgood became president of the Rockefeller-owned Colorado Fuel and Iron Corporation. John used to tell his friends in Lucas about the strange quirk of fate which sent John L. to face Osgood in New York in the 1930s. They were on opposite sides of the negotiating table. Osgood looked at John L. Lewis in a puzzled manner. He did not quite recognize John. "Say, don't I know you from somewhere? Your face looks familiar." "Yes," shouted John Lewis. "You're the son of a bitch that nearly starved my family to death." Such stories show as much as anything can how Lucas, Iowa shaped this giant of the labor movement.

These stories also show how John L. was able to articulate the anger of the many working people who were not in a position to tell off the rich and powerful. John L. spoke up for those afraid to speak up for themselves, and so many of the working people of Lucas and other places could forgive him his ego and his large mistakes. People in Lucas had warm feelings for John L., some counted him as a friend. In the mining towns still digging black diamonds with human sweat, the miners *worshipped* John L. Many miners' cabins would have a picture of John L. Lewis and a picture of the Virgin Mary on otherwise bare walls.

Lucas, of course, was "played out" by the early forties. John L. Lewis was just getting his second wind. He was hurt and angry at the American people who didn't understand his struggles for the miners. In 1943 the most crushing blow of all hit John. His wife, Myrta, died. The miners idolized John L. Lewis, but only his wife had traveled the miles and years from Lucas with him. With her death he had only the miners, and it appeared to them that John L. was their only defender.

In that year of the war, the miners were walking off the job in Pennsylvania. Wage and price controls were supposedly holding down inflation but in reality, prices of all manner of things, including coal, were increasing drastically. After much futile negotiation, John L. told the members of the United States Senate that the miners were not getting medical care, and that their families were unable to buy meat. The mine operators brought in a vegetarian nutritionist, who said meat was harmful anyway.

On April 22, 1943, John L. called the miners out on another strike. In the midst of the World War, Lewis was villified with charges of treason in the daily newspapers all over the country. Cartoons showed him stabbing an American soldier in the back. The Republicans and the Communists alike attacked John L. as a traitor and a saboteur. It was clear that the half million coal miners in the country saw John L. Lewis as their "Commander in Chief" and they would only go to work "when John L. tells us to." *Stars and Stripes* printed a commentary on John L., ending with this: "Speaking for the American soldier, John L. Lewis, damn your coal black soul."

The half million miners on strike watched John L.'s maneuvering for nearly eight months. Finally, John L. won the battle for the miners. They were awarded $1.50 more per day. And John L. was the most hated man in America.

He found solace in coming back to Iowa. The *Des Moines Register* did another check on what the home folks thought of John L. in August of 1945. With a byline of "The Old Hometown and John L. Lewis," the *Register* concluded that "just a wee bit of the shiny paint is beginning to peel off the idol of this one-time thriving mining community—just enough to reveal some flaws." The worst Tommy Hopkins would say about John was that he was a bit too extreme.

Herb Owens, the reporter for the *Register,* quoted Norm Baker, the owner and cashier of the Farmers and Miners Bank, as saying, "Lewis is a likeable man personally, yet I think he's one of the worst men the country's got. He wants power and he's bull headed." Norm's son, Gerald, was angry about the quote attributed to his dad. "He didn't say that and Herb was out to get John L. He had told Herb that if he were to print anything bad about John L., that he would not be welcome in the bank again." Many years later when Herb came to do a story on the Lucas Farmers and Miners Bank, Gerald Baker told Herb that he meant it. Herb was not welcome in his bank. As for John L., he was used to the bad press.

John L. would often come back to Lucas after the war. His daughter, Katherine, would say that a great man could not afford to have many close friends. That may or may not be true, but John L. did have many old friends in Lucas. He would drive into town slowly in a black Lincoln limousine. He would visit Don Stark and Marion Mitchell, and about lunch time he would visit Albert and Irene Baker. Irene cooked a fine lunch for John L. and reminded him of the way he used to tease her when they were young. John would laugh the same way he had done when he was a freckled-face kid in Lucas.

John L. spent most of his time in Lucas visiting with his old friend, Norm Baker, and his son Gerald. It was Norm who had arranged the wedding party for John L. when he was just another Lucas miner. John L. and Norm stayed close all through the years.

One morning in the summer of 1949, Everett Roberts was leaving Baker's store with his nine-year-old son, when John L. came in the door. "How is old Ed Roberts doing?" John L. asked. "Oh, he's down fishing at the pond today," Everett said in a hushed tone his son had never heard before. "Well, I hauled many's the load out of the Big Hill Mine with Ed. He was a damned good miner." "Yes, he was," Everett said. Then John L. spoke to Everett's boy. "This your dad, is it?" "Yeah," the boy murmured with his head dropped. "He ain't much good, is he?" John L. teased. "Probably better than you," the boy said in a flash of shy anger. John L. mussed up the boy's hair and moseyed down the aisle, laughing to himself. Everett whispered to his son that that was a great man they had met. "Not as great as my dad or Lash La Rue," the boy thought.

John L. continued his loyalty to Lucas. He got union jobs for lots of Lucas men—Marion Mitchell, George Griffiths, Rabbit Evans, and John White. Then, too, John L. would try to make amends if he had offended any of the Lucas folk. He did not want to be without honor in his own town.

John L. had gotten in a fight with the Corum boy when they were both young in Lucas. Nearly fifty years later, he would apologize to him for the fuss they got into over a girl. John didn't want enemies from his hometown. He had enough everywhere else.

In November of 1950, the *Register* took note of John L. again. "Lucas' 'Own' Lewis and Moses will Decide Pay of U.S. Miners," the paper said. It pointed out an oddity, namely that the two principle opponents in the coal industry's wage disputes for all of the United States were Iowa boys. Even stranger, they were both Welsh boys from Lucas. John L. represented the United Mine Workers at the conference table. Across from him was Harry

Moses, whose grandfather, Tom, was killed in the Lucas mines in 1886 and was buried on a hill in a cemetery north of town. Harry Moses had risen through the ranks a good deal since his family left Lucas. Harry's father had become a vice-president of United States Steel and Harry had become president of their massive coal operations. Both John L. and Harry had followed the career of the other, and both were paid more than $50,000 per year in 1950 dollars to stare the other down. They both said that their personal Lucas-born friendship would outlast the conflicts of capital and labor. Maybe it did. Both men were living well by that time.

By the 1960's, John L. was getting too old to come back to town. Lucas folks would sometimes visit him in his apartment in Alexandria, Virginia. John L. would occasionally send back money to the Saints Church. He was in his eighties and feeble. The old people of Lucas didn't forget John. Every couple of years they would repaint the sign overlooking the highway, which said "Lucas, Birthplace of John L. Lewis." Sometimes people from far away would come and take pictures of the sign. Then they would stop in at the Farmers and Miners Bank to find out where John L. used to live in the town. They were retired miners and steel workers who worshipped John L. Lewis. Most people drove by too fast to see the sign or worry about it. The people in Lucas kept it repainted anyhow.

Hard Luck and Mud

People in Iowa tell you that small towns are good places to raise kids. It's hard to say if Lucas was good or bad. What is certain is that it was peculiar. It is always a little peculiar when there are more poor people than rich because the poor kids have to be more creative in their leisure time than the rich kinds.

One resource Lucas had that other cities didn't was dirt to play in. It was useless dirt, too, not the kind that represented neat gardens necessarily but the kind that replaced sidewalks; the kind you just tracked in to someone's new-scrubbed kitchen floor. That kind of mud.

Everyone underestimates how much kids love to play in the dirt. Everyone that is but the makers of Play Dough. Dirt is workable, unresisting, whatever size you want it to be, very tactile, colorful in its own way, and it is forbidden. Not only that, dirt rightly formed can proximate weapons (such as mudballs), race tracks, snake holes, small dams of small creeks, and animal droppings. Much dirt in Lucas had ancient animal droppings mixed with it.

Harly and Melvin had a good bank of clay and mud right next to their yard. It was eroding steeper every Spring and it was a good mix of brick-colored clay and deep-brown earth. In the 1950's their friends gathered around the dirt bank for many days with tin and plastic implements to turn it into a cave; no, a superhighway; no, a fort; no, an airport; no, a big mud slide; no, a car wreck. Whatever it really was, it was always unfinished—as every child's world should be.

Harly and Melvin had one sister, Fayrene. She was a couple of years younger than the boys and was totally excluded from playing in the mudbank. Harly and Melvin would scrap a lot. Harly, the biggest, and Melvin, the oldest, would fight and lose their tempers over the gawdawful silliest things; namely stuff like whose turn it was to do this, that, and the other.

It could be said that the boys and their little sis had quite a bit to be angry about. It's no use saying Lucas was poor, which it was and is, because the boys were in the poorer category of Lucas citizens. The Welfare Lady from Chariton would come down about twice a year to visit the tarpaper-covered house on the west hill where they lived.

Their aunt had taken care of them for a very long time, in fact since they were all babies. What had happened was this. Their pa was sent to prison over at Fort Madison. He burned down his grandma's house for the insurance money and that just wasn't right. Now the mother of the children, she took all three to some larger town such as Newton or Marshalltown. She went to a hotel on the square and walked right out and left the two little boys and their baby sister in the room. She locked them in. Then she left for good. No one knew where she had gone. Melvin, the older of the two boys, climbed out a window and down a drain pipe and he hollered for help. Course people came and let the children out but a person can understand that Melvin had kind of gotten to be independent at an early age. In an odd sort of way, he stayed that way, too.

Their aunt took the children in and got them signed up for welfare and there they were—momma gone for good and daddy doing time. Their Aunt Effie was a singular and peculiar person. She was the sort that a person might use as a model for a bad cartoon about Old Maids. High cheek bones, she had. Black hair pulled back real severe. On those rare times she smiled her front teeth stuck way out. Thin and upright she was, too, and the way the world had treated her it was no wonder she looked like a flinty person.

For it wasn't just her brother's children Effie had to raise. That was just the half of it. She also had to take care of her fragile, blue-veined and senile pa at the same time. He was so old he scarcely knew where he was a good deal of the time. He didn't speak and didn't seem to listen. He was in his 90's and had run out of things to say. It got so that Effie had to dress him, sit him up, and finally feed him bite by bite. Sometimes he would sit there by the old, wooden kitchen table next to the cook stove and he would be snoring with his eyes open. One day she found him sitting there dead.

People around town were right when they said that Effie had quite a row to hoe. Still, they didn't think too much of it. When sacrifices had to be made it was, by gawd, the women who made them. Except, of course, for Harly's and Melvin's ma, who was gawdknows where doing gawdknows what with gawdknows who.

Effie had a few peaceful moments during those years, like the times she would snap beans on the front porch. Then she would hum some old, lonesome-sounding hymn without opening her tightly closed lips. But most of the time the two boys would be fighting and Fayrene would be having a temper fit, and she would just say "one more sound and I will blister all your little asses till you can't set down for a month." That was no idle threat either.

You could get a picture of the kind of life Effie was trying to live by looking at her outside toilet. Now this was the 1950's not the 1850's, and most people in America had flush toilets. Lord knows, even some in Lucas had them. The best way to understand what those toilets were about is to imagine yourself in one, on say the 5th of February in the dark of evening. Snow and wind whip around the door, the latches made of bent nails and a hook that doesn't close them completely. The wind that came in was a sign that maybe folks weren't supposed to even be living in Iowa in the winter. Nature didn't intend it.

Effie's toilet was one of the very worst in town. The high side of outdoor toilet life was represented by the W.P.A. varieties (government made) and the fancy, three-hole variety (with the small one in the middle) with wallpapered insides. That was class and that was not what Effie had. In fact, there were more holes than wood in the structure she and the kids used. Finally a storm just sort of collapsed the whole building over the hole.

Harly and Melvin got to be resourceful boys pretty early on. They peddled the Des Moines paper and Christmas cards, picked up scrap metal, too. Work was the only way they ever got any change, and it was a way, too, of getting away from Aunt Effie.

She didn't really mind the boys being away although she was strict and upright in their raising. It seemed she had accidentally fallen into the role of the older female martyr, sacrificing what little happiness she could dredge up in the town for her brother's children and her pa. The boys would be gone on some winter's evening adventure, maybe with a chance of earning a quarter. Effie might just sit in her kitchen with the half-linoleum, half-bare floor. Just sit with her head in her hands, after feeding her pa his cornmeal mush with milk, after wiping his blank face, just sit there. After you were in the house awhile you wouldn't even smell the coal oil stove in the kitchen. She would stare out the window at the frozen winter and think about her bed upstairs, the restfulness of it and the cold first ten minutes of it. She would take her rest when she could. She didn't pray at night because she didn't believe in God or at least not in any of the religious stuff you would hear at the town's churches. Work was her religion and work was what ground her down. She had to be hard, flinty even, to keep those rapscallion, heathen boys and their younger sister under control. When a person has to be that tough and hard-working and lowdown poor, too, it's just natural they wouldn't have as sociable a personality as they might have otherwise. Then with her brother in jail, too. . . .

She had some few moments of rest in her kitchen and she had her pride. She had a clean house, she was satisfied of that. The fact is she never did get much respect. People said she was an old maid and hard looking and her brother was no account, stuff like that. And people would tell their children not to play with Harly or Melvin or Fayrene. They would say "now I'm not saying anything bad about them but you should play with somebody else. I don't believe they know how to behave." If pushed to the limit, the parents might even fall back on the bad blood theory that maybe that kind of a fellow who would burn down his grandmother's house might pass that on to his children, and gawd knows what the mother was like.

Well, the boys and their sister still liked their pa whose name was Delbert, and who on rare occasions sent the kids handtooled billfolds and belts from the prison over at Fort Madison. Lots of the other kids at the Lucas Public School kind of wished their fathers would make them something as nice. On the other hand, Melvin, Harly and Fayrene didn't get much for Christmas since they were on welfare.

In the Spring of the year when Melvin was in fifth grade, Harly in fourth, and Fayrene in third, their pa came back to Lucas. He didn't come straight back. He went to work in some town in Missouri first. He came into town with a new red Ford Pickup, picked up his two boys and a couple of their friends at lunchtime and took off like a bat out of hell, spittin' gravel and peelin' rubber out of the school yard. "Geez," one of the boys thought. "This is exactly how somebody from the pen drives in the movies, dangerous and crazy." The boys bounced around in the back of the pickup and Delbert headed for one of the old, steep roads in Lucas which was going to grass and mud and rut. He slammed the pickup up over the bumps and mud, up the unused road and veered this way and that, then fishtailed. He spun those tires, hit a rock, and nearly threw his boys and their buddies out. When he finally made it to the top he asked his boys how they liked the ride. Harly and Melvin claimed they loved it. The other town boy was too scared to eat lunch. "Goodgawd, he'll kill us all next time," he whispered to himself. Later he did see where it could be fun to have a pa like that.

Effie didn't see the fun in Delbert at all. She didn't trust him. More than that she could throw him out, and she told him just that. He told her he could live without her giving him just any shit at all. He didn't hang around the boys much after his run-in with his sister. Occasionally he would take the boys somewhere. More often he would tell them he would take them to some stockcar race or livestock auction and then he would forget to do it.

Something else happened about that time. A preacher from the Holy Roller Church began to show some interest in Effie. Nothing too much came of it. He was selling commentaries on the Bible parttime, and after Effie bought one his interest began to lag. People thought that was easy enough to figure out.

Harly was the most good-natured of the boys. He had a rounded face, pleasant it was, with glasses over his big eyes and his mouth open just enough to seem relaxed but not enough to let flies in. He did stutter. He did that in an odd sort of way. When he would get to a word he couldn't say he would substitute the word "other". When he would say, "I aint walking on no graves at the graveyard. I told Melvin that and he said I was *stuperstitious*—er I mean *stupidsti* . . . er other."

Melvin was always a better dresser than Harly. He seemed to be smarter too by quite a bit, although Harly did pretty well until third or fourth grade when the kids began to tease him more and his stuttering got worse. Melvin got himself a Des Moines Tribune paper route, and by the time he got in high-school he had bought himself an old Ford sedan. Harly claimed he had put money into the car, too, but he never got to drive it even after he had his permit.

Often as not, the old car would not be in running condition. It would sit under the tree in the front yard. They would sit there in the car and dream. Harly would say, "When I get this car running and get it running right, and when I get new upholstry in this thing, I'm gonna get me a rubber and put the make on some girl. Get her in the car and put the make on her. I will, too."

Harly would say, "If I had me the money, I'd go up to the A & W and see how many chili dogs I could eat before I would—other—before I would barf. I could eat probably twenty before I would—other—barf." "That's why you are a fat hog," Melvin would say, smelling the new upholstry in his mind. "I could handle more women than you could coney dogs." "No woman wouldn't—other—wouldn't fart on you," Harly would say—and then he wouldn't say anymore.

As the boys grew older they did less stuff with each other. Harly dropped out of high school. He didn't keep himself up, didn't wash and began to smell bad. Didn't try anymore. They said he was lazy—born tired—was what people said about him. That wasn't true. The kids in his class remembered how anxious he was to read in first grade and how he was good in arithmetic. Something changed in the boy and he lost something.

Melvin figured he had better get himself a job where he could make some money, and he went to Des Moines to do it. When he was nineteen he got a job with a Ford dealer up in Des Moines, and he got himself a brand-new, baby-bird's-egg-blue Fairlane convertible. Three days after he got it he took off work to see the big rodeo at Sibley, Iowa. He drove his new Ford as fast as she would run—sometimes the speedometer would be buried on 120 miles per hour. He only had break-in oil in the car, and it was only supposed to be driven 50 miles per hour for the first few hundred miles. Melvin figured he would limber up the car a little quicker. He ended up burning the engine right up—the metal just froze. Ruined it good. Then it seemed that his boss hadn't given him the time off from work so he fired him. Of course, he didn't come down to Lucas very much at all after that.

Fayrene got pregnant and married a boy in the Service and they moved to Colorado or Arizona, or someplace like that, to live.

The last people heard of Harly, he was living in some institution where they took care of people. He didn't seem right, people said, but they just didn't know how or why he was that way.

It really was a big surprise to people when Effie got married to some farmer who lived way over on the other side of Des Moines. People were even more surprised when her man died and left her the farm and quite a good deal of money. "Well," people would say, "she's had a hard life. I reckon she deserves it." Effie didn't seem surprised by anything, and when she was an old woman she would sit in her chair by the window of a winter's evening and she would look out on the frosted ground—just like she had done in Lucas.

Minnie Comstock

She used to be Minnie Jones before she was married, but she was old when we knew her. Her house was on the corner just as you would go down the big gravel dip where the hill turned and went east. Claptrack shack it was, built when people walked the board sidewalks. No paint on the two-story, dark house; it would scare kids to kingdom come and the kids would run between lightning bugs to get off that corner and make the shivering stop. Sometimes the lights were bright in her house, sometimes not. Nobody knew her well, though folks were kind. But she got awful odd as her body got more crooked, with her face all under scarves like maybe she looked like pictures you'd see of a witch.

But Minnie did have spirits in her house. That's what she said. They got noisy, wouldn't let her sleep. Finally she just moved down to the basement, let them have the upstairs. But they were so noisy and they danced up there, having a time. One spirit came all the way from Ottumwa, and she called him Jim Hoxey. She didn't know the rest.

The mayor, Everett Roberts, got called up in the middle of the night to go and see what the old lady was yellin' about. He was brave to do it. She was just yelling out loud to drown out those spirit noises upstairs. They took Minnie to the hospital and when she got home, Albert and Irene Baker (good-hearted souls) took her in their house like they had done with other people. They asked her to stay two or three weeks. "I just can't do it, I just can't do it. I'm never going back there no more." Talking to herself when she wasn't talking to Albert and Irene.

She said she'd go to church with them but about six o'clock she went down to the toilet and said, "I just can't go to church with you. The spirits won't let me." Albert told her that wasn't the right kind of spirit to tell her that. But the spirits wouldn't leave Minnie alone.

One day when Albert and Irene had their TV acting up and visited the neighbors to see a program, they saw where she had trudged through the yard to her old house—the dew of her tracks led right there. And she was in there, all right. Oh, she was dressed up. She had an old, black dress on. Sittin' there all stiff and formal. Somebody was coming after her. She was plumb gone. She was going to get married, she said. Jim Hoxey was coming after her. She had $1,200 in her knarled hands. She had a strange distant smile about her eyes.

They took her to a nursing home. Folks said when she was a young woman she was engaged to a rich man. Her mother broke that up pretty quick. She had told some people that she didn't want to be buried out there at Goshen with her mother, cause she had ruined her life. They found money sewed into her coat. They got her a guardian. Albert and Irene went up to the nursing home to see her. She wouldn't speak to them. It got to be pitiful before she died.

Daniel Evans

The masquerade ball held last Saturday evening was very well attended, about twenty couples participating. Good order was observed and everyone seemed to enjoy themselves. The prizes were won by Miss Maria Evans, representing a wingless butterfly, and Mr. Daniel Evans, a negro comedian. The prizes were a gold bracelet and a pair of cuff buttons.
Lucas Ledger, 7 February, 1902.

Board by board, Daniel Evans' place had begun to let light and outside darkness in the cracks and undone windows. There weren't a lot to cry when the old man died alone. If he'd been alive still, his two 1951 Kaiser-Fraziers wouldn't have rusted out so quick because he would have kept waxing them and he would have hung around the barbershop. He had owned the shale and slag hill that had been the Big Hill Mine. The last time it closed was 1914, so Evans didn't do too well with it.

He'd sit in the barbershop and argue about the best fruiting raspberries, car engines, and just how many patents he did have registered with the U.S. Patent Office. For Daniel was an inventor. His inventions were not profitable, to be sure, but they seemed as real and important to him as his Kaiser-Frazier autos. No one knew much about his patented inventions; they seemed to have to do with nozzles and couplings and such. Others of Daniel's creations people did know about and it set the teeth of child and parent on edge.

For Evans had constructed three plastic coffins—one for a large man, one for a small woman, and the last for a child. They were said to be standing upright on one of his second-floor rooms. Several trustworthy folks had testified that he had asked them to try one on for size. No one did. Such is the stuff of small-town legends. He had a pool table in the living room. *What does he do in there every night alone? Plays pool with himself? Yeah, pocket pool. Yeah, plays with himself, I'm sure.*

Parents told their kids to stay away from Daniel. They looked at his little, round face with the strong bifocals and said they'd heard things about him. *Heard what? Just things. I just don't want you going around that place day or night. What things? Well, he's a pervert. How do you know? I just do. Stay away from there or get the tanning of your life.*

Something happened years ago with Daniel. Was it when his wife died or because his sons didn't come to visit him? Something a long time ago. Most wouldn't talk about it. He was bitter, unappreciated, and just felt like he had to fight for any feigned respect down at the barbershop. Since he lived just next to the school yard, he could sometimes be heard debating loudly with the school janitor, Albert, who was an elder in the Saints church. Daniel was an atheist by decision or affinity. Loud talks they would have. School kids didn't pay too much mind to all that. Some adults did. Lots of people didn't care.

It was only a few years before Evans' death that the greatest scandal of all spread through the town. Talk was that Donnie Mark, the retarded boy, had spent the night with Daniel. *Put some vaseline in my . . . he did, uh. Started poking his thing up me, he did. Hurt like hell, it did. Wouldn't let him do that no more, huh. Ran away right there, I did, uh.*

Daniel was still lonely. Died just a few years later. When the Centennial Book came out for Lucas a few years later, it listed the "Ones Gone Before" in the town and it listed the dates of their passing. Daniel Evans was listed but without a date. No one, it seemed, could remember exactly when he had died.

How Time Passed at Baker's Store

The long, floor corridors at Baker's store smelled of oil because of the oil and sawdust mixture used to the sweep the place at night. The building was a tinsided "L" with a feed storage "lot" at the back of the place. Most people would trade at Baker's store in the 1950's although there were two other grocery and general merchandise stores to choose from. Everyone knew old Norm Baker, who owned the store and the Farmers and Miners Bank. And, of course, they all knew Jerry and Frickie, his boys, as they respectively helped in the bank and in the store.

Open the side "Colonial is Good Bread" screen door and a person could walk over to the counter where Ethel Angove was stacking the Butternut Drip Coffee cans (the kind the old men loved as spittoons) and taking orders over the telephone and bagging groceries. She worked from 6:30 in the morning to 7:00 at night every day except on Saturday nights, when she dreaded the 6:30 to 11:00 work-a-day grind.

Six or seven kinds of lunch meat from the basic kinds, "big bologna" to the fancy ones with pimentos or olives you could have sliced. Three or four kinds of cheese from the very sharp New York to the Velveeta-almost cheese. Cottage cheese with chives. Anderson-Erickson milk. All these things were stored neatly in the big display case with the cooling unit. A fellow could also get real butter or the kind of oleomargarine which was white with red dye in a dot that you could squeeze and squeeze so it would look enough like butter for you to eat it.

Another display case had cookies in the bulk, with individual glass doors for gingersnaps, marshmallow creams, chocolate-covered graham crackers, and other wonders too numerous for children to completely fathom. Good children were sometimes allowed to pick out a cookie by Ethel; she, tired on her feet after seven hours, still thinking of the pleasure cookies give the little ones. Especially the poor little ones. She made a point of allowing one or two surreptitious cookie borrowing to take place by a needful child before she would pretend a bit of righteous anger and remove the little one from the sweet and gooey temptations in the cookie bin. But she did exhaust herself during the days and later on into the evenings.

Not everyone worked hard at the store. In say 1955, it would be the very place for the spit-and-whittle crowd to move into from the old bandstand on a midwinter's day. Outside the old men could, but usually did not, spit out of the bandstand. In the winter at Baker's store they spat toward the big-bellied, cast-iron coal stove. They would arrange their clothing—caps, coats, scarves and gloves—depending on the heat of the potbelly. If it was red-hot, as it often was if Ethel had recently filled it with coal, their spit projectiles would instantly vaporize on the metal, and the young children would be amazed at the chemistry and physics of it all.

The old men in their four-buckle rubber boots were not ill-at-ease with Ethel Angove's near feverish work around the store. It seemed to make them relax even a bit more. It should go without saying that the old men would talk about the weather. Weather talk was important because it would routinize and smooth out social relations, and it gave the social world a sameness the weather did not have. It was also true that the weather comments by the old men were usually not very creative. "Hot enough for you?" may have been the all-time-champion weather cliche. But others such as "We're a gonna wish we had some of that hot weather come February," or "All winter I was cold and now in July I just don't appreciate the heat, never satisfied, I guess," followed closely. "Yep" would be considered response enough. "Too wet to plow, too cold to cut butter," someone else would muse. "That sure is right," someone would agree. Everyone's blood pressure would drop a notch or two with each weather cliche and if in the winter the stove didn't warm the frontside and freeze the backside, a meditation-like state very close to sleep was possible about midafternoon.

To see the weather talk at Baker's store as pure superficial noise of a soothing and tedious nature is true but sometimes beside the point. Sometimes, however rarely, discussion of the weather from the paintless rounded chairs around the stove had bits of creative thought behind it. Often as not a young boy would say, "Think the rain will hurt the rhubarb;" "Not the canned rhubarb, I'd reckon," the inevitable reply.

Yet some of the older, alert denizens of the store might hit upon creative discussion of the seasonal variations that would cause eyeballs to roll. One old man whose chaws of Redman Chew was tellin bout the time "back in '31 or was it the summer of '32, I'd guess it was, when it got so dry that the fish swimmin up Whitebreast Creek could leave a cloud of dust behind em. And I'll tell you that was a hot one that summer; it got so durned hot that I'd tied my mule up to the fence in a field of popcorn, and it finally got so allfired hot that the popcorn was poppin and flyin around that mule's face and body to where he thought it was snow and jest laid down and froze to death."

"Well, I believe it was the winter of '36 that it was blizzardin so hard we couldn't get into town," sez another chawer. "It was hog-killin time so we was boilin a kettle of hot water on the fire. We set it outdoors a minute just to cool it off a little bit, and that there water froze so durned quick that the ice was scaldin hot."

Ethel Angove was sweeping dangerously near the chairs of the geezers and, with some effort, they would lift one or two feet up so she could sweep the red-oil sawdust under them. "Well, I'd better go up the hill," one bib-overalled man would say. "The old lady will be a wonderin what I've been a doin." "She'll know you've not been doin no work," another would say. "Well, it's like that old song," the other man would respond, getting the topic back to the weather where it should be. "Whether we get her, whether we got, we're a gonna have weather, whether or not." One last spit against the cooling stove and a slower sizzle, and another old man would amble up and out the front door to Baker's store.

An Unpleasant Surprise

They moved into town, I believe it was from Missouri, bought the gas station down there on the flats of Highway 34. It wasn't a bad building, ce-ment block with room for a good-sized garage, then the gas pump out in front. The front part of the building was where they sold groceries—Big Bologna, lunch meat, cheese, Colonial bread, Cheese Kurls, and milk.

They were little, slight people all of them, Donald, Ella, the two boys and their baby sister. They all were pretty good workers including the two boys but, like I said, slight of build and not too talkative. Well, Ella worked right along side her husband. She could not only hoist a car up and change the oil but she could install mufflers and do a fair brake job. Never smiled, always pretty serious they all were, except that Ella was the most hard-working and serious of the family. Nobody ever saw her hair let down because she usually wore a dark green cap on her short hair or sometimes the kind of bandana farmers would have in their pockets.

Seemed like they got along but, of course, several towns folk were in to them for money. "Just put that on my bill", they would say but they wouldn't say when they would pay it. Donald put a sign up in back of the food cooler that said, "All accounts must be paid by the end of the month." Well, some people in town wouldn't even pay attention to that if they got hit in the head with a shovel. But they did pump a lot of gas, being there on National Highway 34 that runs coast to coast, clear out to California.

People weren't too surprised when they hired a fellow in his twenties to help with some of the work around there. Donald moved kind of slow and Ella would be running back and forth between the garages and the gas pumps. This fellow was a good worker, too, people around town said. Had some pep in his walk, laughed about something or other more than Donald would. He slept behind the garage.

And the kids were in school all day and Ella looked more like a grease monkey than god knows what. Good worker she was. People did get a surprise, though, in the early fall of the year when the guys at the DX station started talking around that Ella had run off with the hired man. I guess people just forgot she was a woman in the first place. And then she left all those kids for Donald to raise in the second place. The little girl was only two years old. People said, "I always knew she was trashy and the kids are the ones I feel sorry for." People did feel sorry for the kids. Except the other kids didn't. The boys were seventh and eighth graders. They didn't weigh but about 100 pounds, if that. Kids knew enough not to tease them about their mother but they would pick on them, anyway.

Donald, Jr. and Willie would puff themselves up to their full height and bluff. Nobody believed their bluff for a minute and the other kids would take them down, just for the unboring fun of it. But they would fight back and lose, and finally people got to thinking they were good boys, hard workers they was—besides sticking up for themselves.

Four years later in the early, overcast drizzle of spring, Donald, Sr. was working on finding the low leak in a truck tire inner tube and working like hell to get it off the rim with three tire irons. The boys were in the upstairs rooms of the station and the little girl was playing with a rubber car on the loose gravel just right next to the chuckholes full of grey lime gravel water. Donald was cussing the tire some, probably wishing he had the equipment of the big garages. The old Chevy Pickup pulled in and it was goddamned dollar to a donut if Ella hadn't come back. Got out of the truck, looking maybe slimmer but probably better off looking than when she left. Sad as ever. Not speaking.

Donald just looked over at her for two seconds, started cussing the tire a little bit more than he had done before. Ella walked half-way to the pumps when Willie came out of the door. He looked at her and he looked at the guys gettin their tire fixed. Ella told him to get his brother. He went in and came back with him. They didn't look at their mother though, just looked at the wet gravel as Ella stood there. It was a hell of a time for strangers to be there. But the little girl with dark blond, short hair, she ran to her mother and hugged her. The guys gettin their tire fixed said they'd leave and just put a new tube in it anyhow, to Donald. Donald didn't move, didn't speak. The boys looked at their mother sideways a couple of times. Ella said she just wanted to see how they's doing. All right, the youngest said, and they walked right away from her and into the station. Donald, Sr., he stood there with the damn tire he couldn't just quite fix and asked her what the hell she was doing there. Just to see how they was doing, she said.

The little girl was in Ella's arms and Ella kissed her two or three times. "Well, I reckon you've seen," Donald said. She put the little girl down and said, "I hope you're all doing okay." She got a funny look, then went over to the car and sat in it for a long while. The girl cried a little and her father made her to come over with him. Ella drove off slow towards the east and Donald commenced to cuss that tire some. The little girl went into the station without looking back.

It wasn't too long after that that Donald, Jr. joined the Marines and the people who had made fun of him for his stickout ears and skinny body said, "I reckon they'll take anybody now." But he was a gritty little shit and when he came back a year later in his uniform, he had put on some weight and muscle. Willie got a cancer of the eye, it was called a blastoma, and they removed the eye. But he was cheerful and friendly and a good worker until it spread, and he died just a month or so before the graduation. So they dedicated the school yearbook to him.

After the boys were gone Donald, Sr. sold his station, took his girl and moved away. Nobody ever did hear what had happened to Ella or where she had gone to, but a lot of them thought that the trouble with the town was so many trashy people would move in and out and you wouldn't even want to keep track of them.

Family Honor

Some people passed through the old town with their lives running smooth and quiet like an iceskater. Some of the very old were like that, also some of the very young. These were the people grateful for even the slightest unintended courtesy. People were aware of them at only those rare times when they would go through changes—illness, marriage, death, or some other drastic relocation.

Flossie Gerken was not one of these smooth-and-quiet-living type Lucas folk. She was what people called, among other things, a "go-getter." It may be that she had to be a go-getter. Delbert, her husband, didn't work. He got a pension from the war. He was in his forties, Flossie slightly younger. He had a bad heart. In fact, he had it well into his seventies. Flossie was in charge.

She wore her hair very short, very curly, and very tight to her head. She wore clothes from the World War II period, and the blouses with their puffed sleeves made her large shoulders even more impressive. She seemed always to be angry but it was hard to say why. She didn't like being poor and having troubles paying the grocery bills at Bakers Store. She didn't like the talk that her old man was a loafer. She didn't like it when people would treat her kids—Reuben, Trixie, and Sue—badly. Lord, she was a tigress where those kids were concerned.

She did not treat her ancient mother-in-law with much respect. The old lady was as frail as a dry leaf, quiet and uncommonly kind. She lived with the Gerkens out of necessity. They took her pension check for her room and board. Flossie would yell at Mrs. Gerken and insult her in ways that made the old lady feel she wasn't worth her old-age pension. Sometimes the old lady would cry of hurt and loneliness.

Flossie was always in a great hurry. There was no great reason to hurry in Lucas in 1956. That is unless something inside you commanded speed. Flossie drove the family's old Chevy coupe wildly. When she would hit the brakes at their house, the mulberry-stained gravel and chicken droppings would spray. Stray chickens would show the world they could fly at those times.

She would plunge into the house and tell Gramma Gerken to get her lazy, old carcass out of the way. She would then fry Big Bologna lunch meat, make a sandwich for the kids, slap Trixie for teasing little Sue, sit down and kick off her shoes, roll her Big Mac coveralls up, roll her eyes, and cuss *"them damned snotty people in Lucas. Most of them don't have a pot to piss in and, oh my, they're so nice to your face and Flossie this and that, and you turn your back for just one minute and, oh, they are backbiters and hypocrites. I'll tell you,"* she would say to her husband or to no one in particular, *"there's a lots of people in this town that thinks I don't know what's a goin' on. I know who does me dirt and who doesn't. They had better just watch who they are foolin' with. And, Trixie, you can just straighten yourself up this minute, Miss Missie, or I will slap you silly. I will."*

Then Flossie would quiet down until one of the kids rocked the old lady's rocking chair on the tail of the mongrel pup. Then it would be hell to pay again. Delbert and his ancient ma would not speak up to Flossie. She would not allow it. They did not have the energy nor the inclination for it. Besides, Flossie was the only real hard worker in the family.

She worked for people, wallpapering or doing their wash. She would deliver the Sunday paper. Different things like that. She didn't work much on her own house, and what with different animals in the place and a lack of plumbing it smelled worse than it should.

Still, Flossie was admired in town in a peculiar way. It was a fearsome admiration because she could huff and puff in such a way as to put a dent in any townfolk's placid day. She seemed to have the world by the tail; that was the front she put on. People in the town humored her, cajoled her, and once in a great while even laughed with her. "Oh, you dirty pup," she would say to her children the rare times they made her laugh.

She had some notion of family honor and she believed (for it was true) that her family was constantly on the edge of ghost-town disgrace. Her children were always in trouble at school. Her girls were prone to let fly with some insult to a classmate. Her boy was more placid, like his pa. Both of these situations incited violence from the local roughs, and they would insult or attack the boy or the girls—pestering or shoving or taking away their caps.

Flossie was near-crazed about the way her children were treated, which was badly. The day they threw her boy into the shower with his clothing on, she called the sheriff on the culprits and pulled her boy out of school. He had hurt his back in the struggle, she said. He would not come back to school until the superintendent, *who don't have the sense God give a goose, would throw those nasty little snots out of the school. Oh, he was nice enough when I talked to him about it to my face. . . .*

In one sense Flossie was right to be outraged at her children's treatment at the Lucas School. In another way, well, all the kids were teased and roughed up except the very biggest and toughest. Nevertheless, after Flossie had counter-attacked the local bad boys, they counter-counter-attacked by throwing firecrackers on the Gerken roof—and rocks as well. Here again, someone else may have taken this noisy assault more in a philosophical vein. After all, the bad boys threw rocks on the school superintendent's roof nearly once a week. They did this in the middle of the night and they did it for no known reason. Flossie called the sheriff and the mayor in on the case and the situation cooled down after talks with a few active boys.

The battle for the Gerken family honor moved to a second front. Flossie attended the Presbyterian Church until she had a falling-out with the elders over a teaching assignment at Bible School. She marched her troops over to the Assembly of God Church and was saved in no time at all. They allowed her to play the piano, and she played it in the way she walked or drove her car. She hit the notes accurately, awkwardly, and hard with all the muscles in her impressive shoulders called into play. She like the noisy sound of the church and she liked the sing-song praying and shouting. She could do that with the best of them.

It wasn't long, only a few months later, that Flossie had been insulted. She would never set foot in that place again if they paid her one-million dollars. Then she attended meetings at the Saints Church. The visiting ministers convinced her that it had the truth going for it. It was the one for her. The Saints didn't know exactly what to expect from Flossie and her children, but they couldn't turn away converts.

Sometimes when the regular piano player was sick, Flossie would play the hymns hard. The Saints had trouble keeping their singing in touch with her playing but they were patient. Some of the ideas Flossie brought to the Saints Sunday School class were from the Presbyterians, some from the Assembly of God, and some were her own. She also picked up on the Saints' ideas from time to time.

Flossie was helping with the Christmas Program, and when Mrs. Roberts got a bad chest cold Flossie took it over and gave Trixie a starring role. Trixie did a good job singing, reciting, playing angels and the Virgin Mary.

The Saints would often have visiting preachers on Sunday evenings. Here it was the last of April and Flossie had not thumped the piano in church since the fortunate Christmas Program. A visiting minister had come up from the church college. He was an educated man and the Lucas folk all hoped he would be impressed with the inside decor of their old church, as well as by their faith and humility.

The regular piano player was sick with a sore throat so Flossie took charge of the pre-sermon services that evening. The visiting minister sat between two elders from the Lucas Church, crossed his legs and straightened his blue suit.

Flossie went to the piano and announced that Trixie was going to be singing with her. The older members of the Lucas congregation were beginning to get uncomfortable, not knowing exactly what Flossie would do in front of the out-of-town minister.

She plunked the first chord even harder than usual, really put her shoulders into it. Then her daughter opened up with a nasal-slammed note and she sang as loud as she could "Dust on the Bable; on God's Holy Word; Dust on the Bable. . . ."

She was singing a daggoned Holy Roller song in the Saints Church. No, wait. It sounded like a hillbilly song—or maybe it is something from one of those Missouri radio stations. Oh Lord, that preacher must think we are fools in Lucas. Unfortunately for Flossie, a long freight train on the CB & Q tracks drowned out the mother-daughter harmony. Some of the congregation considered that a thoughtful gift of a gracious Lord.

It wasn't too long after that Flossie pulled her family out of the church. She cussed them out real good before she did. She lived in town for several more years till her kids got all grown up. She stuck it out there in town—protecting the family honor.

A Kind of Sexy Laugh

She moved up here to marry the fellow that ran the gas station—the one on the four corners. It was the DX, I believe. She had three daughters and came up to marry in the early spring. Here it was the last of April and snow still settled on limestone gravel around the driveway. The two daughters were pretty girls, twelve and fourteen. One had red hair like her mother. I don't believe they went to church anywhere in town, which is all right people said, but you'd think they'd send the children off at least.

The Mister was a hard working, big man who drove a truck like several fellows in town. He owned his truck and was well thought of. His mother was a sweet person; people always admired her.

The high school kids got to hanging around the station later that spring. They put a jukebox in the place and played a lot of that loud Hank Williams country music and that rock and roll, which seemed to be designed to irritate the eardrums of the people who would come in to pay for their gas. They would fix flats, change the oil—kind of light mechanical stuff. Later they hired a high school boy to do that and sometimes another boy would pump gas.

There were only two gas stations where the kids could hang around and this was one. Over across the road at the Standard Station the older men, and sometimes their wives, would eat a chicken-fried steak. The men would amble into the feed store part of the station and argue politics and whether professional wrasslin' was real or put on. One fellow had been to Chicago to the Marigold Gardens and said he had seen it in person and it was real. He saw blood coming out of the mouth of one of the wrasslers. Another guy, though, pointed out that he just wondered why they would always pin one of the fellows just a second before a commercial was due on the TV. So the argument was a standoff.

But the younger boys that first spring, they would more likely hang around the DX. They liked the hamburgers and the jukebox at the DX, and they might have liked Joanie's raspy, easy laugh and her girls, too. They would sit there on those aluminum chairs with the blue plastic back straps, playing cards or shootin' the breeze. Or they would go out and time their cars or just put some peanuts in their Pepsis and let them fizz up. Maybe they would look at the out-of-state car licenses once in awhile.

The year went on and Joanie was doing all right. Her man just let her run the station, with the help of the high school boys. They did a good business. The year passed and another sloppy spring, with some new rockabilly songs on the jukebox. Joanie and her husband bought a new 1957 red and white Chevy Hardtop. They weren't selfish about it; they let a couple of the kids drive it. That was the thing of it. They were hard-working folks but they seemed to know how to have a good time. Never had more than a beer or two at a time. Lord they did like to laugh. And as another summer or two went by, the boys started getting interested in the sisters. Their mother was fairly strict with them but they knew how to laugh and flirt and gossip in ways everybody enjoyed—pretty much in a coquettish kind of way.

The high school boys liked Joanie because she seemed younger than her thirty-some years. She was thin, well built, red-headed and lively. And she had the best belly laugh in town. Some of the women folk in town were ever so slightly put off by Joanie because she smoked cigarettes, which caused her voice to be husky, deep and raspy. The boys thought she was a livewire. And indeed she was.

She had to caution the boys about chasing her daughters (cute little vixens, they were) round the station for it might give people bad ideas and chase away timid customers. And indeed it did.

In the evenings the kids might dance at the station or buy enough gas to get to a neighboring town to cruise the town square; there perhaps to be driven out by local territorials from the county seat. The jukebox would play Ferlin Husky, Fats Domino and Little Richard and the kids would boogie and maybe someone would cop a feel of one of the daughters.

Joanie would dance, too, and laugh. No more than two beers for her. She enjoyed herself and that was okay. One night she danced with a young married man, Lloyd Burns. He was a tall, dark haired man who looked enough like Gregory Peck to be his cousin, and he and Joanie danced to a Patsy Cline song, holding each other close. They kept on dancing until they danced right behind the counter and into the kitchen. Young tongues clucked. Shame on you, Joanie. "We were only in there less than a minute so you guys just get rid of your dirty minds." That was what Joanie would say. "A guy may try to get friendly with me but, believe me, I know how to cool the critters down. You'd better believe I do." Lloyd left—smiling some, some drunk, too—in his Ford pickup. Some of the Lucas kids began harmonizing with and making fun of the jukebox songs, and it was getting time to close up for the night. There were pretty good grins that night.

When the teenaged boy was pumping gas at the station three weeks later, he saw a Ford pickup slide into the midafternoon silence with a gravel-splitting crunch. Two women came out of the truck with a slam, intentionally slamming the door hard in a way that was difficult to ignore. Joanie and her daughter were upstairs asleep in the apartment above the station. It was siesta time at mid-afternoon.

"Now, where is that trashy woman?" they yelled at the boy sitting half crouched and semi-conscious on an aluminum chair, leaning against the blue-painted cement wall. "Who do you mean?" he started, knowing full well who they meant. "Well, she's taking a nap and, hey, you can't go up there. That's private property. Hey!"

Oh, lordy, the boy thought, this is some kind of a dream. Good god, them women might be packing guns. Lord, they were angry. One of the women was Lloyd's mother; the other his pretty young wife. No weapons on them but there was homicide in their voices.

The voices drifted down the stairs. "Just what do you think gives you the right to mess with my husband? By god, I know what's going on and I swear I will wreck you. I will let you have it." "And if she don't do it, I will," shouted her mother-in-law in counterpoint. "You leave my son alone, you no-good hussy!"

"I never did mess with your husband, and if you can't keep him home it's your problem. Now you get the hell out of here before you wake my little girl and I get the sheriff on you. Ronnie works here and he knows I haven't been messing with your man." Six angry eyes searched the boy's face. "What about it, Ronnie?," Lloyd's mother demanded.

"She ain't been messing around with him. I would know 'cause I'm here every night. No messing around. Just talking. People just hanging around talking; that's all that's going on."

"Was Lloyd out here?"

"Yes, but he never messed around. Nosir. He was just kinda talking and stuff." The two women left, bouncing more threats off Joanie. Joanie was near tears but she cussed the women out and thanked Ronnie for sticking up for the truth. Some could question the boy's answers since he was, in a sense, defending the honor of his employer and indirectly his dollar-per hour salary. That wasn't it, he thought. Mainly he liked Joanie's laugh and her energy and he thought, well now, they were only dancing in that kitchen for about a minute. I don't really supposed they could get enough messin' around done in that short of time to be worth talking about. Even if they did get some kind of a grope or, lord knows, a quick French kiss.

That was a wonderful event, even if the folks didn't happen to be married to each other. He had never thought people in their thirties could ever be that glandular. It was something to look forward to.

Joanie and her girls worked the station for several years after the blowup. Folks still had fun out there at the station. Joanie and her husband had some kind of falling-out but it seemed she thought he had been stepping out on her. Nobody knew if any of that was true, but Joanie's station closed. When it closed the Jukebox left, and the lube jobs, and the teenaged Romeos. But the worst thing was that Joanie took her laugh out of town. She became a licensed practical nurse, and when the boy thought of her in later years he was hoping she could still laugh in that hoarse but generous way. And that maybe, somewhere else, she could still find a place to dance in the kitchen.

PART 4

Winter Kill: Visits with the Old Folks (1890–1967)

Don't Never Get Old

Well, it is a haunting image. The old and humble folk at the Saints Church singing *Jesus, Lover of My Soul,* or *Let the Lower Lights be Burning.* The time was drawing nigh; they could feel the cold, stiff winter of the end of their agedness and the end of the town; an end to families. And so they sang, dirgelike, boring, and unimaginatively to an outsider. Secure in the ritual of the tragic. Not caring about the world of the Kingdom of God on earth but "my heavenly home" and "my waiting plot" at Goshen Cemetery. Who could blame them? The young. Who could understand the tidiness of the graveyards counterposed against the disorder of the town? Who cared? Who pulled weeds? Kept the sidewalks clean until the arthritis set in? Who said "don't never get old?" Were they suggesting suicide or the second coming? Who appreciated the nice breezes in the summer's failing light but had to go in before it got a little chilly? Who fell to wondering over geneologies of townfolk when no one else cared? Who spoke unthoughtful rhymes again and again, comforted by the sameness of it all? Who tolerated the rest of the world but didn't want it? Who would laugh at distant stories and laugh at distant cryings? Who wanted children to be happy for their times of happiness? Who? The old folks who sat in the back center-sections of the church.

Duke's Winter Evening

It was a cross between a waddle and shuffle that old Duke Edwards did that December evening, coming down Highway 34 from Chariton. He had been up there to apply for a grocery order from the Welfare Office. He had some kind of a foul-up in getting his old-age pension from the state. They couldn't find any evidence that he had been born. There was his physical presence, of course, but the state wanted a birth record. And that was hard to come by.

Duke was just a mite tired as he stepped into the Conoco Station for a bottle of Bubble Up. It was getting harder for an old man to hitchhike even though he almost always got a ride with somebody he knew. He got into the station out of the cold wind and said "Howdy" to the fellers and they "howdied" him back. The rumor was that Duke didn't smell too good. Lucas folks

didn't get close enough to find out. It wasn't a serious bad smell. It was just an old-man-living-alone smell, and you'd allow for him not taking as many baths as he should.

Duke's clothing was a little odd, also. That probably came of him living alone. He had what looked like a corduroy shirt over a wool plaid shirt, and that over a faded, pink garment with big buttons. He had at least two or more pairs of coveralls with the white and blue stripes on under that. "Weather don't bother me much. I'll just put on another layer of clothes. I'll be just fine." The rumor went around that old Duke would put on a new layer of clothes when the outside layer got dirty. That may have been because he had the layered look in the summer when it was hot as well as in the snowy months when it was cold. He would pick up work whenever he could, which wasn't too often. A little farm work here or there, a day's work unloading a railroad car, not really enough to keep him in pipe tobacco.

He had been a hardworking young man—a mule driver in the mines and later a gandy dancer on the C. B. & Q. Railroad. He was husky with strong shoulders and a turtle-thick neck. He would tell the men at the station stories about when he was in the prime of his life, and how in those times he was a professional wrassler. He had a cauliflower ear to prove it. Wrassled all over the midwest, Duke did. "I was strong as a bull in them days," Duke would say. "I'd wake up in the morning so hungry I could eat a sow and her litter of pigs. By golly, I would work it off; two or three matches a day sometimes. Well, I wrassled some of the meanest customers you would ever want to meet. Some of them would use a choke hold on you. You know that's illegal but, by god, I broke a fella's arm once who pulled that on me. I can't remember the name of that town where it happened. Up in northwest Ioway, it was. Way up there. I'll remember in a minute here."

The boys at the station weren't interested in the name of the town; they had heard the story a dozen times before. That late in the afternoon they were more interested in teasing Donnie Dilly, one of the several retarded residents of Lucas.

Since Lucas had no minority groups in town in the 1950's with the possible exception of a Catholic family, retarded people were often the brunt of the jokes put forth by the town wits. Donnie was good to joke around with because, unlike Duke or the other old folk in town, the retarded boy was unpredictable. He was not wise in the ways of the town wags, and they used that fact for the entertainment of the gas station loafers.

One time the boys down at the station had fed him Ex-Lax, telling him that it was chocolate candy. The results of that joke were all over town. It made the boys laugh for months. Old Duke didn't laugh. He figured it was cruelty pure and simple. The boys down at the station would ask Donnie about his sexual habits and he always would respond in the same way. "It points up every night, it does, uh. When the morning sun hits it, it goes right down, it does, uh." Laughter and more laughter from the good old boys.

Duke didn't like that teasing of Donnie. He didn't believe that was the right way to behave. He would have whipped thunder out of them fellers if he was younger and, by god, he could have done it, too. As it was, he spit his chew on the wood floor and on the cuff of his pinstripe coverall legs. He ambled out the door of the station, across the highway—walking through the slush across from the W.P.A. pond. A chilly wind was blowing right through his layers of clothing, and just as he got to the railroad tracks he met another old man, Rabbit Johnson. Rabbit wasn't just right in the head, and Duke didn't trust him at all since last summer when he passed Rabbit mowing the lawn with an old push mower. It wasn't working just right and Rabbit had just picked up the helpless machine by its wooden handle and smashed the blades and wheels down onto the cement sidewalk—yelling some words only he understood. He crashed that mower down on the sidewalk three or four times and Duke had to walk around the broken pieces of the damned thing. Rabbit could have hurt somebody. No sir, Duke didn't trust him at all.

"Did you order up this weather we're havin', did ya?" Rabbit asked Duke. "Not so's you'd notice," Duke said, walking a wide path around Rabbit. Rabbit seemed all right but you never could tell about him. Duke turned the corner of the Hooker's Harness Shop and looked in the window at the saddles and whips and the newly-soled shoes. He would have to have Old Man Hooker put some soles on his shoes when he got the money. It wouldn't be cheap, he reckoned. The old man was tight as the bark on a tree. Did good work, though.

Duke would pass Roy Palfreyman's *Trash and Treasure* Store on the block across from the hardware store. Roy was in there playing cribbage with a couple of other older Lucas boys.

Duke stuck his head in the door of the junk store. "Howrya doin, Roy?" he offered. "Just going broke as fast as ever," Roy responded. Roy was a few years younger than Duke and half Duke's weight. He had a sharp, angular face with wide-open, searching eyes. You had to have those kinds of eyes to be successful in the junk business.

Duke got to listening to a story Roy was telling about how he had left Lucas, looking for gold in Alaska and way down in Nevada. Then he commenced to recollect that orange grove he had owned down there in Texas. Duke had heard the story before but he figured to warm himself a little more in Roy's place before he went on up the hill.

Duke got to looking around the store and Roy continued weaving his stories. He looked at the dusty glass case of eye glasses, the sixteen-pound spittoon, cracked porcelain pitchers, shaving strops, meat choppers, pre-electric wash tubs, an apple drier, large picture of wolves howling in the winter snow, odds and ends of furniture. It was all covered by Lucas dust from a few decades before.

"No sir, I figured I'd live out my days in Lucas. I could have lived anywheres else I'd a mind to. 'Course my folks was here. My folks always told me. . . ." Duke's mind trailed off Roy's speech about coming back to Lucas.

They had both come back, all right. They didn't come back to much as far as that goes, Duke thought.

"Hey, I seen that new whirly-gig thing you put up in your yard t'other day, Roy. It sure is somethin'." "Well, it is, isn't it?" Roy agreed. "People go by my yard and they will stop and look at my homemade inventions such as my combination roulette wheel-bird feeder or my windmill scarecrows, and they will likely say they've never seen the likes of them. I believe I've got twenty-four of my wooden inventions out in my yard now. Purtiest things, brightest colors a fella could want—greens, reds, purples, golds and blues. When the wind blows, say there's more action in my yard than any other place in town. 'Course it takes a lot of skill to do the woodworking part of it. If a fella has ideas and never carries them out, just what the hell good is he? Yes sir, I do believe I've got the most exciting front yard in the state of Ioway."

Duke agreed. "Well, Roy, I believe you're right. I've never seed the likes of sitch." "No sir, you haven't," Roy confirmed. "I believe I'll be gettin' home," Duke said, feeling a wave of fatigue, and he ambled out the door of Roy's *Treasures and Trash*. That Roy was a nice old fella but he could wear a body out.

Duke waved at the folks in Hookers Barber Shop and began to lug himself up the hill to his house. Well, it wasn't exactly his house. He had had a house over in the Jericho hills in the north part of town, just above the old Skidmore Mine. He was more able to work then, of course.

It was dusk as he plodded up the schoolhouse hill, walking along the street where somebody with smooth tires had left tracks in the grey snow. The snow was the same exact color of the sky and Lucas seemed a lonely, familiar place. Duke met a couple of kids with skis at the top of the hill. "Where did you get them things?" he inquired. "What in hell are they anyways?" "Well, they're skis," the boys said, laughing a little at old Duke's unworldliness. "Sheeot," he was going to tell the young boys about the wooden sled he had as a kid but they were off, laughing and talking, before he could get it out. Standin' on poles and sticks and ridin' down hills on them. Crazy devils, he thought to himself. There's a lot I never will see—nor would want to.

It was around the corner he walked toward the old Lorimor place. That was where Duke was staying. When he ran out of money Everett Roberts had let him move into the shack for free. The shack had once been part of a new house that the fella over there was building. Well, he got run over by a semi and never did get to finish the house. It was one room with a large cement foundation attached to it.

It was dark over at the acreage where Duke would rest and there wasn't electricity in the shack. He didn't mind that too much. Some people had a notion that the place was haunted because of the man who had died over there. Everett had told him, too, about playing on the place when he was a young fella near the deserted house, when it was raining on a spring night long ago. Everett and his buddy had tripped and fallen over the body of an old woman who had lived there and had died of a heart attack earlier in the day.

None of this stuff worried Duke. He had lived too long to believe in spooks. He believed that Lucas was a lonely place, though, for an old man with no family. He heard a rattling on the outside screen door which did give him a start. He asked who it was and opened the door to see a couple of kids. Mae Roberts had sent them over to bring Duke a hot meal of roast beef, potatoes and gravy, homemade bread pudding, green beans layered in a kettle with a broken plastic lid on the top.

"Bless your doggone hearts," Duke said. "That is a real nice surprise," and he turned up the oil in his lantern to see the kids better. He asked them to come in but he said, "The place is a mess. You know how an old man is." The kids were frightened of the dirty, one-room shack with the bed and table and one chair. They said they should be gettin' back and Merry Christmas.

Duke thanked the children and Mrs. Roberts and said, "Well now, thank you 'till you're better paid." He began to eat just after the children left. He thought it was a wonderful meal and he began to remember that, by god, it was gettin' close to Christmas after all. He got to remembering one Christmas evening when he was a boy. The half-formed memory he drifted into saw the winter sky all pink and deep red turning dark blue and his ma was laughing about something, he couldn't recall what. Her laughter was fading out on him as he dozed into the aged winter night.

Two Long Lives Together

A handful of the old folks around Lucas in 1986 remembered the mining and the polyglot, the babble of Scots, Welsh, and Swede. There was Albert Baker, 93 in that year. His family had come from Pennsylvania to settle in 1858. His older brothers, Chris, Noah and Pete did various jobs around town. Chris drank too much. His sisters stayed in town, too, for the most part. There was Lillian, who had married at fourteen to Chris Hawkins, the English miner. (She survived him and two other husbands.) There was Annie, who married Charlie Woods and spent her years in Lucas weaving gigantic rugs on a loom which took over her basement. And there was Katherine, who became Katema later in life. She had married the Welsh miner, Ed Roberts. But they all lived in Lucas for most of their lives. They seemed contented there when they got the chance to be.

Albert married Irene Evans in 1913. She was part of the many sets of Evanses which came to the town from Wales. In 1880 there was the family of John E. Evans, John L. Evans, and John R. Evans living in the mining camp. John R. had been converted by Mormon missionaries and migrated to Utah but, like many other Welshmen with strict nonconformist views, he was shocked by polygamy. John R. had one child in Wales, one in Utah, one in Missouri, and one in Iowa during the 1870's. There was the Thomas Evans family and

84

the Evan Thomas family. In 1880 David Evans, another Welshman, showed the other unpuritan side of the Welsh character. He ran the Miners Home Saloon.

Irene's father was not John L., John R., or John E.; he was John T. Evans. (It was more important that they kept each other sorted out than that you do, dear reader.) Well, John T. had come over from Pontypool, Wales, because he, like John R., had been converted by the Mormons. (Not only did the Welsh copy each other's names, they followed each other's experiences, it seemed.) But John T. had gone to Utah with his brothers, Dave and Bill. He also found celestial marriage to be a shock to his nervous system. It was even more of a shock to his wife, for she had never been too keen on Mormonism from the first. When John T. was approached by the elders to take another wife, he took flight instead.

John T. had gone through the Temple Ceremonies and had received his Endowment from the Church in secret ceremony. Mormonism was very, very much like Masonic ritual and one took a blood oath to secrecy. When John T. left his Utah home for his new digs in Lucas, he told his family that he feared his brother, Bill, was to be put on his trail for the Church sanctioned vengeance of blood atonement for apostates. Finally, several of the Welsh miners, including John, joined the Reorganized Latter Day Saints, which did not believe in polygamy, and felt relaxed enough about their Mormon brethren to be philosophical about it. "Well, maybe they need polygamy out in Utah for it may take a man six or seven women to find one worthwhile." This was the point at which the womenfolk would look daggers or Bowie knives into their eyes. What teases the Welsh were.

But this was the stock Albert and Irene had come from, and in 1986 they had together accumulated about 184 years of Lucas experience. Too much, some would say, for such a small place. Living in Lucas that long a person just naturally gets over restlessness.

It may be that at some time and in some ways, Lucas escaped the meanness of spirit of some small, desolate, midwest towns. People looked after their own, more or less, depending on just who their own were. Some did more. Maybe feeding stray dogs, for the town was a great place to dump off unwanted dogs. Maybe helping neighbors even more than baking pies and cakes for the after-funeral get-togethers the older folk seemed to like so much.

Some folks took in all sorts of folk who wouldn't have survived in a city or in an institution. Not that lots of the folks didn't know how to be cruel when they got the chance. But there were the others, such as Albert Baker and his wife, Irene. Strict and proper they were about the Saints Church. And Albert kept his older adult Sunday School class wandering about in the Old Testament for twenty years at a time. And they were strict with their kids and with the boys and girls at the Lucas school where they janitored. "Wipe your feet, Don't be tracking in that filth" they would always command, as the children would troop in from fifteen minutes of exuberant freedom at recess. The children would do it.

Hardrock Republicans they were, too, of the kind who traced their loyalty to the Civil War. They also were kindly in a rare and brotherly-sisterly kind of way when the need arose. In Lucas in the 1950's and 60's, it arose. It was the old, the sick, and the slightly off that Albert and Irene cared for. There was Sophronia Goben, an old, widowed lady whose back bent down with the time. There was something wrong with Sophronia's spine. It had been bent from the time she was a young woman. (Although few people could believe she had ever been a young woman in 1955.) As she aged she became more crooked. When she would walk down to the post office or to Bakers Store, the loafers and spit-and whittlers sitting there in the band box would watch her slow movements and make comments on her shuffle. She was looking like a question mark, one would say. "Well, it sure does cause her to look ahead," another would comment before spitting a stream of Snoose tobacco nearly out of the band box, but not quite.

But Sophronia was in pain. She didn't care how she looked so much as wanting to stop the pain and wanting to get around. When television came to town in the early 1950's, Sophronia saw the Oral Roberts healing show, and a few years later when he brought his huge tent to Des Moines Sophronia went up to get healed. She believed with all her heart that she could be freed of her pain and the sorrows of her earthly body. And when Oral laid his hands upon her back she felt something happen. When she got home, she told folks that she had felt something happen and the healing was beginning. But the healing never did get going too well. Her back got a good deal worse. Albert and Irene were right there on the block to take care of her. They brought her soups and lit her fires, and they bought her groceries when Bakers Store didn't deliver. They were there for her.

When Sophronia died, they played at her funeral:

"Jesus, lover of my soul,
Let me to thy bosom fly.
While the nearer waters roll,
While the tempest still is high;
Hide me, O my saviour hide:
Till the storm of life is past;
Safe into the haven guide;
O receive my soul at last."

That seemed to be just about every older person's favorite hymn, whether they were R.L.D.S. or Presbyterian, or whatever. But a lot of the older folk leaned on Albert and Irene until they were safe in the heavenly haven.

Albert and Irene took in people, too, such as Johnnie Johns. And they had him for eleven years. Johnnie Johns was the son of Thomas Johns, born in South Wales in 1840, and Mary, who was two years younger. Thomas Johns had come over to work in the mines of Pennsylvania in the 1860's, and when he had saved enough money he sent for Mary and his seven children. The children caught a fever and all seven died on board the ship. Thomas met his wife, Mary, at the docks in New York. She was crying and he said, "Mary, where are all my children?" She said, "We buried them at sea. They are all gone." They started over again. They had four children in Pennsylvania and three more when they got to the coal camp at Lucas. It is easy to see why Mary never did get a chance to learn to read or write. Yet she was a midwife and delivered Albert Baker, and for that reason had a special fondness for him. Albert and Irene took old Johnnie Johns in, in a friendship born of tragedy.

Thomas and Mary had not yet seen the end of tragedy, for their son, Jimmie, born in Lucas, was killed by inhaling black damp (carbon dioxide) in the Cleveland No. 4 mine. As Irene Baker would remember it: "It was an awful day, the day of the funeral. It was raining and we had two funerals to go to. Jimmie's service was at the Saints Church in the morning and they buried a young girl, Sylvia Rotheset, in the afternoon. I took care of the children in the morning and went to Sylvia's funeral at the Presbyterian Church in the afternoon. Sylvia's mother would not accept that she was dead. A long-time after that they had to dig the girl up to show her mother."

On the day that Johnnie Johns died, George Sloan, a spit-and-whittling hangerout at the white, peeling-paint bandbox, came up to Albert and asked if he could move in and board with them. Albert said he didn't believe that would be too good an idea for they were wanting to have some time to themselves, he and Irene. They had raised four children to adulthood. Besides, while George was a harmless fellow, he still wasn't quite right in the head.

The next Sunday Albert and Irene drove over to the Saints Church for Sunday School and Communion Service. When they got back to the house, George had moved in. He was in his sixties and not an old man by the Lucas standards of the 1950's. But just a little strange he was, and some of the younger fellows such as Everett Roberts and Hal Polser would tease him just to see what would happen.

Albert would say, "It used to tickle me so. He was always sweet on some young girl. He liked them all. Well, he went through all the Hoffman girls. Had a crush on every one. He was in his sixties but, my, how he admired the girls. He was sweet on the youngest sister of the Hoffman girls, and they used to tease him so. The youngest one told him that she sure was fond of a man with a black mustache. One Sunday we came home from church and George was standin there and he taken shoeblack and brushed it on his face with a shoebrush. It was drippin here and there and all running down his face and he says, 'Albert, it don't look like nothing, does it.' " Albert couldn't think of anything to say.

Albert and Irene's lives stretch back to the times when the mines were roaring; the busts and booms produced the movements in and out of the town and, of course, the movements of the living to residency in one of the town's cemeteries. Irene liked a story she heard as a girl in the town. "Well, they buried a woman over at Fry Hill Cemetery. And the husband, he went home after the funeral and he went to bed that night. He heard a knock at the door and he got up. A voice said, 'This is your wife, let me in, please, let me in.'

He ran away from the door, sure it was ghost. It turns out some graverobbers had dug up his wife after it was dark, and when that cool air hit her, she woke up and they pulled her out of there. You see, they didn't embalm them at that time. She finally had to go spend the night at a neighbor's because her husband wouldn't let her in. That was before my time, of course."

Irene remembers being a young girl sitting on the front porch, listening to a Welsh family sing after the workday was through. Soon the family next door would pick up the tune, and eventually the entire street would be harmonizing some Welsh air. The outdoor singing left with the Welsh.

The Welsh used to love storytelling, and proof of the truth of tales which would stand up in court was not always required. It was more important that the tale be interesting. It was also helpful if the story poked fun at someone, not excluding one's self. That has always been one of the unwritten codes of life in Lucas.

"When I was a kid," Albert remembers, "I loaded my sled up with kindling wood for the fire. I pulled it through the snow til I came to a fence. Well, I got down on my knees and prayed to the Lord to unload that kindling on the other side." Since Albert laughs when he relates the tale, we all assume the Lord did not carry out his boyish desires. Nevertheless, he has missed very few Sundays at the Lucas Saints Church in his over-ninety years on earth. This, even though there was no miracle with the kindling wood.

In 1983, after seventy years of marriage, Albert and Irene got the flu so badly that they had to go to Chariton to the County Hospital. "They put us in the same room," Albert says, "so we could make faces at each other." In Lucas, people would tease until the last day of their lives.

Les and Gwenneth and Whether to Take It Serious

They both died in 1965. He in September and she in December. He was 72 and she a couple of years younger, not terribly old by Lucas standards. Her name was Mary Gwen but everyone in town called her Gwenneth or Gwennie. She was born to the Welsh miner, Tommy Hopkins, and his wife, Hannah. Tommy had worked in the collieries in Wales at nine years of age, and he came to Lucas to work in the pits there. He roomed and boarded with Elder John Watkins, John L. Lewis' grandfather. He met Hannah in the mining camp where the Cleveland Mine had just started operations. In 1896, Hannah gave birth to Gwennie.

Gwennie grew up in Lucas and early on she married the Irishman, Les Ryan. Les worked in several mines in town. The last one he worked was the Iowa-Nebraska, where he worked with John R. Evans, Ed Roberts, Jack Griffiths and Slim Williams.

It didn't surprise people in town when Gwennie and Les died within a few months of each other. Les had a bad heart and Gwennie had been sick for a long while, anyway. Besides, it was difficult to imagine them apart. On the other hand, it was a little difficult sometimes to imagine them together. That was because Gwenneth was a quiet and demure woman and Les was always on the rowdy side. He could talk pretty rough and he would speak his mind.

It may have been that Gwennie was a pretty woman in her youth, but in her later years she had lost a few teeth and her eyes looked large and round as hazelnuts, magnified by her thick, wire-rimmed glasses. Then, as she got older, she lost a good part of her hearing as well. This was not entirely a curse since she taught half the kids in town how to play the piano. Indeed, her piano was the centerpiece of the house where she and Les spent so many years together. It was a mahogany upright piano with carvings of a subtle and flowing line. Gwennie's cats did sometimes forget and abuse the finish of the piano. Cats. There were always more than a dozen around the place. Les would cuss the creatures under his feet; called them all sorts of names, which bothered Gwenneth a great deal until she lost some of her hearing later in life.

Gwenneth was the recording secretary for the Town Council and for the School Board, and this was because she wrote with a grace and flourish, letter upon line so that a simple check which said *Pay to Bearer on Demand: Four Dollars and Sixty-Five Cents* became a work of art. Gwenneth's written work of art was readable as well as aesthetic, so while everyone admired the beauty of her checks written for the town or for the school they cashed them at the Farmers and Miners Bank as quickly as they could.

Gwenneth went to the Saints Church. Les wouldn't go. She sat next to Aunt Lillie Woods. Gwenneth would smell of Rose Water and Aunt Lillian smelled of Lilac cologne. Gwenneth smiled so often and so long at the people of the congregation that the smile lines got permanently etched in her face.

One thing Gwenneth would not do, however, was join the Saints Church. Of course, her parents had belonged and she believed in it well enough. She even paid her tithes and offerings. The problem was that the Saints baptized by total immersion and Gwenneth was afraid of the water. No one made too big a thing about it. The elders could have chided her about it; in fact could have worried for her eternal soul. But no one did much. They were glad to have Gwenneth in the church and people may have thought there was some chance she would eventually go into the water. By the time Gwenneth had become an old lady Lucas did not demand more of its people than they could give. You could call it fatalism or easygoingness, but Gwenneth was accepted on her own terms—she with the ready smile, the many cats and the lifelong fear of immersion.

Even when half the Lucas population had moved out of the town to work in the new, booming coal mines at Hiteman, in Monroe County, in the first decade of the new century, Les and Gwenneth stayed in the old town. Later, when other miners left for the new town of Buxton, Les and Gwenneth stayed on, finding work about town to do. When another migration left town for the mines around Melcher, Les and Gwenneth stayed on in Lucas. That was in the 1930's. There was still talk then about the mines opening up again and Les may or may not have believed that, but he stayed in any case.

His off-and-on work at the Big Hill Mine and the Iowa-Nebraska pit kept Les busy. When old Tommy Hopkins died he left his daughter and son-in-law all his possessions, which weren't much. But in Lucas not too much could be quite a lot.

Gwenneth and Les were not so tight that coins screamed out in pain from being pinched but neither were they free with their spending. Thus they spent the last years of their lives in the sometimes-comfort of the dying old town. It wasn't often that Les would come out on the front porch of their roomy but perfectly square house. With its four lathed pillars and fancy woodworking attached to the front of the house, it was more plush than most in town. But you would be more likely to see one of Gwennie's myriad cats on the porch than Les Ryan rocking away the hours and years. Les was a doer. He worked for the town.

Les first met the Roberts boy when the boy, with a friend, had been experimenting with the relationship between a Daisy BB Gun and the tin halos around the town's street lights. The Roberts kid claims to this day that the other boy shot out the light and handed him the gun the moment old Les appeared on the scene. There he was, standing slightly bowlegged, in coveralls, with a green tie up at the top, corduroy cap and dark grey, cotton work jacket. "What in the hell are you doin there?" Too late to run and rushed with panic, the boy replied idiotically, "Just standing here." "Who in hell are you?" "Everett's boy." "Well, you're no damn good to me and you're going to pay for that street light and go to jail for awhile, too, I'd reckon." Les didn't move but the boy had the righteous hell scared out of him and he fled, trailing shame and guilt.

It was a few years later that the boy and Les started working together for the town. They worked on the streets. The streets of the old town were part shale, part gravel and part mud. Since the town was built on several hills, the water drained down the ditches in a hurry through the metal culverts under the driveways and street crossings.

Les knew how to use a shovel from his days in the mines. He taught the boy to use it, scooping gravel into chuckholes in the streets, digging up culverts, cleaning out ditches—all good, honest work. The boy as a teenager worked in Levis and an old T-shirt in the fierce July mornings with the steaming sun and the sometimes tree shade, an inexpressible luxury. Les wore bib overalls, a heavy flannel shirt, and seemed not to sweat or in other ways be bothered by the heat. His only concession to the heat was to leave his corduroy cap at home, leaving his pure white hair flopping in the breeze.

Les was a small man, maybe five foot six or seven. His slightly bowed legs moved him around as if he were in a hurry to get somewhere. All the same, he was not in a hurry to leave the town. The fact is, Les wanted to fix the town up and he struggled mightily to do just that. He was not much for the high technology of the town—a one-ton truck and a road grader. He felt more at home shoveling dirt and gravel or supervising the operation.

This dog-day morning in July Les was directly the teenage boy, who was driving the road grader along the ditch of one of the several steep hills just east of the ruins of the Big Hill Mine. The object of the activity was to lower the grader's blade at the proper angle to deepen the ditch without destroying the roadbed with deep cuts or scraping mounds of dirt into places they shouldn't be. Neither Les nor the boy quite knew what they were doing.

"Back it up and cut her this way, this way!" Les would shout to no avail. The grader was as noisy as an ancient tractor, which with a few modifications it was. The boy couldn't hear him and kept on with his futile efforts to get the grader and blade at the proper angle in the ditch. "No, cut her thisa way!" Les would shout haplessly, for none of the laws of physics seemed to work for the boy as he at once dug yet another hole in the already pocked street, and simultaneously filled the ditch with gravel.

Les began to cuss, which the boy could tell by the motions of his mouth and the rolling up of his eyeballs. Disaster again. This time Les was swinging his arms in short, chopping movements to the right and left. Then he would make smooth, graceful, angular movements with his arms. He was giving the boy signals, violent ones and sweeping ones. Sometimes it looked like Les was giving semaphore signals of a special kind; at other times he could have been conducting a brass band. The boy noticed that Les's hands were tapered, unknotted and gnarled like most of the miners. Soft and pliant hands he had for a working man. The words coming out of his mouth were not soft and pliant. Les was so frustrated he could have spit rivets. It was time to take a break. Les and the boy sat under a Mulberry tree, trying to figure out what was wrong.

The boy was finishing high school and he told Les he wanted to get out of the town, probably go to college close by. "Yeah," Les said, wiping his forehead with a red bandana and putting it back into the chest pocket of his bib overalls. "Well, what do you think of going to college?" "It's all right, I reckon. It's all right if you don't take it serious." "What do you mean by that?" "I've spoke my piece." "Does that mean you don't think it's a good idea?" "I already told you what I thought of it; now let's grab a couple of shovels and get that ditch cleared out." Les knew about appropriate technology before the idea had caught on elsewhere. They did scoop the ditch clean. A few years later, the boy would tell Les that he was getting married. "It's all right if you don't take it serious," Les said again and he wouldn't explain. When the boy was in college he found the word *laconic* in the Merriam-Webster Collegiate Dictionary, and he thought of Les Ryan.

Still there were ditches to be cleaned out that July afternoon, and continuing up the hill they found a steel culvert all silted in with mud, gravel and weeds. "We'll have to pull that one up," Les said. "You go and ask Miss Dulbert if its all right to pull that culvert out from under her front yard." He sent the boy to Miss Dulbert's tarpaper and grey-shingled house on the hill. Zinia had never married and was a good and upright forty-year-old woman, raising her brother's children and taking care of her elderly mother. She wouldn't have any of this ditch digging in her front yard. "No, I don't want you two digging and messing with my front yard. I don't believe you know what you're doing, anyway."

The boy went back to tell Les. It was hot and it had been a bad day for the pair. "Why that old . . . ," Les spit out. "I'll bet her . . . is as dried out as. . . ." Les felt better after he said that, and the two workers for the town went on to other ditches.

Several of the high-school boys would work with Les on the roads, and they would work hard and be paid the minimum wage, which in 1960 was one dollar an hour. Some days the boys might move a small mountain of gravel on and off the town trucks; other days not so much work was done. It always seemed to the boys that townsfolk would drive by slowly on those slower days, glaring at the waste of their tax monies, or teasing the boys about their shovels taking up roots and growing right into the dirt if they weren't moved faster.

It could be that the boys profited by the criticism of their work. It could be that the criticism produced more responsible adult citizens. Maybe not. It was both a rare and odd thing to hear Les Ryan criticized for working at too slow a pace on the streets, or mowing the John L. Lewis Park with too many breaks. Les was not a young man working for the town; he was in his late sixties. Moreover, Les was working for the town with no pay. He loved the work and he loved the town, and he worked for free, and that was the way it was.

He worked for the town as it was going downhill—losing people, losing houses, losing stores, losing money, and losing the fight against mud and weeds and decay. Still he worked for the town for free. And although Les was a strong and agile old man, his own body was losing against time as well. The situation was hopeless but not serious.

In the last four years of his life, Les bought an old Plymouth for fifty dollars. It had a leaking differential. A wooden peg held the grease in pretty well. Les junked the car a year or two before he died.

Gwennie failed fast after Les died in later summer; she didn't last until Christmas. Nothing much to stay around for except her cats. Since she and Les had no children, Gwennie left all her money to the Saints Church, but it went to the headquarters in Independence, Missouri, instead of the local branch in Lucas. That was a little bit of a shame because the foundation of the local church was crumbling, and they could have fixed it up. Les and Gwenneth liked the town so much.

This Here Good Old Man

It was a small, green house wanting paint like most of those in the town. It was out on the way to the old Cleveland Mines, a company house that had outlasted the Whitebreast Coal Company by many decades. Large elm trees on either side of the street. The house looked kept up but closed up, too. The lawn was neatly mowed. The wood was piled in an orderly way on the north side of the house. Yet the windows were closed tightly, even on summer days. The shades were pulled down. That was not the look of a deserted house in Lucas. They were open and naked to the look of outsiders, with the faded wallpaper turning tan and grey. No, this was the home of someone who did not often venture out.

In fact, it was the home of old Don Stover. He had been the telegraph operator and Station Agent for the Lucas depot of the C.B. & Q. Railway from 1911 to 1949. He was an old man in the 1950's. His family had lived in the town since its inception. N. W. Stover, his grandfather, had begun a drug store in the town in 1877 and manufactured four patent medicines, which were surely a boon and comfort to the customers of his day. But, alas, the formulas for Black Crow Liniment, Iowa Condition Powders, Healing Stypic, and Poll Evil Ointment are gone forever. This may indeed be a lack for there are still far too few remedies for Evil, Black Crows, and Healing, to say nothing of the Iowa Condition.

The July 19, 1899 *Lucas Ledger* reported that: "For the second time, N. W. Stover's Drug Store was burglarized last Saturday night, the thieves effecting an entrance by breaking out a glass in the rear door. About $7.00 worth of clothes brushes, books, etc., were stolen. In both cases, a decanter on the counter half full of whiskey was undisturbed. An effort was made to get Mr. Stover to hire the Chariton blood hounds." While we have no way of knowing what the elder Mr. Stover did about the crime wave at his store, one imagines that there could not have been great hordes of well-brushed, teetotaling, book-loving thieves in the mining town at that time. Surely bloodhounds were superfluous.

At any rate, N. W.'s son, Fred, took over the telegraph office in 1908, the year John L. Lewis left town. Then three years later his son, Don, took over. He rode to work on a bicycle regularly as the trains rumbled by. His wife, Anna, died in 1947, and two years later he retired. Don, Jr. took over for a couple more years when the depot was abandoned and torn down, as happened in towns all over the country. The country needed telegraphers no longer by the 1950's, and by the 1980's people had begun to wonder if they needed the railroads.

Don would have been forced to retire, anyway. He of the soft speech and gentle manner. He was beginning to find it difficult to move his arms and legs and hands, for arthritis was setting in. It seemed that his hands and the art of telegraphy were retiring at the same time. His affliction he suffered in silence, but he knew he must fight the affliction to keep going at all. So he rode his bike around town. Not up the several hills in the town but down on the flat, he rode his old black, girl's bike.

Local kids thought it was a funny sight. This old, bald, white-haired, fragile man riding awobble around the bumps and ruts of the downtown shale and gravel streets.

The twelve-year-old boy came to deliver old Mr. Stover's *Grit* paper every Thursday afternoon after school in the early 1950's. He would knock at the door in the early winter chill with the sun nearly down, hoping against hope that the old gentleman would get to the door faster than last week. There was a sharp and cold breeze, and the sun was threatening to go down in the west especially early that day.

Maybe he's asleep. Or dead. He looks so frail. A sound, muffled, comes through the door like a voice or a table bumped against. In another lengthy minute, Don Stover had come to the door. "Come in, come in. I'm glad to see you. You'll get too cold out there." The boy agrees. As he walks in he is hit full face with intensive vapors of steam. No less than four kettles are on the cook stove and the heat stove. Only one electric light illuminates the dark and it does so in a very partial way. The boy is reminded of ghost scenes in spook movies with artificial fogs fragmenting and blurring the lights. "I hope it's not too hot in here for you," the old man says. "I keep it so hot for my arthritis. I couldn't get around at all if I didn't keep the steam going." "No, it's just fine," the boy says as the pores in his face open like thousands of damp umbrellas.

Old Don shuffles into the other room to get change and the boy looks around the sparse, clean room. A Bible and some other religious books of no significance to the boy look well worn. Some turn-of-the-century, popular art framed—not much else in the way of decoration.

When the boy sees the old man again, he is slightly shocked by his emaciated body, the prominent bones in Mr. Stover's head, his delicate white hair, his ears protruding out beside his sunken eyes. He is wearing a white shirt and tie tucked neatly into his shirt, and his grey suspenders hold his dark green work pants half way up to his boney shoulders.

Mr. Stover gives the boy a dime extra "for coming out on such a cold day. I look forward to the paper and you're a good boy. Very regular. That's the way to be." The boy is embarrassed by the extra money and feels a tactile shock when the old man touches his hand to give him the change. The old hand is soft and translucent; soft, as they would say in town, as a baby's behind. The softness and smoothness of the old man's skin does not reconcile with the aged face and the fragile body. It looked to the boy that if he would exhale too hard the old man would fly across the room. Yet his hands were so soft, covering the hardness of the joints which now were bending permanently. Another few pleasant words and the boy was out in the cold again. A dime to the good.

That was just like old Don Stover, people would say around town. He would give anybody the shirt right off his back. Kids would go there on Halloween and get money. Not treats, money. If they waited on the porch long enough for him to get there.

All the churches in town claimed Don. In one sense they were all right in doing this, for he made the rounds to the Assembly of God, the Presbyterians and the Saints Church. Said nothing but kind things to everyone in a voice scarcely above a whisper. When he died in 1966, he left his money to the churches in equal proportion, not wishing to offend any townsfolk even upon his death.

People might wonder why old Don was so kind to folks around Lucas. Was it because he was so slight and fragile and weak that he feared the world? Would that have meant that if he were young and healthy and big and strong, he might have been tempted to be less afraid, more assertive, as we might say today? One would like to believe that it was not fear that made the old man so kindly towards the residents of the old town. It may be that his frailty, which really began at an early age, taught him something other than fear. It may be that it taught him something about the fragility of life in general. And because his body seemed to be in the process of losing life for so many years, perhaps old Don knew what most of us find out much later, or not at all. That is, that our bodies are transient like old coal towns. We are all fragile and unfinished. We have only each other and that only for a time. Perhaps old Don Stover recognized that truth from his friends in Lucas, and from the premature and gradual loss of his body.

PART 5

Confessions of a Ghost Town
Narcissist (1948–1960)

Lucas Apologia

It's a gawdurn dirty old town, the boy thought, walking along the tracks. It's a dirty, old, brown, fallin'-down town. He was satisfied with the rhyme and thought for a minute or so that he could be a famous song writer with a little bit of luck. Maybe quite a bit. The streets are not even paved and the people are old, not like in Urbandale, but they're all your relations—purt near. And the insides of the houses smell different than the new-pine smell of new houses where we used to live. Those old people in the old buildings. Train rumbles distant. You can put a penny on the track, the boy thought, or on a dead man's eye. Too weird to think about. It's a dirty, old fallin'-down town. Next verse. It's fallin' down all around, the dirty, old town. Nah, forget the words, he thought. Passengers going by so fast look at us and think, they don't amount to much in that town. And the boy thought, "Yes we do; if they only knew," and started making a song out of it. He couldn't tell if the people sliding, carupeting by were dressed up but people here could dress up—It was no use, the comparison didn't work.

The boy began to walk up the hill to his house. The train was gone. And his poems, too. He could walk in the middle of the road until a car came by. Then he'd have plenty of time to get out of the way. Home to be with his baby sister. A funny looking kid he was in a dirty old town, he thought. More comic books to read when I get home but there's hardly anyone to trade them with here. That's another problem with Lucas.

What were the good things about Lucas? That could take some thinking. The boy saw a fallen, dry leaf being crawled on by a fuzzy wuzzy. Well, one good thing was that not too many cars come up the hill and the chances of a fuzzy wuzzy or a caterpillar surviving the hour or so crossing the street were pretty good. Better than fifty-fifty, I'd guess. The boy waited ten or fifteen minutes. He hunkered down and nudged the fuzzy wuzzy insect along its path when it got too complacent. Then he gave up. The caterpillar was on its own. One good thing about the streets of Lucas was clear. They were safe for caterpillars.

The place was good for stray dogs, also. They got dumped on the highway like human tramps. Now a human tramp might come up to a house in Lucas and say to the lady of the house, "Pardon me, ma'am, but I've not had a meal for two days. I believe I'm so hungry I believe I could eat grass." Well, there was one old lady in Lucas who was known to tell the tramp to go to the back-yard for the grass was longer back there. Same with dogs. Lucas people didn't want to let the dogs go hungry but they didn't want them to get too comforted by charity. Anyway, the stray dogs seemed to like Lucas. They hung around in scruffy packs. Still Lucas was probably better for them than most places.

The boy thought about those lucky cousins, the ones who moved to California when he had to move to this place with the musky smell of woodrot and old folks' liniment. One of his cousins had seen the real Jay Silverheels, who was the real Tonto, in a supermarket buying vegetables just like a person.

In truth, the older folks liked the place more than the kids. The older folks could sit around in their backyards and play devil cards and laugh at each other, sometimes kindly and sometimes not.

In time the boy would leave Lucas but he knew he would be scared to do it, feeling a little like those stray dogs that could have been treated better in the town. There wasn't too much sense in going somewhere where life was more cruel. Life in Lucas moved too slowly to make intentional cruelty very intense. So it wasn't so bad that the stores and the homes smelled musty. Decay wasn't really in that much of a hurry and neither were the Lucas folk.

A Spiritual Tramp in Lucas

He was feeling the sun on his eleven-year-old neck. The Roberts boy was sprawled out on the tin roof of the abandoned chicken coop at his dad's acreage. It was late May and the sun shone directly on his face and neck and bounced its rays off the corrugated tin through the breezy air onto his shoulder-blades. That was the second good feeling the boy had experienced that afternoon. There were six abandoned buildings on the place and each had a different boyish use.

The half-built house on the acreage was devoid of any window panes whatsoever. Thus its open windows were perfect receptacles for thrown green walnuts. Why would anyone throw them through an open window? The possibilities are legion for a semi-bored, eleven-year-old Lucas kid. The primary purpose was to enact the role of a baseball pitcher in some future World Series game, or at least the last two innings of such a game. The Roberts kid could whiz the green, near-baseballs into an empty window with fair speed and pretty good accuracy.

In truth, he was so accurate with his throwing—a ball thrown in the window is a strike, one hitting the stucco side of the house is a ball—so accurate that he had to throw wildly by intent to walk an imaginary enemy batter. The imaginary batters were all from the National League.

It was a game in which he could have nearly perfect control. Once in awhile, it must be admitted, he would throw a walnut wildly so as to splatter green, sunburst spots on the stucco wall of the abandoned house.

Earlier that afternoon he had thrown the walnuts wildly and lost an imaginary series game against the Chicago Cubs. He had lost the game to show, no to *prove* to himself that he was fair with himself. If he had only won games, he might have stood accused by his ego of only playing games he could win. He didn't consider throwing the game with himself as cheating. Quite the opposite, it showed himself to himself as a decent and honorable game player.

So he had come to climb up to the roof of the chicken coop, convinced of his own goodness by his trick walnut-throwing. He was lying flat as a prairie on his back, thinking about his essential goodness. Not only was he good. So, too, was the world. School was out. No bullish boys nor bullying teachers, no rows of long, long, long division, and none of the hellishly misnamed "story problems" in his arithmetic book. He had no bellyache from overeating. No one was looking for him. He was not sorry that Mr. Lorimor had been killed in a truck accident years before and that his dad had purchased the rundown haven. All that had happened long before his time. He was content.

As he lay on the roof he imagined himself falling up into the sky, falling through the sweet cirrus clouds into space. If you looked at the sky long enough, it could be done. The clouds were wisps, spirals, and meanders of soft white, gauzy air. A person could see shapes in them if a person tried; here a great chest, there a snake, more to the left an earring, and above that something resembling a turnip.

He stared at the rapidly moving clouds for nearly ten minutes, feeling the vastness of it and the beauty of it. The clouds were moving faster now and a slight wind moved over his face and neck and forearms. He saw the clouds forming in the southern sky and they were forming rapidly. It seemed to have the form of something like, with a little imagination, a person—a person with outstretched arms. It could be—but he couldn't think that—it could be Jesus.

He had heard about Jesus coming back out of the sky and this could be. . . . Maybe this was the day they talked about in school, the day Jesus was returning. He was alone on the tin roof and Jesus was returning. All that he heard was the wind. He was ready for heaven. The cloud formation looked more and more like a white-robed man and the winds were picking up. The boy was ready. He didn't hold his hands skyward, just out at his sides. If this was Jesus, he wouldn't have time to say goodbye to his little sister nor his mom and dad. He experienced panic for a split second. Then the clouds began to dissipate quickly into formless frizzles and rolling, white sky pebbles. His cloud Jesus was gone.

He wondered for a moment if he, this eleven-year-old kid, had stopped the whole thing with his doubt. Not likely, he figured. Maybe somebody's doubt would mess up walking on the water or something like that, but nothing this big. It was just that some clouds began to look funny. He didn't need to remind himself not to tell this story to his relatives, the religious kind or the not so religious. He got teased enough far as he was concerned. He began to walk home. Along the path he pulled out a dry, tallish weed and threw it across the road. It was a good sailing throw. It was a good day even with the world not ending.

Lucas was a good place to learn lessons. It was a good place to ask questions, too. "Why was I fool enough to think I saw Jesus in the sky?" is not the type of question to ponder for too long a time. The answer could be too obvious. But for a boy, gaining manhood atom by atom, in a town which is falling down year by year, there are other questions. Important questions. There are, for example questions about dogs.

The Roberts kid always wanted a pet and Everett and Mae always had good reasons for not getting one for him and his sister. Only a few weeks after his cloud delusions, Everett brought home a medium-sized cross between a collie and a spaniel. Ronnie loved it. He named it *King*. The dog was a bit wild but the kid petted, fed, and nearly lived with the dog for a month. Then one night it ran away. No one ever saw it again.

Everett told Ronnie about another dog that was wandering around a dirt road and the farmer thought he might have to shoot it to keep it away from his stock. He brought it home to Ronnie. He loved it. He named it *Queenie*. She was a sweet dog and he petted her, fed her and nearly lived with her for several weeks. When the Robertses came back from vacation in Moline, Illinois, the dog was gone. Someone had seen it in another part of the county, sucking eggs.

It was then that the Roberts kid began to see a pattern emerging. You get a dog, he thought, then you do all these nice things for it. Then the damn, ungrateful thing runs away—just like it is somekind of a play where they say— "and now the dog runs away." It was more frustrating because the kid didn't know if this was some test by God, some random event, or some basic character defect in dogs. Maybe it was some organizing principle for all of his future life. Maybe not.

He named his next dog *Prince* just because it seemed to be part of the whole parcel of unfaithful dogdom. Yes, yes, he petted him, he fed him, spent hours with him. Prince was a good dog, skinny a bit. It did suck eggs from the neighbors—nonetheless a good dog. It also chased cars. That was all right as long as it didn't catch one.

One day the boy was sitting on the back porch, petting the skinny dog's black and white head, while Tom Thumb and his kids were driving an old tractor with a flat wagon down the street past the Roberts' house. My God, those kids were calling to Prince! He perked up his skinny ears. As they rattled down the gravel road, Tom Thumb's kids started calling the dog again. Again Prince perked up his ears and stood up. The Roberts boy grabbed him and held him in place. Then the dog lurched away and ran for the wagon. When he got down the hill across from the high school gym, the Thumb kids picked the dog up. Ronnie kept yelling, "Come back! Come back! I love you more than those guys and I'm richer." The dog was not a sentimentalist nor a snob; he never looked back. I knew this would happen, the boy thought to himself.

100

And that was true. What to make of it? A philosophy that life is nasty, bitter and short, and that you can't trust any living thing. Naw, he just figured he'd wait awhile before he got another dog. And that is what he did.

In between crises with dogs and the day-to-day chores of small-town living, which weren't many, the boy would read everything possible—sometimes hiding from his parents who had ordained yard or garden work for him. He would hide in the back yard behind the garage or in an obscure corner of the school-house yard. He liked to read outside, in any case. If he weren't hiding he would sit under one of the elm trees where his pa would sit in the summer. Or he would read on the well curb in the back yard. It was a wooden curb and underneath its weathered boards was a thirty-five-foot well. The boy never had any cavities in his teeth all through grade school and high school. Now it is true that his mother, Mae, let him have very little sweets and he certainly had no money to buy them with. Still he liked to think it was the bird droppings from the old pump filtering down into the well water which caused certain chemical changes which prevented tooth decay. That was what he liked to think.

With few kids his own age in town it was natural for him to spend a lot of time thinking, so he did. This is what got him the reputation of being lazy— this and his pa calling him a no-good playboy, not worth the powder 'n lead it would take to blow him up. What an odd thing to be called, the boy mused. (He could muse a lot for neither of his parents whipped him at all. They just yelled sometimes.) I understand that I am a playboy, the eleven-year-old thought to himself. But what I don't know about is that powder and lead thing. It sounds like some kind of gun from hundreds of years ago. I reckon dads have been saying that to their boys for maybe a century or maybe two centuries. Seems like dad could cuss me out with something newer. Oh, the "no good" part I understand. When I was a real little kid, dad And Uncle Bill Angove and Grandpa Roberts would all sing to me:

"Ronnie Roberts aint no good;
Chop him up for kindling wood.
But he's too green to burn."

Beings as the boy was thoughtful or lazy, as the case may be, it was only natural that his mind would turn to things of a spiritual nature. They always had. When his family had lived in the suburbs of Illinois, his mother took the children to a pentecostal church which had a woman minister much in the image of Aimee Semple McPherson. He recalled Miss Nita Watts talking about Aimee's salvation and how she had gone down into a gravel pit to pray and had been saved. Miss Watts wished with all of her heart that we could all get what Aimee got down there in the gravel pit that night.

When they had moved back to Lucas, the Robertses started attending the Saints Church, although Everett seldom went. The boy found the Saints Church to be slow moving and formal compared to the rocking, handclapping pentecostals.

At first he decided he would go to the Assembly of God Church, which provided a lot more heated activity than the saints. He went several times when he was ten years old and his parents, to their credit, let him do that. One of his aunts said he was a spiritual tramp for going to different churches. He supposed he was. When a fight broke out in Sunday School class at the Lucas Assembly of God and the teacher kicked all the kids out of the class, the Roberts boy decided he would accommodate his worship to the faith of his fathers, even though his father didn't attend. Thus it was that he came back to the Reorganized Latter Day Saints. Slowly he accommodated to the slow hymns and the even-voiced sermons, and he was baptized when he was eleven in the same year his mother accepted the faith.

The Saints did not believe in smoking or drinking; movies and dancing they left to one's own conscience. They didn't preach hell much at all but rather the building of the perfect city, the Kingdom of God on earth. The old folks were a gentle lot, all but the pre-teen Saints were hellions who used to beat on each other without much caring about the Kingdom of God one way or the other.

Ronnie had seen the slides showing that the Reorganized Church, or R.L.D.S., was the *true* church on earth restored in its purity from the time of the apostles. Still he heard and read so many things. . . .

In his twelfth year he was sent to the R.L.D.S. Church Camp, where he experienced the emotional and spiritual highlife he had been expecting. Much singing, much fellowship, and maybe just a pinch of the Kingdom of God on earth. One eventful night he heard a minister say to test God, that if one wants an answer from God to experiment, to ask him any question and wait for a definite answer to come.

The boy was feeling very, very spiritual and very good—indeed, everyone was saying just what a good boy he was. Secretly, however, he was going to experiment with God. He loved the idea but was also afraid of it. He had heard of God experimenting with people—like Job, for example. To do it the other way around was scary. How to do it and what questions to ask? Since he felt he knew pretty much everything else of interest to a twelve-year-old boy with the exception of sex, he figured he would just up and ask God if the R.L.D.S. Church was the true one or not. He gave a good deal of thought to the problem. He could throw a wooden farmer match down on the sidewalk and if it lit, it would mean that the Saints was the true church. He had practiced a lot and most of the time the matches lit when he hit the sidewalk with them. Would he do three out of five with God? Somehow the experiment didn't quite fit the problem.

Finally he hit upon the correct method. At the camp, the early-morning wakeup call was sweet and pure organ music piped through a loud speaker. It always woke the boy up. "If it wakes me tomorrow, God, I will know we have got the true church here." This was a good experiment because the hymns were truly beautiful in the dawning hours and because he didn't want to make the experiment something God would have to put a lot of energy into. Besides, he always woke up to the organ music.

The night of the experiment he prayed especially hard and then cut off communication with God to make the experiment more valid. He had a difficult time getting to sleep. He was very excited and his heart was beating fast shortly before he closed his eyes and lay back on the camp cot.

It was a dreamless sleep, and when the morning light came he awoke with a start. There was no organ music playing—none at all. The boy was shattered; there was a lump in his throat. He felt betrayed. He felt that it was very early. He went back to sleep.

When he awoke a second time, it was to the glorious chords of the electronic organ playing hymns of praise and adoration. God had answered him! Then he remembered that he had awakened before the organ music. Did that count? Was God talking out of both sides of his mouth? Was God being excessively legalistic? "Yes, Ronnie, you *did* wake up to the organ in the morning." "But I also didn't," the boy answered in his imaginary dialogue. "It just goes to show," Ronnie Roberts thought, "but what does it go to show?" "Anything you want it to," he reckoned.

Still Not Worth the Powder'n Lead It Would Take to Blow Him Up

The far, sweet sound of the semi's tires whining up the mile-long hill in the early moonlight. That was on the edge of the Roberts boy's mind as he swung in the schoolhouse swing, chest down, knees flapping in the recent dark. He would hear the semi's shift to low or super-low, but even the faraway revving engine had a lazy sound about it. He saw the bats diving in and swooping out of the chimney of the school house. He had heard they were bats. He wasn't sure. And the longing would come over him. Undefined, probably not too unique either, he thought, or maybe it was and he was. And being different was just the beginning. He didn't know.

The swing creaked back and forth with unhurried rhythm of protesting metal. Alone he was and ready for anything that required sincerity and average size. He was sure of that. Well, maybe he wasn't ready for death. Not for other peoples mostly. His own seemed centuries away. It would be even. Born in 1939, he would probably, likely even, die in the twenty-first century. Unless he died sometime, popping out from behind a tree and saving the life of a beautiful, helpless girl who had fallen through the ice some winter and got saved by him after a heroic struggle, during which he literally threw her to safety as he went down for the third time. If he hadn't died, she would have let him make love to her just out of gratitude. That would be sad all right.

He felt his thighs and felt their fine, strong shape, and wondered when his legs and other parts would sag like his grandfather's or uncle's. He let that idea ooze out of his mind like silly putty squeezed too tightly with a fist. Feeling the texture of his Levi's, he sauntered up the hill to the brightly lit patchwork house. Past the elms and box elders. A dog barked a hill or two away, and the gold tin-shaded street lights shone through the high flying bugs down onto the gravel and grass. It was too dark and still to look over the road to Fry Hill Cemetery and too strange to look at the hill across the road where his dad, as a boy, had stumbled over the body of an old woman lying in the wet grass and fog down near the well. It must be time to take a leak and watch TV. Good god. A guy wonders where his erectile tissue will lead to.

Stepping around the side of the house to take a leak, the wind comes up as he pees on the tree. The tin and wood door moves on the tin and wood garage. It always needs more than paint. The boy is tired but to go in will mean struggling with sleep. He closes the screen door silently and smells the old newspaper, varnish and pine odors of the painted grey back porch. The old door to the kitchen always opens with a thud and screech, announcing the completion of his early eve meandering, and he is tired and ready to go. He sees the fatigue on the faces of those who haven't left and now never will get farther away than Goshen Cemetery.

And the buildings are tired, grey-weathered board, coarsened by the seasons; one Main Street shop held together by a big cable. That was Roy Palfreman's doings, he reckoned. So the town took a while to die. Maybe it would take longer than he would. His grandma said, in a defensive mood, that there always was a Lucas and there always will be. But then the farthest away she ever got was Missouri. It didn't matter about that, or the town's roads closing, one every few years. What mattered was to get out. To leave sometime in the cool of the morning to places you could take pictures of, or places where you could be beyond those clumps or trees on the horizon. Somewhere with a different pink and rose sunset through the awkward green box elders.

The sheets were clean and stiff. The van vibrated the window sill and he thought about the Flamingos' *I Only Have Eyes for You.*

Next morning broke with the Kansas City rock and roll station blaring out noxious, antiadult tunes. He sat on the well curb, hating the music as it syncopated in his mind. The music fit his morning mood—hot, muggy, repetitious—and full to the hilt of no redeeming social value. The trees at the top of the old hill were plush with greens, but the grass dusts were bone dry, promising with the orange sun a sweaty, unworkmanlike day in southern Iowa. In the room where he slept, the one put together by Uncle Charlie and Uncle Pete, the doors closed cheaply and without a real carpenter's fit. The chiffonier's circular mirror reflected back his young and tired profile. The lawnmower running down the street made him jump inwardly. It was the sound of his father who mowed in anger. Anger at working alone after hours. And alone without the boy who hid in those few places in the house to be alone—to read about the outside world and prepare for it inwardly. Do my legs (hairless as they are) look like a girl's? *No goddamn help around here—I've got to do everything myself. Buncha lazy bums—just a lot of birds in the nest waitin for the daddy to feed them. You're not nothing but a worthless playboy. Not worth the powder and lead it u'd take to blow you up.* It was true. The boy believed what his father said. An unhappy world for adults out there. They work too hard and don't live long enough to enjoy it. I've got to get up and hide for awhile, and I will.

The seven north-south streets of the town began at the chuckhole pocked railroad tracks next to the pond, a hand-dug body of murky water commissioned by the W.P.A. in 1936. The storefront buildings faced one side of the main street only, and the used-to-be gas stations, grocery stores, harness shops, and barber shops had transmogrified to other uses before they were shut down. The town, like others of its kind, was overchurched with four churches and scarcely 500 souls left to care for. It was probably no accident that the poorest and most lively church was located at the bottom of the hill. The Holy Rollers, as the unbelieving young called them, congregated on Sunday and Wednesday nights, making a joyful noise unto the Lord and to his people for blocks around.

To the left of the Assembly of God church, as the rollers preferred to be called, was the shambles of a grey, black ruin of a house which had been occupied by the Phillips family. It was said that Mrs. Phillips was frightened in a dream by an apparition and frantically tried to dispel it by emptying three bullets into the horror. It was a dream, she had said, but in the morning her husband was dead and Mrs. Phillips was taken away. They had gotten along fine, the old timers said. Now the rubble of their collapsed house gave urgency to forcefully cadenced hymns about the "power, power, wonder working power, in the blood, in the blood of the lamb."

Near the front of the church were two 60 feet elm trees which grew together in front of old Doc Bell's long deserted, two-room office. Between the trees was a thick, wide board which provided a bench for spectators of the actively godly holy rollers. The boy often spent evenings there with other boys, ridiculing the mind-numbing and excited cadence of the preachers. *We laughed so loud in the dark at the Jesus jumpin shuffles because we guessed the thumpin sounds carried through all the hills in town. Edgewise and anyways, the Jesus stumpin stopped and its sounds mingle with our now long-gone laughs somewhere long ago in our ghost town.*

The public drama in the town was here. Poor folks from the countryside came in to partake in the emotion and the boy and his friends waited between the two trees for the roller girls to come out with passions so deep and full that their fears of sin would be left for other days or times. Rarely did it happen. Once though Buzz Skinner put his hands on Betty Hayes' knees, edging upward with a musical question—how much farther can I go? Slight slaps of the hand took him a bit at a time to the musky delights undreamed of in our poor philosophies. Finally she bruised her thighs on the gearshift of the pickup escaping from the confusingly sinful rush of wonder working power. The boys talked about this close call for a time and gave urgings and secret doubts to Buzz's next adventure.

The boy listened with the skepticism and the smugness of an Anglican highchurchman, though such a person would have unnerved him completely had one come into the insular world of southern Iowa. The boy's family were Latterday Saints of the Reorganized species, and while they gave everyone to know that they were not Mormons of the Utah persuasion, they were suspect by the up-the-hill churches representing Presbyterians and Methodists. The boy could not keep those denominations straight since both seemed to drive better cars than the Saints (to say nothing of the rollers) and both cooperated on chili suppers and bake sales. The boy knew he and his family's church was different, and it was because of the persecution, the longing for Zion the beautiful, new revelations, baptism by immersion and slide shows which led to the ineluctable conclusion that the Saints were true, even if the truth had needed to be reorganized. An awkward sound and thought. But no mind. It was the true church.

Saints Church didn't smell too much of pleasure but of serious scents of funereal wellbeing, cared-for wood paneling, fine white altar cloth, mud on the back-row boot stack. The washed out gravel—round, grey green, rose, white and small—slowly spilled over the sidewalks while the Saints opened their hymn books to Page 53 to sing the first and last stanzas.

It was a place where visiting preachers showed the old Jerusalem gospel by way of slides. Aunt Lillie would pop up on Wednesday nights and say, "Now if I've said or done anything to offend anyone in any way, I want to ask for your forgiveness." No one needed to forgive her. Prayers happened so long they could suffocate a boy counting silently for the end; the elder saying, "Now Lord, we know that you know what's in our hearts." The grain of the walnut wood of the pew in front was memorized but forgotten with the next joyful kid moment; out of the building with the buggy, round, lights shining on the laughing going-home-to-bed people.

They were still under the influence of the hymns and they hummed them. "Let the lower lights be burning, cast a beam across the way. Some poor fainting, struggling seaman, you may rescue, you may save", and the still more mournful "Work for the night is coming, when man works no more". People hummed and sang softly as they drove off to home, and there was still an hour or so of TV to watch before resting for the workweek.

On that Sunday evening in August the boy sat with his best friend, a sixteen-year-old, who shared lust of girls, antique cars, laughable people and a sense of inferiority slowly transforming into a shaky, articulated superiority. In the front door of the Roller Church the boys could see the preacher's sweat-rent shirt, his spastic gestures of sincerity, and his breathing cadence, "Jesusa-Jesusa-Jesusa—donta the nama Jesusa make you feela bettera already? Scream yesa to the Lord."

The boys felt the power of their ridicule. It was growing and it would later be called an acid tongue, but as of now they wouldn't have wanted to share the bright lights of the Roller Church with the ranter at the pulpit. They still had room for embarrassment. Finally, the boys felt strangely sad and out of phrases and scenarios with which to whip the rollers. It was time to go home. "I'm glad our churches don't scream and act obnoxious." "They're about the same", said his friend. The boy blanched in the dark and replied that "Yeah, they both sing the same kind of slow, draggy hymns." But he knew deep down in his soul that the restored gospel message of the latter days had only to be had from the grey shingled, little church on the east hill. He had betrayed his faith in the dark and no one save God knew. He had chosen friendship over the truth and he was sick unto death, or at least a little embarrassed.

It was three years before in history class. He, the only Saint in the class, was listening to the history lesson on the Mormon trek across Iowa. The seventh-grade boy in the seat in front of him seemed to be winking at the others in the class, sensing the discomfort of the Reorganized Saintly boy. The discomfort mounted uncontrollably. God was no immediate help. The boy tapped the normal, unstigmatized Protestant on the shoulder and said, "Hell, I'm awful religious, aint I?", at once calling attention to his internal bad faith and his self-explanatory hypocrisy. The terrors of the seventh grade were not all hypermuscled retardates or the viciously innocent advocates of long division.

The school had no rooms or halls large enough to echo but it did smell of new wax and varnish in the fall, and for the youngest of us, glandular, ignorant and graceful in our white country ways, the expectation of drama mingled with the immergent and infinitely reproducable boredom. *Ms. Dales, she got married to a kid she taught in eighth grade. He was a big kid and had flunked a couple of times and husky he was. But they were out with her sister and they went out and parked and she got a blanket out and her sister's boyfriend claimed he stepped right over them in the dark. It was funny, too, because she lost her glasses and her folks was so religious.*

The boys would sit around the big cement well curb or on the sidewalk and say, "Hay, Donna, you want to go out in the weeds with me?" It was always the weeds even when there must have been flowers or clover to go to. Weeds aren't good for nothing else, the boy supposed. The girls didn't laugh and sometimes even if they were older they said just as they should have to the boys, "Don't be thinkin you can diddle me." Though sometimes the boys did. You could tell in the dark when a girl's white socks were upwards in the front window of the car. Some boys were pretty, some had dried sweat, some girls had bad breath, some gave boys dreams. We are all pilgrims, the boy thought. I wonder where my erectile tissue will lead me next.

Fighting for a Bad Conscience

They lived in the Jericho Hills, just a block or two north of the town and later south of the school. Some said the father drank too much. He wasn't a big man but it was still odd to hear a grownup person called "Tom Thumb". Tom and his wife never had a car. He would work as he could though. He had a wagon and a team of horses he would drive into town. A very odd sight that was in the mid-1950's—the couple and their two boys sitting in the wagon following the two discouraged, old horses up the hill to home.

They were poor people probably because the old man drank too much, people thought. Their two sons weren't growing up to be too big, skinny and smallish as they were. The older boy, Darwin, had bright red hair and a matched set of freckles. Being a poor kid, Darwin didn't do too well in school. Like other poor kids, he seemed to be distracted in school. He had things on his mind—or could it have been that he was hungry.

The teacher got on him a lot, anyway. So did several of the kids. But it was true that he could stick up for himself. He might mouth off to a kid and run fast as a little redheaded streak for open ground, and if he got caught and pounded by a bigger kid, he was still sassy. That was the way he was.

But if anyone would have thought about it, they would have had to realize that he didn't have an easy time of it. Nobody really did think about it very much because every kid had his own problems. Darwin hung around with the Lawler kids. They were on the small side and got into trouble with their teachers just about every day. They were all good runners though and they were also quick on the lip.

One day the boy came into school to start his ninth-grade day by putting his rusty brown suede jacket in his locker. Darwin was in the boys' room just walking away from the urinal. The Roberts kid was in an expansive and teasing mood, and he greeted the smaller Darwin with fast footwork and faked punches to the head and shoulders. Bobbing, weaving, and punching with two fingers, the boy was pestering Darwin beyond the latter boy's endurance. Without warning Darwin shot a right cross to the larger boy's eye, hard, which provided a summer night's view of the stars, in the course of a second.

Darwin knew it was time to run and he was fast, but in the second that the stars had exploded in the larger boy's eye, the nature of the horseplay changed. The ninth-grade boy pounced on Darwin, "pummelting him", he would say later "with many blows to the head and body." As Darwin crashed out of the restroom with the other boy on his back, they both plowed head and head-on into the substantial corpus of the school superintendent, B. W. Burnison. This immediately ended the scene, for it was not a good thing to butt the body of a higher authority in the morning or even later in the day.

Appointments to meet with said official were set up on the spot, as it were. And the two boys made their way up to their third floor classes quietly and thoughtfully. Indeed, they were thoughtful. What Darwin thought was probably that he was in a no-win situation again. Perhaps he was used to it. Perhaps he never got used to it.

The other boy sat in study hall praying and full of remorse. He was not praying with remorse, however. He was praying in that time-honored way sinners have of making a deal or contract, if you will, with the Good Lord. "Dear Jesus, I know I don't deserve it but if you keep me from having a black eye, I'll never fight again." It seemed to be a reasonable contract, but since the Lord moved in mysterious ways one could never be sure if he had assented to the deal. It could be that the Lord would find the social humiliation of a black eye to be an educational experience for the boy. It could be that the boy was meted out justice for his early morning teasing and tormenting behavior. The eye hurt, it stung. But by the end of the day the verdict was in, and the Lord's mercy had evidently sensed the ruinous consequences for the boy's social life. The eye did not swell.

Darwin was called into the office first and there came forth an awful yelling, the kind of yelling adults do to terrorize children when lowered-voice threats fail to accomplish the purpose. Darwin was getting reamed. He came out of the office with his face as red as his hair but he purposefully bounced as he walked to show that he was not made meek and mild by his experience. He was a brave kid and he reminded his classmates of the time when Little John Little (no relation) had been taken into the boys' showers and got all his hair shaved off. "I aint gonna worry 'bout it," he had said when he emerged, newly bald. And he said it with such power that everyone believed him. That's what the boys would call being a tough sonofabitch, and that was what Darwin was like.

When our boy went into the office, hoping not to tremble behind his blackened eye, he was greeted in quite a different way. B. W. told him that he wasn't the kind of boy to usually get in trouble, which was true. And as the boy looked at the shiny oaken floor, B. W. reminded him that he was the mayor's son and thus must be circumspect about his behavior. The boy began to look up at his adult superior because he could see that he was getting off the hook. With a contrite heart and gratitude to the good Lord, he promised never, never to fight again. This time the promise was to B. W., since God had already come through on his part of the bargain. "I've sure learned my lesson, Mr. Burmison," he murmured to the older gentlemen with the white hair parted in the middle.

Of course he was sincere, contrite and, of course, he had learned a lesson. Yet his feelings about the lesson were more complex than he would have imagined. The unexpected feeling he felt after relief was guilt. He had started the fracas innocently enough, it was true. But he had started it. Yet it was the smaller, poorer boy who was yelled at, and it was made clear that he was labeled at fault by the official authority of the Lucas School. So the boy felt relieved and guilty at once. Relief was relief and guilt was what he felt about something all the time anyway. So what.

As the year went on, things got back to normal and the boy made a temporary peace with Darwin. Soon it was nearly Christmas and the boy brought to school a Frosty the Snowman pin which would light up if you pulled the chain on its bottom. There was some risk in doing this since he would have been the laughing stock of the school had it been seen on his person. The object of the game was to give the artifact to a girl, Helen Deaton—to be specific, to win a favorable glance or word from her. He had planned to show the marvel to her, nonchalantly pull the chain, light it up and say with feigned indifference, "Here, you can keep it if you want to."

But that damned little Darwin saw the pin and, quick and rascally as he was, he grabbed it and was off like a red-headed flash, turning the light on and off, flaunting it in front of all the boys and heaping great red hot coals of shame on the boy who brought it. The worst had happened and this time it was Darwin's fault for sure. And when the boy struggled to take the Frosty away from the smaller boy, he was subjected to the outrageous slings and arrows of early-adolescent jeering. He was mad.

He met Helen back by the lockers and gave her the object just as he had planned. And she seemed to light up as much as the plastic snowman, but he was still mad. And he was waiting until school let out. He was going to get Darwin no matter what. His promise to God was not greatly on his mind for this was righteous indignation. His cause was just and the other boy was smaller. God would definitely understand.

There were two-and-three-foot snow drifts between the gym and the school in the flat area where the boys played softball in the summer. The sun shone on the snow in the wicked blinding early afternoon day as the school buses loaded up the country kids for their rides home. And there was Darwin, taunting, teasing and yelling at the boy, ready to fight or make tracks as the occasion demanded. It was not a violent fight. The boy was somewhat larger and stronger than Darwin but Darwin was quick and shifty, a talent probably learned from ducking blows at home.

Still the boy pushed him into the snow drift and up again they plunged at each other. They were more irritated with each other than truly angry, but the fight went on with the larger boy getting the better of the going. It was then that an unexpected, sardonic voice came from across the road a few yards away. "That's the way to go, Ronnie, beat the living hell out'n of him. It will save me the job of doing it when he gets home." It was an adult and further it was Darwin's father yelling, was it possible, words of encouragement to the boy fighting his son. The boy stopped fighting and felt nearly at once terror, shock, and finally on understanding what Tom Thumb had said—a kind of sickness he had never known before. The boy was stunned. Darwin's dad not only didn't stand up for his son; it seemed he wanted him to get the hell beat out of him.

Darwin wandered across the street, seemingly embarrassed by his father's loud remarks. The boy trudged up the hill in the snow-bright, late afternoon sun. He felt weak and more than little nauseous. The world wasn't right. Fathers don't do that. It isn't fair. What did he do to deserve such a betrayal? Maybe it wasn't a betrayal; it just seemed like for some random purpose the world had ganged up upon the smaller, poorer boy. The way of the world is that everyone gets a fair chance and if they don't, you pretend that they do.

The boy remembered how at Christmastime the teachers would ask the kids what they got for presents, and how he would lie out of embarrassment for, with all his relatives, he had an embarrassment of riches in the most literal sense. Darwin and the other poor kids were uncomfortable, too, for they couldn't pretend to have received much. But that was it; you pretended. You covered up the inequities in the town. But this, this was impossible, and to the boy's emotional life it couldn't be covered up. He wondered as he trudged up the blue-snow-shadowed hill, what would have happened if his father had cheered for the other kid. It made him even sadder when he couldn't quite imagine such a maddening possibility.

About a year later he was on the school bus with Darwin, and both boys seemed exceptionally happy for some reason or other. Darwin offered the boy an apple, maybe to make up for being such a pain in the ass. And the boy accepted it from Darwin's dirty jacket. The boy felt good. He couldn't afford an enemy like Darwin. It made the world too confusing.

Bad Boys, Ornery Boys, and Shy Ones

During the forty-eight years the mines were percolating in Lucas, it was a poor town with big ideas and a certain amount of hope. After the mines closed, people's ideas narrowed somewhat. Dreams were partialized and fractured for those who stayed around the old place. It was not that there was no wealth around because there was, with the occasional well-to-do farmer and the Baker family who owned the local bank.

When the people decided they would stay in the town, they found for the most part their biographies narrowing their choices in life and most were somewhat satisfied with that. With Social Security payments beginning in the late 1930's, the older folk could even claim a small bit of safety in their declining years.

But it was different for the young folks. They were as glandular and optimistic as most kids in America but they learned, measure by measure, that the town had little in the way of a possible future for them. Some got married way too early, and it seemed that biological accidents were more prone to happen in Lucas than in more privileged sections of the country. With no jobs around in the 1950's, most would move on to a city looking for unskilled, laboring jobs. Some talked about moving out to California but most never made it past Des Moines. The few that stayed around got jobs at the Chariton Wholesale House, or less likely, worked as section hands on the railroad.

For those more poor than most, the future was fairly clear—poverty follows poverty. There are many ways of dealing with being born poor. It can, in some ways, produce a mutuality of sacrifice and the realization that survival depends on people helping each other. That often is the way of "primitive" peoples in the world. Still, poverty in Lucas was never isolated from the happenings in the rest of the world. For this reason, many poor people turn mean, small-spirited or even violent in America, and Lucas for all its quirks could have existed no where else but in America.

Some poor folks were mean in a dramatic way. The meanness of the rich is often hidden from the rest of us. It consists of breaking unions, bullying employees or doing cut-throat competition in the marketplace. The meanness of the poor is not hidden at all from those who have the dubious opportunity to live with it. School kids at Lucas lived with it every day in the 1940's, 50's and 60's.

Adults many times romanticize childhood years—the innocence, the total involvement of children at play, the exuberance. All that is true, but in the childhood of the poor in places like Lucas there is another memory to be dredged up, and that is terror. In the early 1950's in the Lucas School, terror was Elmo Snethen.

Elmo came from a rather large family, several brothers and sisters. They all were as poor as he, naturally, but they all turned out rather well. There was a vast anger in Elmo from the very beginning. Did it have to do with the impoverished nature of his family? Maybe it was the bickering and violence that went on between his parents. Maybe it was the lack of any future to be seen in the town. It is true that some of his kinsmen had not done as well as they should have. His Uncle Delbert was currently spending time in the penitentiary for burning down his grandmother's home for the insurance money. His grandmother was not in the home at the time, but no one in town was certain that he might not have considered that a minor obstacle to his activities in any case. But that was Elmo's uncle.

Elmo may not have been too bright; no one knew for sure. He was kept back in the fourth and fifth grades for showing a lack of appetite for scholarly pursuits. He did come to school regularly through the eighth grade, and during those years the Lucas School yard was not an entirely comfortable place to be.

To understand why, it is important to construct a mental picture of the boy. He was of average height with long, brownish blond hair. Even at the age of twelve, Elmo had the body of a very well conditioned, very strong adult male. His back and arm muscles protruded out of any old work shirt he happened to be wearing at the time. His face, with a perpetual scowl etched on it, was outlined by a strong set jaw and formidable cheek bones. All this was attached to a thick and muscular neck. In a word, Elmo looked mean and appearances were not deceiving.

"Elmo", the fifth-grade teacher might ask, "Where is the rest of your homework? I told you to write the names of two European countries and a draw a map of the countries. All you have given me are the names and one is spelled incorrectly. Where are the maps?" "I didn't hear nothing about no maps." "You will do those maps now." "You never told me nothin so I'm not doing nothing." "You will do it now or have a three-day vacation from school." "Sure as shit, I'll take the vacation," Elmo would say.

The fact was that for those three days, the school, the teacher and the students were on vacation from Elmo. He was the kind of boy who could give the word "bully" a bad name. Once in his cousin's barn, Elmo lined up the seven or eight smaller boys who had been playing a form of makeshift basketball. "All right, you morons, pull your peters out of your pants. I want to look at you stupid jerkoffs." When some, out of fear of God, failed to do it, Elmo told them that he would personally take a pair of pliers and crack their nuts if they didn't. They did. Elmo walked by all the boys, making disparaging remarks about their private parts such as, "Yours looks like a fish worm, but what fish would want it?" and the like. All the littler boys ran towards home, stopping a safe block and a half away to shout at Elmo things such as "I'll be glad when you're dead, you rascal you." And they meant it, too.

It was at school where Elmo's anger at the Lucas version of the world came out most viciously. He had beaten all the smaller boys into submission and even intimidated the larger ones. Recess was the time of the great terror. Elmo would pick out a hapless boy, preferably one prone to tears, and pound on him until he had frightened him nearly to death. Each boy watching knew full well that he could be that boy.

But Elmo was not satisfied with merely beating the boy into tears. His next step was to order (in imperious tones) every other boy to go and club the hapless victim as well. Each boy was forced to make a decision. College professors and their ilk might call it an existential dilemma. To do further punishment to a victim of Elmo's vicious whims or to risk the same treatment for oneself. The boys knew that in the movies a hero would step out of the crowd, grab the bully by the neck, swing him around and say, "If you're looking for a fight, try me." That was in the movies. The boys had a good grasp of reality, and the kindly ones hit the victim as softly as possible and hated themselves as cowards for the rest of the afternoon.

By the time Elmo was in the eighth grade, his scholarly ineptness and physical viciousness were at their zenith. It was at that unfortunate moment that Wendell Moon moved to the old town with his father. They moved to a farm just south of Lucas on the other side of the railroad tracks. Wendell was slightly overweight and slightly shy and new; in other words, a perfect target for Elmo. Elmo's rage was directed at the hapless boy and he pounded him again and again. Often Wendell was too frightened to come to school.

Wendell started riding the school bus home although he could have walked. But Elmo would be there, beating him in the face and threatening his life. Wendell's dad began to wait for his son at the school bus drop, and Elmo said he was going to beat shit out of him, too, or take them both on. One day late in the afternoon Elmo went downstairs to the boy's toilet, and Wendell was down there waiting for him with a baseball bat. When Elmo came in the door, Wendell cracked him on the shoulder with the bat just as hard as he could. He hit Elmo a glancing blow off his left ear and Elmo would have torn him apart, except that he could not get his hands on the bat. Wendell hit him in the stomach and on the shinbone, and that's when someone called the sheriff to come down from Chariton. Elmo was pretty badly hurt but nothing got broken. Wendell and his family moved away.

It wasn't as though the worm had turned; it was that the victim had gotten as crazy as his oppressor for a little time. And in their secret heart of hearts, the other boys wondered if they would have picked up a bat against the vicious boy. Most all the boys were glad they didn't have to find out. The boys tried to get along, just get through the days. Like the miners in the town seventy years before, they looked for ways out of trouble. Trouble would come, nonetheless, and when it did some stood up to it and some backed away. But mostly people would do both at one time or another, just like Wendell did with Elmo.

Elmo left town soon after the ballbat incident. He was sixteen, anyway. Before he did, however, he got another test of his meanness. In May of that year, 1952, the district manager of a feed company was driving into Lucas to see one of his salesmen. As he came in on the road past the ruins of the old Whitebreast No. 1 Mine, he saw a man hanging on a barbed-wire fence. The sun had barely come up that morning but it was a bright and gentle kind of day. He stopped the car and went over to the man. His insides had been blown away by the sixteen-gauge shotgun in the grass beside him. It was Elmo's daddy; he had gotten up during the night to chase some dogs away from his sheep. He didn't have a trigger guard on his old gun, and somehow he got his gun tangled in the fence. Folks said he blew daylight through himself and the men of the town who saw him said it was an awful thing to behold.

Later that day Elmo came into Rogers Hardware Store, and they told him his daddy had shot himself in an accident and that he was dead. "Good," Elmo said. "That saves me the trouble of doing the job, myself." Everyone agreed he was a bad boy. The last folks heard of him, he was in the pen in Texas or somewhere down south.

There weren't too many boys in town as bad as Elmo. Most were sometimes ornery, sometimes a little stupid; especially when they were drinking or chugging mixtures of Bubble-Up and Vodka. When the Conoco Station was robbed in the early 1950's, several dollars were taken plus all the candy bars and cigarettes. When the high school boy was handing out candy bars and cigarettes to anyone who wanted them, the sheriff came down and arrested him. He came from a very poor family and he had seen the movie, *Boys Town*. When they took him to the local judge, he said he'd done the robbery so he could go to Boys Town, and he asked please if he couldn't be sent there. The judge gave him a couple of years at the Boys Reformatory at Eldora instead, and he was quite disappointed, people around town said. But he was just an ornery boy, not too bad as Lucas boys go.

The fact is that ornery boys were the rule in Lucas in the 1950's rather than the exception. People might think there is not much to do in a Southern Iowa near-ghost town. People are wrong. The boys growing up in the old town had active minds and sometimes, it seemed, even more active glandular functioning. Take, for example, the Sadie O'Brian incident.

Sadie was a nicely-formed girl of sixteen, a sophomore at the high school. She was a pleasant enough girl and most sought after by the local lads. She did have one character, we cannot say "flaw", but one kind of vulnerability. In this she was not unlike the other girls of her age and temperament. She would, under the proper or rather improper circumstances, shriek. Other girls might scream if excited or disturbed, but Sadie would scream in a profound and exceptional way. It was something to behold.

So the high school boys, being of sound body and less sound but highly active minds, would spend time creating the circumstances under which Sadie would shriek. There was a general tendency among the boys to take girls into out-of-the-way places such as the cloak room, the curtains behind the stage, storerooms, or hidden corners of the gymnasiums to acquire a specific knowledge of the girls' anatomy. Usually not a great deal of anatomy was discovered, as the girls were as shifty as quicksilver. Nonetheless, it was all the more thrilling that many of the girls squealed during the process. Shy boys, fat girls, and those going steady did not participate in these rites. Sometimes, however, willingly or not, Sadie was a participant.

It was an early afternoon late in the winter, when Mr. Howell had left typing class with the instructions to put away the equipment, that the incident happened. Today it would rightly be called sexual harrassment but in 1956 it was called making Sadie scream. About three boys went with Sadie into the equipment room adjacent to the typing rooms. They were teasing her and feeling her up. Sadie did not like it at all. She screamed. It was time for the bell to ring for the next class when Dike Clouse had a fragment of an idea. The boys quickly closed the door of the closet-like room, locking Sadie in.

She screamed even more loudly but to no avail, because the room was in the basement of the school and it was deserted. Everyone had gone to the second-floor study hall, and everyone knew that poor Sadie was padlocked in the typing supply room. "Where is Sadie?", Mr. Howell queried. The boys and girls looked from their fingernails out of the corners of their eyes. "Never saw her," one boy lied. "Maybe she got sick." another fabricated. But the boys and girls all knew and were accessories to the crime. Time passed. Study hall ended. Basic Science class began in another room.

It had been a long time, more than an hour now. Some were actually forgetting about Sadie. Others were wondering what had happened. What had happened was this. Sadie had yelled and pounded on the door as loudly and as hard as possible. Then, perhaps like Wendell Moon, her victimization made her crazy in a useful way. She flung herself against the wooden door four or five times, screaming with the belief that she had be confined to hell. On her last lunge she smacked open not only the door but the casing and door frame as well. It was, in a sense, a magnificent physical achievement. It was then that the real drama began. Sadie called her mother.

Sadie's mother, Blanche, was, to use a non-Lucas word, formidable. This was true in a number of ways. She was married with several other children, and she ran the farm. It was not that her husband did not work. He did. It was always clear that Blanche ran the show. She worked harder than most of the men in the county—plowing, handling animals, throwing around 70-lb. hay bales. She talked rough and she swaggered. She had a set of shoulders on her that any local man would envy. Her biceps did not ripple but they may have been a close alloy to steel. She was five-foot-five and could outcuss most men in town if she had a mind to.

Sadie called her just after she had broken out, her voice broken with tears. Most girls or boys in that situation would have called the County Sheriff. He was used to coming to the Lucas School. It was more serious to call Blanche O'Brian. She was coming to rescue and avenge her daughter.

Meanwhile in Basic Science Class, B. W. Burnison, the superintendent of the school, was trying unsuccessfully to get his students to elucidate the difference between organic and inorganic materials. The students had never heard tell of such because they had not read their Basic Science texts. Suddenly the door in the back of the room arced open and the metal knob smashed into the plaster wall. "All right, you good-for-nothing bastards, which of you did it?" It was not a question that Blanche was asking, with her hands flexing into fists and her legs planted apart. It was the hope of physical combat.

"Now, you sonsabitches," she said, tossing the brown, veneered chairs off and out of her way as she moved through the classroom. "Now, who's gonna come out here and fight me like a man?" B. W. Burnison, a slight, grey-haired man, was not emotionally prepared for this excursion into possible mass violence in his classroom. Therefore, he said to Blanche something which sounded like a line from a "B" movie. "Now, now then, Mrs. O'Brian, let's not act in haste and do anything we'll regret later." He was ignored and fairly cowered up at the blackboard.

"Damn you to hell, Dike, are you gonna come out and fight like a man?" she raged. Dike, who was better than six feet tall and no weakling at that, suddenly got very interested in the cover of his Basic Science text on his desk. The collective heartbeat of the silent class raced on. The big boys in the class who had terrorized Blanche's daughter were humiliated and physically scared for their own well-being.

"You rotten louses aint worthy for me to whip but all you have to do is breathe in my daughter's direction and I'll break you in half so fast, it'll make your head swim." Yes, the boys thought, she would. Blanche knocked down a couple more chairs out of the way with her right hip and exited, slamming the door so loudly that a few of the boys imagined her cracking their fingers in it. She was gone. Class didn't resume. Quite a few of the boys went to the boys bathroom to talk it over. Quite a few more went because they suddenly had to.

In the years that followed Sadie was still a little temperamental. She fell in love with a town boy and later a boy from another town. She pretty much didn't get teased after that.

Most of the things ornery boys did at the school were not as dramatic as that. Sometimes they would put their hands in the pockets of their tight jeans, pulling them up around the crotch, and say to the girls, "See my new shoes." Or they would drive around town, backfiring their dual Hollywood glass pack mufflers if they had cars. Nothing to get worried about.

Some boys, of course, were too shy to be as ornery as they would have liked. So they disdained and feared orneryness such as throwing rocks on the school superintendent's house, which other boys did, or stealing watermelons or getting too fresh with the girls. These boys made a virtue out of their shyness and felt morally superior and smarter even than the ornery boys.

Kynard and Ronnie were shy, thirteen-year-old boys but they were, as it turned out, megalomaniacs. They were not as big and aggressive as the ornery boys, certainly not as the bad boys. Orneryness made them nervous. They laughed a lot because they were nervous about bullies, girls, adults, teachers, other towns, religion, parents, and other things too numerous to mention. They laughed, and eventually they found that it was a strange sort of power to laugh. They made fun of everything, especially themselves. That covered that problem; they had become, to some extent, invulnerable to the tearing of others.

And just for the liveliness of it, they had fallen in love with the absurd. Although they were teenagers, they watched Howdy Doody. And when the Space Ranger on the Captain Video Show was advertising Tootsie Rolls, they would be eating one and then trying to blow the Captain Video secret message whistle ring. When part of the half-chewed Tootsie Roll ended up on the ring, they laughed for days. They developed a secret language. They walked around the old town at night, making fun of everyone they knew. The whole town was an inside joke. They loved it and they loved laughing at it.

One Spring day they got up on the top rung of the fire escape at the school, and in their shy but megalomanical manner began to harangue the younger children with speeches. One of the boys pretended to be W. C. Fields, the other "Oil Can Harry", who was the villain on the Mighty Mouse TV Show. Doing their harangues and imitations gathered a sizeable group of small children beneath them. From time to time they would throw pennies down from the balcony, watching the younger kids trampling and fighting each other for the coins. They made wry comments about human nature and laughed until they got the hiccups. Was this how John L. Lewis got started? Probably not.

One of the boys moved from the school and the other began to play basketball, and the town did not seem as lunatic to him anymore. In one way the boys were not unusual Lucas characters. They knew that laughing at oneself is a good way to avoid that kind of snobbery folks in Lucas called getting "the big head." No, Lucas was no place to get the big head. Almost everyone knew that.

Holding On to the Green Times

The boy had thought summer all the dark, wet, winter-slush long. Summer will come. The town's unpainted buildings got dressed up by the volunteer trees and shrubs, which covered the recent decay. Mowing one's yard was giving order to the place. Some people didn't. Not only did ditches grow up but the yards of the old and poor, the transients from Missouri, the abandoned houses owned by the state because their inhabitants got old-age assistance. The state didn't keep places up.

Some, however, mowed beyond their yards and ditches. A few had orchards and well-kept gardens. They fought a rear guard action against the seeming disorder of nature's return. But with the spring, newness would come to the old town. You could take walks in the evening, though most people didn't. And you could smell the new grass, pick up maple squirters, hooked together, it seemed, like the well-turned thighs of a young girl. The frogs, crickets and birds would come back, and especially the Mourning Doves would come back to town. You could hear their early morning songs—lazy, lugubrious, calming. You could hear them when the washing machines paused and when the early morning smells of bluing and soap and bleach came from some widow's clean home.

But all that said and done, it was the green fuse of leafing days the boy wanted from Spring. If it were Spring, he told himself, slogging through the wet, cold snow. If it were Spring. When it gets to be Spring I will appreciate it. Winter didn't perk you up; it made you tired. Like in this book that said if you don't go to the toilet when you need to, the poisons build up and that makes you tired. It's the same thing. Maybe not the same thing but you get tired of Winter, anyway. If it were Spring, what would he do? Enjoy it. How? Take in the green. Just take time and take in the green. A half hour, maybe. Just sit and look at the trees and grass and the shape of the hills and be thankful. Maybe to God. No, that's not it. Just look at the green things growing. Sit on a step and do it. Just take time out and do it.

When Spring came, in early May, his head was flooded with girls and music and his body, religion sometimes, stuff he had to do. Spring's green got put into the background just like in any technicolor movie. Life is stories, not looking at green. For a second he remembered his Winter promise. He sat on the cement porch looking south, down the hill at the new greened trees and shrubs and grass. He tried to catalogue them all but finally gave up on that.

It occurred to him that he was stupid, watching the green. Things were happening. He had to make things happen. He got his basketball down from behind the tin garage door and practiced sinking jump shots, to the amazement of any imaginary crowd that could be watching. Some other time for this Spring and Summer stuff. And so the thoughts passed. There's time when I get old. But will all the greens still be there for me? And will my eyes take them in? He put the thought out of his mind and rubbed hard on the new pimple on his forehead. He would mow the yard if he had to.

There would be softball practice at the ball diamond if those grey, shapeless clouds would break just a little. The kind of day was emerging that older people would say looked like it could rain all day. They didn't care too much. The boys would say, "Think the rain will hurt the rhubarb?" "Not the canned rhubarb," or a laconic "Too wet to plow, too warm to snow." Older people didn't care that much. Boys did. They wanted to play ball down at the ball diamond.

Ray Polser, Golda's son, had built the ball park and it was just on top of the slag of what used to be the Big Hill Mine. The boys liked teams from other towns to come around to play there. The Lucas boys knew you didn't slide into second base or any other because the remains of the mine—the slag, cinder, and shale—would peel off a good part of the visitors' dermal layers if they tried to slide.

Ray had formed a girls' softball team that put the town on some sort of map because the girls were good. Some, in fact most of them, weren't from Lucas. With the lights on at night and the cars parked all around the ball park, Lucas was, if not bathed in glamour, at least dipped in formal glory for the evening.

The girls' team was the Lucas Blue Belts, named for a local feed store and their white satin suits, with bright blue accessories, glowed an incandescent shimmer of grace when they warmed up. Fast pitchers. They had good hitters, too. They would generally lose to the Greenwood Park girls from Des Moines, who were always the state champs, but they seldom lost to anyone else. They played the men's team, too, and would beat them. Although the men's uniforms were not the reason they lost, they were not as well tailored as the women's. They all had advertisements on their backs from local businesses and people would laugh everytime the guy would come to bat with the slogan, "Fry Hill Cemetery—A Good Place to Rest." Maybe that wasn't too funny after all.

The night games would bring people together from town and the surrounding countryside. They would charge 35¢ for some games and take up a collection for the electric light bill sometimes, but Ray never made any money on his ballpark on top of the mineshaft.

When the boys would go out to practice (if the rain would only hold up a little), they would sing the songs broadcast over the loudspeakers Like *How Much is that Doggie in the Window?*, by Miss Patti Page, the singing rage,

119

or *Beatlebaum,* by God knows who. The boys would have loved to play at night, or even practice then, but there was no money for paying for the lights, so they played in the afternoon when they got the chance.

They tried to mimic the casual catches and hard, straight throws of the men or, better yet, of the Blue Belts. It was hard to do. And the magic of the place wasn't the same in the daylight. Lots of magic things happened at night; girls would snuggle their boyfriends on the hard, wooden benches; drunks would laugh a lot or maybe throw up over by the railroad tracks. Once a woman walked all the way from Chariton—nine miles to the ballpark at Lucas— because her young husband had left her alone for the night and she thought he was down at the Lucas ball diamond, flirting with another woman. She was right. She screamed at him a lot behind the main bleachers and he drove her home like a whipped pup.

Some older fellows did get drunk on beer, and though they usually didn't get too rowdy at the ball games they often did need a place to relieve themselves. One night a drunken, old man asked the boy which way to the outhouse. A small boy pointed to the lot east of the ball diamond over by the C. B. & Q. tracks. The old man staggered in the opposite direction, heading west toward the edge of left field. The boy stood up and yelled, "Hey, the outhouses are out the other way," at the top of his lungs. This caused all the people in the stands to first, laugh at the boy (the nearest adult shussing him) and, second, focus on the drunk relieving himself over by the left field fence. The boy was sobered by his embarrassment but the drunken, old man was not sobered by anything for a goodly time thereafter.

Although nothing much but weeds and scrubs grew on the manmade desert of the leveled slag heap, the boy was reminded that it was summer and the time to be alive midst the green growing sights and smells of the ghost town. How to appreciate it was the problem. How to make everything stop to appreciate it was the problem. And when Ray Polser decided that he had lost too much money on his team and ball diamond, the bleachers and lights were torn down. Some people in the town thought folks should get together and chip in to keep the place going—something for the kids to do, don't ya know. But they never got together for that, or later to save the high school when it closed down. Folks in Lucas didn't really get together that much.

So the ballpark was gone with all its images of lights, music, yelling and playing ball. It was another lesson for a boy growing up in a ghost town. It was a lesson about how things don't last. Folks in Lucas hadn't read Jean Paul Sartre, where he says mankind is a failed and useless passion and that all our projects are incomplete. But given another choice of words, he could have gotten lots of people to agree with him. The boy was still frustrated that he couldn't hold on to the greens of spring and summer when they came. Every winter in Lucas he vowed to do it but every spring and summer he forgot mostly, or fantasied about sex or heroics of some future time. And he forgot about the green, growing images he wanted to save in his mind. There was always another summer. But not always in Lucas, it would turn out.

Lucas Buckaroos

It was the beginning of a great, hot morning. The heat of the day mixed with excitement and dust in the downtown street. It was the second Friday in June, 1953 and it was movie night at Robinson's Movie House and Grocery Store. The kids would get more excited as the day went on—reading the movie handbills, hoping for a Lash LaRue thriller or some kind of *Bowery Boys Meet the Spooks,* or something like that. Anything was good. Toward evening the tension got into all the kids' throats. Then they went and put penny candy and Kist Soda Pop ("Get Kist") and chunks of Bubble Gum all together in their mouths to cool down the excitement.

They shouldn't even be that excited. It was only a Gene Autry movie. Lots of kids could do without that singin'. Still, when they trooped into the theater and crammed into the sixty, assorted seats they were tense. A few moments later when the mystical blue flood light came on, they spoke more serious and low than they had to. During the last song before the movie, a Jimmy Wakeley favorite, girls would shush and slap their little sisters to make them keep quiet.

Finally the movie came on with a glory that was foreign to Lucas. The yodel-throated cowboy was up there on the screen with his sidekick, Smiley Burnett. It wasn't too long before the Lucas kids saw a rattlesnake on the screen just to the rear of Gene's horse, Champ. They screamed a warning to Gene, who pretended not to hear. Champ reared with a sharp jerk that snapped the reins at Autry's elbow. That was all Gene knew before a million blazing, glittering stars burst into his vision.

However, it was not long before Gene was up and yodelin' again. Gene meets the girl. "Now, what would you like to hear?" "Your Last Goodbye." "I know that one." "I picked up the trail to your heart," he sings. The Lucas kids judge the girl to be too scrawny but they like her fringed, cowboy outfit with the cactus sewed on the vest.

There is Gene's comical sidekick at the scene of the crime. "Why, this is an outrage or I ain't a foot-high sapsucker," he yells. The Lucas kids make a mental note to remember that one. Then the kids squeal with the inexhaustible, inevitable chase scene where Gene boffs the archcrook just like he is supposed to do. Evil was a little more slippery to deal with in Lucas, but in Hollywood it seemed like Gene and Lash LaRue and Ron Reagan had the bad 'uns on the run. That was real good.

At the end of the picture and after the projector had broken down its usual number of times, things got sadder up there on the silver screen and more realistic to the Lucas kids. Old Timer, the girl's father, was sick abed, and after Gene had rescued his ranch and daughter, he called all the townsfolk around him. "Speeches are not exactly my strong point so I'd better sing." (The Lucas kids weren't sure that was good logic.) "That's why I'd like to dedicate my next song to the Old Timer." (The old fellow looked like any of the spit-and-whittle crew who hung around the town bandstand—wrinkly with tobacco spit-stained whiskers.)

"Why, the sun's in the west, you've earned peace and rest, old buckaroo.
You old buckaroo, your ridin' days are through.
And when God calls you from off the prairie range,
You're waitin' for the change.
Because you're sooo weary, buckaroo."

Lordy, that song seemed like it could apply to half the old folks in the town that humid, hazy evening. The kids piled out of Robinson's combination grocery store and movie house and commenced to beating on each other to relieve the tension. "Roy Rogers' horse could take Gene's anytime." "Gene don't even look that strong to me. Charles Atlas could take him." "Who do you think you're kiddin'?"

As a herd of ten-year-olds walked up the hill full of Hollywood glamour and justice and music, one said to another. "That there Old Timer looked just like your Uncle Charley." "You've got the gol-darndest imagination," his older friend said and shot him nine times with his plastic six shooter. Gradually they return from the Hollywood Ghost Town to the one they are growing up in. Some wish they lived in the golden west. Some wish Gene could sing better. Some are happy. Eventually, late into the June night, they all fall asleep.

The Last Shivaree

The old men, sitting in the bandstand next to the bank, had just come from behind the tavern to sit outdoors. It was a heat-fogged, blue-hazed evening. It was still warm enough to remember the heat of the day. The old men were watching three cars stopping down at the town park. "Don't reckon those boys have got something better to do, just worthless as teats on a boar, they are."

"No, just drive around and make dust," says the other flannel-shirted man. "Shoot, I don't reckon you was a hellion." "No, I wasn't." "You'd steal watermelon." "I'd druther starve than steal anything." "That's what those boys are doing," the other old man said. "Starving?" "No, they're out a stealing watermelons." "Well, I didn't get your drift," the other fellow says and wipes his mouth on his sleeve.

"No, I believe the boys is going on a shivaree." "Who was it got married?" "I believe it was the Watkins boy. Oh, he give his folks a lot of trouble. I guess he's settled down now. He's the one that married the Ellis." "The one who had fits?" "No, that was the sister." "Of the one who had fits or got married?" "I don't believe you've got a brain in your old head." "I'm talking about the one they are pulling the shivaree on tonight." "Well, they could be stealing watermelons," the other old man said.

The boys parked down at the town pond. They saw the old fellers up at the bandstand. The boys were going to pull a shivaree out west of town. "Let's wait till they're in bed together before we shivaree 'em." "We'll ask 'em, stupid. We'll call up and ask 'em if they're in bed together. What we'll do is wait till their lights go out. I'd hope to reckon. We'll drive out there slow; stir up some dust in the old bandstand. There's several geezers up there."

The boys drove slowly in front of Hunter's store and the tavern and the town pump, then tore off—all three cars of them—around the dust in front of the bandstand. "Good golly, Miss Molly!" one boy said. "Eat my dust," another yelled. A third boy thought, "I sure wouldn't want to get old." Then he said that to his buddy. "I sure as hell wouldn't want to get old like them geezers." "It's either get old or die," his buddy said. "Shoot, that's all right with me—live hard, die young and make a beautiful corpse." Then he spun his tires and kicked gravel and dust up in front of the bandstand. One of the old men said, "Them crazy devils had better get the law called on 'em." But he didn't do anything about it.

The boys drove down Highway 34, turned sharp off onto the gravel road south, and raised three cars worth of dust into the darkening sky. Then they turned off their lights and idled the cars into the driveway next to the farm house rented by the newlyweds.

They kept as quiet as could be as they crept against the house. None of the boys wondered where the shivaree custom came from. It was just one of those things that nobody around town would know. The boys liked to sneak around after dark and they would do it every chance they got. They would spy on couples making out in parked cars. They would bushwhack them, yelling, pounding on the cars, scaring them out of whatever they were doing. Helped keep the population down, they figured. They would steal watermelons and, if they were lucky, get shot at so's they'd have stories to tell about it. At Halloween they would dump over privies or haul someone's car into the entrance of the school.

Then, of course, they would sneak around and shivaree some couple a week or so after they were married. Tonight they carried pots and pans, big steel spoons, a policeman's whistle, a five-gallon bucket, two moon hub caps, and an old school bell. They crept up beside the house, which was dark and quiet within. They waited a moment. Laughter. Somebody yelled "quiet"— then all hell broke loose as it was supposed to do.

Somebody honked the horn of Watkins' Chevy pickup and everybody started beating on the cans and bells and hub caps. They were whistling and stomping and yelling as loudly and obscenely as they could get.

"Hey, you guys, get your sorry butts out here. Quit bumpin the hump and get out here. Yahoo! We know what you're doin in there. Quit it and come out." More banging and yelling. "Don't be playing possum with us. We know you're diddling in there." More yelling.

Finally a light goes on in the shadeless window upstairs. The noise increases. Finally, Jim Watkins appears at the porch door. He is embarrassed, the boys guess, although they can hardly see his face with the kitchen light behind him. "What are you guys all wantin? Doesn't your mammas know where you boys are tonight?" "Shivaree!" someone yells out. "Where's your old lady?" someone yells. "She's just right here," Jim says as Sandy Watkins steps into the doorway. Sandy is five months pregnant and dressed in a blue flannel bathrobe. She doesn't say anything.

"Well, what have you got for us? one of the boys asks. "Got for you," Jim says. "I aint got nothing for you." "You're sposta have beer and cake, crackers and cheese, all that kind of stuff." "We aint sposta bring our own food to the shivaree. You're sposta feed us."

"Feed your guys? We ain't got enough food in the house to feed Sandy and she's going to have a baby here in a few months. We got oatmeal and no milk to go with it." Sandy burst away from the door in tears and they could hear her crying as she ran upstairs.

Then the boys knew that it was true. The Watkins had no food in the house. There was silence for the better part of a minute. The boys were thinking up a way to cover their retreat. Finally one said, "Okay, Jim, we'll let you go this time but, by gawd, we'll be back." "Sounds good to me," Jim said. He was nearly as embarrassed as the boys. He hadn't told them to come out. It wasn't his fault they had come. He just didn't like everyone knowing his business. He went up the stairs to comfort his wife.

They boys drove pretty slow on the way back to town. They cussed each other out on the way. What the hell kind of a shivaree was that supposed to be? It wasn't my fault and I didn't think it up. That was about as funny as a doggone rubber crutch. Then the boys were silent the rest of the way home.

PART 6

Aftergrowth (1867–1985)

Ed and Katherine's Century

Old Ed Roberts would sit on the enclosed porch of the house in Lucas. Ethel, his daughter, and her husband, Bill, lived in the seven-bedroom house on the West Lucas hill. By 1960, Ed had lived in the house rented from the Bakers next door for thirty-five years. To be old was no struggle for Ed and he knew what struggle was. He was slow and thoughtful. He half-way kept to himself. He knew that time would heal wounds and eventually make everything all right, but the way time did that, was by exhausting a person. By the time Ed turned ninety in 1957, he was exhausted all right. He would listen to the news, sitting in his chair, or watch the television when it didn't hurt his eyes. Or he would read the *Des Moines Tribune* or the *United Mineworkers Union* paper or the *Chariton Weekly*. Once when his grandson had gotten an autograph book for his birthday, he asked Ed to write something in it. Ed said he couldn't think of anything to say. The boy's feelings were hurt. A couple of days later he asked again, and Ed said he couldn't see how to do it. The boy's feelings were hurt for a long time until one day he saw Ed make an "X" on his old-age pension check.

Ed had gone to school only three months in his life. He had learned to read on his own but never to write. Maybe that was embarrassing but writing wasn't too much use in the mines where he spent most of his worklife.

Work started very early for Ed and it was no joke. Ed's dad, John L., a Welshman, had come to Tennessee to work as a miller in a Welsh settlement in 1853. John L. came to work in the coal mines of Cass County, Illinois, after he was wounded in the Civil War. That was where Ed was born. John L. tried his hand at farming in Lucas County, Iowa, and with his wife, Sarah, began to raise their children—Cynthia, Catherine, Jim, John and Ed. They were all tall, lanky hard-working folks. It was good that they could work because in 1875, the year the mines opened up in Lucas, John L. died, leaving Sarah and the children to fend for themselves. Sarah would marry again and bear six children by her next husband, a gentleman farmer named Mr. Cackler.

So from the time Ed was nine, he was on his own. He had heard there were jobs up at Des Moines and walked the forty miles with his brother, John, looking for them. Twice on his walks to Des Moines, he saw a ragtaggle band of half-starved Indians. It scared Ed and John when the Indians asked for food. The Indians understood when the Roberts boys told them they had no food. They didn't look much better off than the Indians. When Ed found work on a farm near Des Moines, he stayed there until the work ended. Sometimes he would walk the forty miles home in a day and part of the night.

When he became older, Ed would deny his pa's Welsh blood. He claimed that his mother, Sarah, was half Indian. "I'm not nothing but a big Indian; that's all that I ever will be." At six feet and three inches, and with high cheek bones and a convex nose, he could pass for an Indian, and he seemed to like the idea of it. He would especially stress his Indian background when he sipped rye whiskey with the miners on Saturday evenings. Eventually sipping whiskey was too slow for Ed and he became a hard drinker.

In 1887, when he was twenty-one, he got a job working on the boiler, stoking the engine which produced the steam energy for the mine. It always seemed that his tall frame was better suited to work on the outside of the mine—up where the wooden tipple would not cramp him like the compact "streets" and "rooms" three hundred feet beneath the earth. He worked the old Cleveland Mine for four years until it closed in 1891. He was making $1.67 per day and he thought he might get married if his good fortune continued. He did odd jobs around town for farmers for the next couple of years—then it was back to the mines.

Once he heard the mines were hiring in Eastern Illinois and he went back there for a time. Then it was back to Lucas for mine work again. In 1894 Ed married Katherine Baker, who grew up west of Lucas. When they applied for a marriage license at the new courthouse in Chariton, it was a tough time for Ed and his eighteen-year-old bride. The mines in Lucas were working only one side of the shaft, and Ed could not afford to pay the cheap rent on the company house in Lucas. Katherine was a farm girl and she didn't care for the new insecurities of married life with a coal miner.

Katherine was a head shorter than her husband and round faced almost squat in appearance. She desperately wanted to be happy but she, like Ed, was born into hard times. She knew the things a farm girl had ought to know—to plant potatoes by the dark of the moon, to be cheerful to strangers, not to let a cat near a new born baby (for it would suck the air away from it). She had heard that a person with long fingers will work hard for an entire life. Her hands were short fingered but Ed's were long. Her future was intertwined up with his.

Ed and his brother, John left Lucas the week of Christmas 1893. They went about 35 miles to Hiteman where they were hiring in the Hiteman mines. Ed and John got work. Katherine didn't like moving to the new mining camp and she didn't like moving so far away from her mother. Still, she and Ed moved into a company house at the top of one of Hiteman's several hills. It was a whitewashed, clapboard "T" shaped house with three small bedrooms, two wood burning iron stoves, a garden in the back, and a mud clay and shale road in the front of the house.

They had little furniture, an old commode Katherine's mother gave them, three straight back chairs and a bed.

Hiteman was the place Ed took to drinking and Katherine took to crying. Hiteman was nearly as poor as Lucas, when they moved there in 1894. Two years later their first child, Ethel, was born. Ethel was a strong child and was destined to outlive all her brothers and sisters. Two years later her sister, Laura, with the innocent smile and guileless manner, was born. The baby, Kenneth, was born and died as the new century began. Things were going from worse to something else for the Robertses.

By the summer of 1900 Katherine was confined to bed. She was sure she would not live to see the fall. She called for her mother to come on the train to her bedside. Katherine survived her female troubles as she called them but she was terribly depressed. There was never enough money, Ed was drinking too much, she missed her family in Lucas and usually she or one of her children were sick. She scarcely saw Ed when he got up at 5:30 in the morning to eat and catch the miners train to work.

Ed wondered about his young wife. He wondered why he had married her and once he left her and went back to Illinois. He had intended to leave her for good but he couldn't. She did have a sweet side to her and he could not walk away from his daughters.

In the fall of 1902, Ed and the other miners listened to Mother Jones, the labor organizer for the miners. She gave the operators hell. She told the miners what they all knew and that is that the operators didn't give a tinkers damn about them and the owners would use every trick in the book to cut the wages of the miners. Ed wasn't a talker or a leader but he was a union man. When the old lady with the black satin dress and the rimless glasses spoke of the hell the miners were going through, Ed and the others got tears of rage in their eyes. Yet, it was so hard to organize the miners when folks were moving here and there, and capital was moving in and out of the industry like some random, ghostly force. The miners did what they could.

Even when the miners were not out on strike, times were so hard. When Ed got his wages in scrip for the company store, or in better times in gold pieces, all sorts of deductions whittled away his money before he saw it—house rent, beneficial funds, house coal, company store accounts, carbide for the lanterns, oilskins for the wetwork, tools such as picks or squibbs or dynamite.

In 1904, Ed moved his family back to Lucas for three years, and Katherine produced two sons, Edward, in 1904, and Everett, in 1906. Then the year John L. Lewis left Lucas to start his organizing career, Ed Roberts left the town again for Hiteman, looking for work. The economy was very bad for the miners. Ed was doing what he could to feed his family. Katherine was pregnant or sick all the time.

It would take Ed a full hour of washing himself in the copper wash tubs to get himself free of the coal dust. So he would eat his dinner dirty. He looked like a large dark ghost at those times and he had little to say to Katherine.

Sometimes when Ed did have a good wage, he would give the money to Katherine, with a few coins left out for the weekend's drinking. Katherine would look at the money and, sitting on their bed, she would rearrange it, group it in piles of like coins, and rearrange it again. It was the money that kept hard times from the door, but not for long.

The children were sick so much. Ethel and Laura began to do their mother's work as one tragedy after another hit the family. In 1910, Ed sat down in his "room" in the mine to eat lunch with the other miners. Some were speaking in Welsh. Ed didn't like that at all. His father had spoken it but to Ed it was just jabber. One of the Welshmen was sick and had to leave. It was the smallpox, and Ed carried the germs home with him. Ed was strong and got over the fever quickly. So did his daughter, Ethel. Ed felt good enough to go back to work in a week but the rest of the family was quarantined. Ethel was fifteen and she worked at the Post Office. She stayed home to help the family. Her eight-year-old sister, Phyllis, died of the fever, and no one could leave the house to attend the funeral. A few weeks later, her six-year-old brother, Edward, died of the disease, and the family grouped together to bury him.

Many years later, when Ethel was an old woman, she would recall "that damned old lousy town. They had every disease there. My dad was so particular about us kids. We had an old lady come in. Her name was Longnecker and she took care of us—stayed with us while we were under the quarantine. Dad got out and he boarded with a neighbor, and we got up every morning at 5:30 so he could see us and we could see him and wave at him going to work—everyone of us. The miners' train left at 7:00. What a life. I'd be scared to death and we always knew when somebody was hurt. The whistle would blow in a different kind of way when that would happen. Men used to get killed there. . . . All my troubles began in Hiteman."

Finally there were four of the Roberts' children buried in the Hiteman Cemetery. The other three grew up there and in Lucas. Ethel had quit school in the eighth grade. She never did like Newton J. Hibbs, the old school principal. She wasn't used to anyone being crabby around her. Kate Roberts cried and cried when Ethel quit school. Kate cried a lot, anyway. Ethel became her chief help around the house. Ethel was often walked home from her job by Billy Angove, who was the son of a mining family from Cornwall, England. Most of his brothers and sisters were born in England but Billy was born in Hiteman. Of course, he went to work in the mines early on like the other boys. When they were old enough to marry, Bill and Ethel did. Bill tried to get out of the mines. He knew the work but he wanted something above the ground.

He was hurt two or three times in the mines. Once he was driving a mule, taking coal up from the bottom. As he went to unhook the chain, it slashed him on the hand and cut off his little finger at the first joint. He came home to Ethel with his hand wrapped in a rag full of blood and coal dust. It scared her to death. One of the Welsh miners from Lucas irritated Billy quite a bit when he told him he really couldn't understand what he was crying about. "Losin' a finger isn't so bad; it's just another part of you that won't be hurtin' later." That was one way to think about it, all right, but Billy didn't see so much humor about it with the pain shooting up his hand.

Another time Bill's father-in-law, Ed, picked up a piece of slate that had fallen on Bill. He picked it up before it had a chance to crush him. Bill liked working with Ed, and miners needed to work in pairs.

Ethel and Bill moved from Hiteman to the other small towns around the area. Bill would clerk in a clothing store in Albia. Bill and Ethel had a daughter, Phyllis, named for Ethel's younger sister who had died of smallpox.

Ethel's younger sister, Laura, was the smartest girl in her class in high school. She wanted very much to go to a summer institute in Albia, or another town, so she could be certified to teach. No, Ed would not allow it. It was not right for a young girl to be away from her family alone. It didn't look right. Laura cried about it, but later she gave in.

She married a Welsh boy, John Moses. John had gone to school until he was fourteen, and then quit to work as a trapper in the No. 5 Mine in Hiteman. He opened and closed trap doors between two entries into the mine, and in 1910 when the Roberts children were dying of smallpox, John was making $1.19 per day. Later he would work at coupling empty coal cars, caging coal, and unhooking empties.

Later John Moses, Bill Angove, and Ed Roberts worked the Lucas mines before the coal operators pulled their money out of the mines and out of town.

When their mining days were through, John moved to Illinois with his wife, the youngest daughter of the Roberts. Bill stayed in Lucas and worked at Bakers store with his wife Ethel. They had moved around to several mining towns but Lucas called them back. Katherine had begun to depend on her daughter and Ethel and Bill moved into the large house Ed and Katherine were renting.

Over the years it became evident that the Roberts women were tied to their parents. They would marry but they would place their parents above their spouses. Ethel would give everything she had to her parents and Billy, her husband, would go along with her plans. Then over the years Katherine felt less alone. She was back home. Her sisters were there and her daughter, Ethel was with her. Ethel did most of the work around the house and Katherine cried less often. In fact, she was one of the happiest women in town and with her sisters or with the neighbors she laughed and giggled for hours at a time.

Ethel could laugh as well, but she seldom had time. She worked eleven or twelve hour days at Bakers store and came home to more work to do for her mother and dad. She would often snap at Katherine about some small thing—something which had nothing to do with anything. Ethel was a dutiful daughter and her duties were endless. For those years in Lucas she was an angry sacrificial lamb.

Ed was now an old man and he spent hour after hour fishing at the W.P.A. pond in town. He would take his grandson, Everett's boy down and sit with him. The sun hurt the boys eyes and he was bored. Old Ed tried to tell the boy stories about his life—stories about the Indians he had known or the troubles in the mines or how Lucas had looked when it was a boom town. The boy didn't care at all for whatever happened before he was born.

Ed told the boy to stay away from strong drink and that he nearly died of it and not to stay around with bad sorts of boys as he had done. Imagining his tall ancient grandpa as a sinner did intrigue the boy and he asked Ed about his drunken times. "I used to get in fights, me and my brothers for no reason at all. I hurt a man once when I was drunk. Then I would take money away from your grandmother to spend on whiskey. I stayed away from home just for foolishness. It shames me now—the way I was then."

What made him stop, the boy asked his grandpa? Ed said he didn't stop until he was sixty and that he had made a deal with the Lord about it. What kind of deal? Ed wouldn't say, it was just between him and the Lord. In fact, he would tell no one about it. The deal didn't include going to church for he never did and it didn't include stopping his chew tobacco for he never stopped. It was just between him and the Lord.

For Ed, life got easier and more agreeable as he got older. He lost the strength and appetite of his large young body but there was no more need to struggle and rage and drink as he had done in the mines. It is true that he had worked all of his adult life and in the end was dependent on the state for his small pension. He was becoming placid behind those dark old eyes.

It didn't bother him that Katherine would laugh and giggle about things that did not amuse him. It did not put him off to hear her repeat over and over again the routine sayings that gave structure to her soul. "God forever hates a falsehood or a lie and he'll punish the wicked bye and bye." She said it everyday. Several times a day she would see visitors coming and burst out with inevitable enthusiasm "well look at who's coming to see me, sit down and rest your weary self and don't hurry off this time." The repetitions and rhymes of her speech gave her comfort. The sameness of her life she did not see as a curse but as some sort of guide through the days. She had no real interest in anything outside the town.

A tired parade of Lucas folks came up the hill past Katherine's house every summer evening. Mr. Stark coming in from working on the section gang west of town. Jim Spencer coming up the hill from Baker's store, getting stupid and senile in his old age. Addie, his wife, stopping in the yard to argue her pentecostal religion with Kate. Mrs. Daughenbach coming over after dinner dishes were washed and the Mister following her with his small-town drolleries. They would sit there under the huge elms until the darkness came in with the lightning bugs, and the four o'clocks folded up at eight. Maybe they would go in earlier if the mosquitos were biting; maybe they would go in later if it was beastly hot in the 1893-model home they knew so well.

The young boys played catch until it got dark, and the old people would loop an occasional eye up over the Des Moines Tribune to watch the little devils. When the little boys sat down with the old folks, they thought, "I hope there's gonna be more to life than sitting here in these old metal lawn chairs and talking."

The old folks thought about their newspapers and what they should get done tomorrow, and how they wouldn't always be able to sit in the lawn chairs in the still, cooling evenings—that this would be taken away from them someday. That someday they would have to give up this little pleasure. They hoped there would be more days of sitting in the old metal lawn chairs and talking.

When Ed Roberts was a very old man, his grandson would look at his high cheek bones and sunken eyes and wonder what he was thinking. Since Ed was so quiet, he must be thinking. What about? Stuff from the old days, he supposed. When Ed got pneumonia, Ronnie worried and prayed over the old man. When they had walked down the Baker's store hill, the boy worried that his grandpa walked so slow. It didn't seem too natural to be old.

Then when Ed Roberts was sick, the people around said, "Well, he can't have too many years left," and that was a new kind of bad news to the boy. Death didn't seem natural to the boy. "Wrong, wrong, wrong it was, wrong," he chanted as he pumped water outside the house in the semi-dark of late summer. And he thought, "suppose God would keep grandpa alive just as long as I pumped this pump and when I stopped he would die." And the boy would pump harder for a while.

Once Ronnie dreamed that he came into grandma's house at night and grandpa had died, and he was there on the floor, laying on some kind of white, enameled shallow sink. That was what they did to dead people. The fear welled all up in the boy. He couldn't shake the death dream out of his head and he couldn't talk about it for fear someone would say, "Well, your granddad doesn't have too many years ahead of him." Some preachers said that it was possible that Jesus would come down and scoop us all up to heaven, and the boy thought that seemed more like a comic book story than anything he had seen in Lucas but he was for it just the same.

The first time Ed Roberts got pneumonia he was in his eighties. He recovered. He made his grandson a whistle out of willow bark and listened to the Saturday night fights on the radio. He would sit and box along with the radio reports, and his grandson wondered if it was true that he got into lots of fights when he was young. "I got into a lot of trouble," Ed said, while spitting his Red Man chaw into the Butternut can on the newspaper, "for hanging with the wrong crowd and drinkin'."

"When you get tempted by the devil," the old man would say, "you just say out loud 'get thee behind me Satan' ". The boy was dubious but polite about the advice.

He knew somewhere in some far recess of his brain that his grandfather and grandmother would die. The thought would slip away easily when he wasn't having nightmares. As Old Ed edged into his nineties he spoke less and less. People forgot he was around. He spent the days working on the bunions on his feet and listening to the news on WHO radio. He ate only cornmeal mush with milk in the evenings and he held his head as if it were in pain some of the time.

It was the summer of 1961 when his grandson had gone west to work in the Forest Service that Ed began to worry over the now grown up boy. He worried about the old car the boy drove out. He worried about logs falling on the boy. He sat in the east window wearing his bright red sweater, his long bony legs propped on a footstool. He was waiting and worrying. In the fall his grandson came home and he was glad though he scarcely had the strength to be happy. Six weeks later he died in the early morning with the bright fall sunlight coming in the east window.

Katherine cried as she had not cried in years. They had been married sixty-four years. And when her sister, Lillian came over to console her, Lillian said, "don't worry about it Kate, I've put three husbands in the ground," she continued to cry. Still her life went on much as before. Ethel took care of her. She still had her sisters to laugh with. There were often funerals to go to, which was her favorite sort of recreation. It didn't matter much if she knew the deceased or the relatives, it was an event for meeting people or chatting with other older ladies.

She lost her eyesight and pretended that she had not. She would watch the television for hours and hear the sound but she would not be able to walk back to her room without bumping into the familiar wine red overstuffed chairs and the oil stove in the front room. Ethel would grumble at her while leading her around. Katherine would wince at Ethel's scolding and she will tell Ethel to just wait and she would be old and feeble and to just see how people would treat her then. These small tempests passed and over the years Katherine's mind became less aware of the world. Her mental powers declined with a gentle sort of way about them, unhurtful and unhurried. When she was ninety years old she told Ethel and her son, Everett that she wished she had a man to warm her bed. "Shut up you old silly thing" Ethel said, "what man would want to be in bed with you?" "Just wait—just wait until you're old like me" Katherine whined in a defensive sing song voice she had cultivated over the years.

Finally in her ninety-third year, they took her to the county hospital for congestive heart failure. She was joking with the nurses and laughing and the nurses joked back with her and she had died like a happy child.

Ed and Katherine's Children: Ethel and Billy

Ethel had taken care of her mother for so many years that she found herself old when her mother had passed on. Ethel was the person who kept the family together, who worked without stopping or giving a thought to it. And although she had worked outside the home until her seventies she was not eligible for Social Security payments. She received her Social Security from her husbands work and it was not much.

When Ethel took care of her parents, her daughter, Phyllis insisted that they all live together when they could—grandparents, parents, and children. Ethel loved Billy Angove, her husband and Phyllis loved James Thompson her husband, but the women's tightest bonds were with the family and the husbands realized that early on. They went along with that reality gracefully.

Ethel was a small woman but she was stronger physically than most men. She would lift, cart, carry, wash, clean, organize all day at work, inside or outside the home. When she washed for the family, her white sleeves rolled up to her strong shoulders, she wrestled the clothes from the steaming soap sloshing machine to the wringer to the bluing tub and the steam condensed on her hair and face and clothes. She moved rapidly because her days were timed to the minute.

Bill Angove had worked in stores since his mining days. He had worked in a clothing store in Albia for a time in the 1920's and his boss made him join the Ku Klux Klan as a condition of work.

Billy didn't think much about it at the time. By temperament, he wasn't good at hating Catholics which was the Klan's target at the time. Moreover, he thought a better class of people belonged to the Masons. He liked their ritual better anyhow. Then he heard about the high Klegal something or other leaving the country with lots of loot, he figured job or no, he would quit the bullies in pillowcases.

He had been taught by his folks to fear being poor. He saw mining as a dead end life. He believed in the union and he would never cross a picket line but he figured with people saying he had such a good personality that he could make something of himself by clerking, selling, that sort of thing. Since Ethel was determined to live with her family in Lucas, he would have to do the best he could there. Maybe, he kind of half thought in his mind, maybe the town will rebound a little bit so that if a man works hard. . . .

He lived and worked in Lucas all through the depression years. He saw things get a little better during the second world war. In the 1950's, he was working harder than ever. He was even able to afford a new car. Still the work was hard on him and he was not as strong as his wife.

Billy was only about five feet, six inches but he was a meticulous dresser. He liked the polyester clothes that came out in the 1950's and his pants were always well-pressed, shoes so buffed you could see yourself in them. Suspenders over a nice nylon shirt, short-sleeved and light green in the summer.

Bill was a fast mover and a go-getter. He and Ethel had worked in Bakers Store as a team for many years. It was a shock when he had his first heart attack and had to go into semi-retirement for a while. Even then he was making the rounds in town, fixing someone's water pump or toaster or installing cabinets or cleaning up yards. The doctors told Bill he would have to slow down—no excitement, no basketball games with the yelling and carrying on. He was going to have to change his lifestyle, folks said. Naturally he couldn't do it.

For a while he did. He put two camp cots out under the huge box elder trees, strung an electrical cord out from the house, and listened to his favorite Chicago Cubs lose close ball games. He would drink ice tea and sit for as long as he possibly could. That wasn't long. Soon he was off fixing, cleaning, and organizing parts of Lucas.

In fact, the town depended on Billy to get things done. He was the spark-plug of the Paul Revere Lodge of the Masons. Whenever Lucas put on a celebration, Bill was the one everyone leaned on. He got things done. He talked to people. He made them feel good about themselves. He had a way about him.

His mother-in-law, Katherine, adored Bill, or Billy Butt Cut, as she affectionately called him because he would do anything for her. He helped fix up and restore the huge three-story Baker house where he, his wife and his in-laws, Ed and Katherine Roberts lived. It would be hard to say who worked the hardest, Bill or his wife, Ethel, but anyone who knew them would say that they never let any grass grow under their feet.

When Bill bought a watch, or a car, or a sweater, it was his view to keep it until hell froze over. He would waste nothing. He would organize everything. The walls of the old garage by the house were covered with boxes and hooks and shelves and drawers to organize his tools with a precision that astonished everyone in town. He would give guided tours through it and comment on the handiness of reach and the ease of getting one of the many tools he had accumulated. "Just always put them back where they belong." He was a perfectionist.

When Bill and Ethel lived in Lucas, their daughter had moved to Des Moines and married her high-school sweetheart. Bill put all his interests and skills into helping his nephew. Told him all about good grooming, which side your hair should be parted on, how to train your hair so that it would always lay down, how to tie a necktie, how to spit-shine shoes—all that and more.

One Sunday afternoon all the family was seated around the huge, oak table. It was the one left by John L. Lewis when he left Lucas for Panama, Illinois. Heaps of mashed potatoes, dressing, ham, baked beans, green beans, scalloped corn, white bread, carrots, gravy and desserts crowded the table. Bill was sitting next to his teen-aged nephew. In the middle of the feast cooked by his wife, he got up from the table. "Come with me, son," he said to his nephew, "come out on the porch." "Oh," Ethel said, "*What* are you doing, Bill, right in the middle of dinner?" "I know just what I'm doing," he said, as he led his nephew away from the dozen kinfolk at the table. He led the boy to the porch. "Now, I just want to tell you, that when you get into your teens like you are now, you know, glands start opening up and you begin to sweat." "Oh," said his nephew. "So I want you to use this deodorant everyday," and he showed the boy how to apply it. "But you have to wash under your arms every day or it won't work and if that happens you'll offend somebody for sure." "Oh", the boy said again, acutely aware of his offensive pits.

Ethel chastised Bill as he and the boy came into the large dining room. "You're embarrassing him; now leave the child alone." "I'm not embarrassing him and he's not a child. He's sixteen now and he should smell right." The boy agreed, looking furtively at his peers. He agreed that he was not a child, at least. That was the way his Uncle Bill was. He saw an imperfect world and he tried mightily to correct it. He *was* a go-getter but, Lord knows, even he couldn't perfect all Lucas. Still the town was painted up, trimmed up, a little more ordered and, yes, the town even smelled better for Bill's efforts.

After his heart attack, Bill tried selling Watkins products, and though people liked to visit with him they didn't have much money to spare around Lucas. Even as handy as Bill was, it was hard to make a living in town when he had a bad heart.

Bill was itchy, edgy, and ready for work even if his body needed rest. "Well, I won't die in bed. You've got to get up and get at it. Most people die in bed— it's too dangerous for me," and he was off in search of work.

In truth, he was one of the few perfectionists Lucas ever knew. The place was naturally frustrating for perfectionists, especially in the 1950's when the weeds were taking over the town and the company houses were tumbling down, and in, with every new season. Bill kept trying to fix things. Something inside him was driving him, some sort of internal bourgeoisie driving and using up that proletariet which was his body. "Heart attack or no, I wouldn't want to be alive, to just sit in a chair. That's not me."

Billy had several sides to him; not all were evident to everyone he knew. He had joined the Saints Church and was called to the priesthood, and he threw himself into church work the way he did anything else. John Blackstock, the big, booming high priest of the Church, called Bill in one day for a talk. Bill came out fuming and angry. John had said there were rumors about Bill, rumors which compromised his integrity and his morality. It was some rumor about Bill and a woman in town. John told Bill he couldn't function in the priesthood until all this got cleared up. *"Nobody* talks to me that way," Bill would say later, "and I don't care for John one bit. I will never forgive him and I will not set foot into the Church again until I get an apology." He never got one. He was friendly with all the other Saints. They were friendly with him. If they needed an errand run or cabinets fixed or an old ice box toted away, Bill would do it. His religious career was at an end save for singing the Saints hymns.

Bill would sing. When he and his wife, Ethel, were in their fifties, he would sing to her in a romantic and intimate way like he was a teenager trying to get her to fall in love with him, or trying to get some buried affection from her. He would sing "Beautiful, beautiful brown eyes, I'll never love blue eyes again", or he would sing "My buddy, my buddy, your buddy misses you," and he would sing it with all the melodious sincerity at his command. Usually his wife would show no visual emotion but Bill believed that he should win her heart over and over again. He was an unceasing romantic, Bill was. That was part of the reason he loved being alive—it was love and work. Finally, there was no work for him in Lucas.

He went to Des Moines. The only job he could do there was to park and wash the cars of the very rich who lived at the Commodore Hotel on Grand Avenue. He felt a little funny around the rich, but he knew he could do the work with a spring in his step and a good word for the patrons of the hotel. The rich were interesting to Bill and he knew how to treat them. He didn't feel inferior to them; it was just that life had dealt him a different set of cards.

He got himself a new car in 1957. It was a Ford, the least expensive model, and he said he might as well enjoy the thing as long as he could, for no one lived forever. It had been ten years since his heart attack and he knew forever was close.

He brought his new car back to Lucas on weekends and cleaned it with the same immaculate concern that he gave those expensive cars at the Commodore. His wife was still working long hours at Bakers Store and they had scarcely a moment to relax even in the Sunday shade of the big elms outside Ed and Katherine Roberts' house. They had fewer moments than they liked to watch the occasional slow parade of walkers up the Lucas Post Office hill. Neither Bill nor Ethel thought life was created to put them at ease, and they were right.

Once when Bill was putting in cabinet work for a Lucas family, he recalled the death of his mother, Bessie, on a cold and rainy night in the Hiteman mining camp. "She could have died in peace," Bill said about Bessie, "but the

137

doctor kept trying to revive her. He kept flicking his fingers at her eyes and trying to start her heart again. It was a horrible, horrible thing. If I have anything to do with it, I will never die like that."

Bill had a massive heart attack at work in Des Moines. They took him to the hospital and kept trying to revive him for what seemed hours. He had a hard death. And then he was gone and buried at the Goshen Cemetery south of town. His daughter, Phyllis, became hysterical, couldn't believe her father was dead. People stood around town talking about Bill's death. It was a victory for the weeds around town, a victory for the chaos in Lucas. His heart had enlarged and broken with an excess of work and love.

His widow lived for a time with her daughter but came back to Lucas to care for her father and mother. In fact, her entire life was devoted to taking care of family members—her daughter, her parents, her sister and brother. All were nursed through the last days of their lives by Ethel. Bakers Store, where she and Bill had worked twelve-hour days, had closed in 1955. When the building was shut down it began to deteriorate very rapidly. Ethel missed the people at the store and she missed the work. A few years later the floors had rotted so badly that the oversized cash register, made of half a ton of brass, crashed through the floor of the building into the unfinished basement. Lucas was becoming more of a site for an archeological dig than a town.

Ethel worked for Pete Woods in his small grocery store well into her seventies. At night she would come home and care for her mother. They had lived in the Baker house for more than thirty-five years. The walk up the hill from the store to the house was becoming impossible for Ethel. Both her parents died in their mid-nineties and Ethel knew that she must close the house and move. She couldn't clean its seven bedrooms anymore, and she couldn't afford the heating oil to keep it warm. She would move to Des Moines with her daughter, who adored her. And though it was impossible, she wanted to come back to Lucas.

When her daughter came back one grey November day to attend the funeral of Ethel's brother, she cried out "damn this town to hell. I will never come back again. There is nothing but sadness here." And truly she did not come back except to be buried in the town. Then, when Ethel's daughter died and when the funeral was over, Ethel cried but she also laughed. It was over and she had survived the funeral and survived this new blow to her life. She could still laugh.

When she was nearly ninety years old, she reflected on all the people she had loved and nursed and cared for and how they had been taken from her. She, remembering the pain and exhaustion of life in Lucas, blurted out, "Oh, Lord, I should of never been born. I do wish I never had been born." But later she was remembering Billy Angove and how they had met at the coal camp in Hiteman and she was saying, "Yes indeed, he was the best boy in the town, yes he was." And her eyes lit up as she thought about it. And she laughed deep down inside her. It was the laugh she had laughed for years; it was strong and it was still inside her.

Ed and Katherine's Children: The Mayor's Story

Since only three of the eight children born to Ed and Katherine reached adulthood, those that did were given extra portions of affection. Ethel and Laura stayed close to their parents even though Laura wanted to become a school teacher (Ed forbade his daughter to attend summer school out of town. It just didn't look seemly to him).

Then Everett being the only surviving boy was seen to be his mama's favorite. When Everett was in the eighth grade at the Lucas School in 1920, he decided to drop out. His dad had gone to school not much more than one year in total, so he didn't mind much. What made Everett want to drop out was his teacher, Miss Ethel Sanders, who would later be called an "old maid". Ethel believed in discipline. She locked children in the coal shed in the middle of winter for minor offenses. When she was angry she would stare down at a frightened boy or girl and with a startling voice she would promise that "If you don't straighten up right here and now I am going to break your arm off at the socket and beat you with the bloody end of it." She had never done that to anyone's knowledge, but the schoolkids who lived in terror of her said they "wouldn't put it past her." Anyway, no one laughed when they talked about it.

Everett didn't like it. He was growing up with the perfect body for a coal miner—a long, powerful torso with massive neck, chest and back and short, but equally powerful and thick, arms and legs. He didn't know exactly what he wanted to do with his life. He played in the town band and sang in the town chorus, and he like to wrestle. He was good at his wrestling and claimed he had wrestled the State Champion of Iowa at sixteen and wrestled him to a draw. He was strong enough, to be sure.

That same year while wrestling in the basement of a friend's house, he was thrown against the basement wall and knocked out cold for nearly an hour. When he awoke his injury had produced a cross to bear—*grand mal epilepsy.* In those less enlightened times, epilepsy was seen as only slightly less shameful than V.D. A doctor prescribed Phenobarbital for him and he took it for most of the rest of his life. He took it in secret. Each month a brown box came to the Lucas Post Office addressed to Katherine Roberts from Western Medical Supplies. It was Phenobarbital. Fortunately, it worked.

Everett didn't tell his bride about his affliction. He was in his thirties then and hadn't had a seizure in years. He stopped taking his medicine. When Mae was greatly pregnant with her first child and naive about the disease, he had a seizure and it was horrible. They were alone on the farm he was renting south of town, and Mae worried that her upset with it might mark their child. When Everett regained consciousness, he promised her that he would take his Phenobarbital the rest of his life, and he did. It was hidden in the closet and never discussed with his children. When it was discovered by the teenaged son, Mae explained it to him and swore him to secrecy.

The first job Everett got out of the eighth grade was working with his father, Ed. Everett was still a teenager and his pa was in his fifties but they worked together digging coal from the Big Hill Mine for the school. They had contracted to deliver all the coal the school would need for the entire school year. That lasted one year.

Everett had the wanderlust and he rode the rails, looking for work and adventure. He worked for farmers; later he helped build highways for the W.P.A. Finally, in his mid-twenties, he got a job with John Deere as a traveling salesman for tractor parts. He would recall later, "Oh, the women were after me in those days. I had to beat them off me with sticks. Sometimes big women would take a liking to me, half a head taller than me. Then there was several Belgium women after me in those days. (To his son he would relate this mysterious aside.) "Be careful of Belgium women. Oh, they nearly were the death of me. And Swede women and Chinese, too. Oh, they were after me."

Later he would explain thousands of times to his children that "there I was in Rudd, Iowa selling for Deere's when your mother proposed to me. Oh, she wanted to marry me so bad." "I did not, Everett. I just said we should either get serious or quit seeing each other," Mae would say.

After marrying Mae Blue, Everett thought he had found the right mate. She looked pretty and delicate to him, and she was a school teacher. That was something Everett admired and resented at the same time. They had a son in Lucas and Everett tried to make a living selling milk from his few cows to the people of the town. That kept them alive, barely. So they moved from the old town to the factories on the Mississippi River at Moline, Rock Island, and Davenport.

Everett quickly got assembly-line work, and by the time of World War II his family had a nice house, a decent income, and a new suburban lifestyle. For eight years he worked in the massive noise and inhuman demands on the never-ending assembly lines. You couldn't talk, you couldn't relax, and you couldn't think. It wasn't what he had imagined his life to be, even though he was doing better than anyone ever had in the family. His dad, Ed, had never gotten an eight-hour-day in the mines with time-and-one-half for overtime. It wasn't enough.

When Everett got the chance to come back to Lucas he knew he would. His folks were there and life in the Illinois suburb didn't fit his style as well as it could. Everybody liked him there. That wasn't the problem at all. In fact the kids used to gather round him in the front yard for stories. He *could* tell stories. "So then those Apaches had me cornered up in the rocks. There was hundreds of them—a couple dozen at least. Finally, they had me surrounded with Tommy Guns and bow'n arrows. I told them that I was part Cherokee on my grandmother's side but they said; 'Sorry, we've got no mercy.' They was coming closer and closer and I was totally out of ammo for my six-shooter. I reckoned I was one dead buckaroo. They was beating the drums hot and heavy, and they was the kind that would eat a sow and her litter of pigs for breakfast and ask for more. The drums was coming closer and closer. There was only one chance I had to get away and I took it." "What was that?" "I took the drum and beat it!" "Aw, that wasn't true." "It sure was; you ask Buffalo Bill when he comes to town. He'll tell ya. He didn't know the front from the rear of one of those bison 'till I showed him."

The kids were fun and the neighbors were good but Everett didn't like the work, making International Harvester tractors or John Deere tractors or clocks for tanks during World War II. The money was good but it was too damned noisy, ,and the work was so hard and routine and slow-moving that Everett would come home, fall asleep before dinner and snore so loudly that the neighbors could hear. Then he would wake up feeling pretty awful, eat an evening meal and mow the yard and collapse early in the evening. Even at that, the work was better than the mining had been. Still, for eight years he had done it with all the regimentation and bossing and routine and he never did like it.

He wanted to come back to Lucas like his folks did. He could live there cheaper and he knew everybody. Half the people were his own kin in some way or another. His wife, Mae, wasn't too keen on the idea. She liked her suburban bungalow. The house they had was new and it smelled and looked new, and she could keep it that way. Still Everett would move. The houses in Lucas were pretty run down. She knew that. Still Lucas would be closer to her folks, and it would be good to get away from those damp vapors and draughts from the Mississippi River. It might be better for Kay's and Ronnie's health, she thought.

Everett accepted a job with Solar Aircraft in Des Moines. They asked him if he had any experience or knowledge about drafting. "Sure, I do that all the time," he told them. It wasn't true. He knew nothing about it. But he figured, "I can learn enough to get by until they decide to keep me. You don't get jobs by telling folks what you can't do even if you can't." Nevertheless, he couldn't do the work.

The family had moved back to old Lucas town. Everett tried to find more factory work in Des Moines but 1948 was a hard year to do that, and the forty-five mile commute was too much. What Everett wanted was a business where he could stay in Lucas, be his own boss (everyone wanted that), and meet people to pass the time of day with. He would have liked to be a farmer but the cash money wasn't there to buy the land. He bought a house up on school house hill from Mr. Riggs, and paid cash for it from his equity on his Illinois, suburban home. It wasn't much of a house. It was more or less a company house from the mining days, with a room added on. Mae didn't care for it too much. Still, it was all paid for.

The roof leaked—it always leaked. The pump for the indoor plumbing broke down once a month or so, and there really wasn't a basement. It was at the top of the highest Lucas hill, bordering the schoolyard to the south and overlooking "Old Jericho" where the Skidmore Mines had been to the north. The Robertses cut down several elms and a plum tree in the back yard and settled in Lucas for the duration.

Everett believed he could get a restaurant going in downtown Lucas, his second year in town. All it would take was hiring someone to fry burgers, make malts and homemade pies. He hired a woman who made good pies. He made pretty fair malts. There was only the one obstacle to entreprenurial success. That was the fact that almost no one lived in Lucas in 1950. The population had straggled down to less than five hundred. Those who were still there didn't have dimes and quarters and dollars to spare. Everett worked as hard as he could in the Lucas Cafe, came out about even financially and gained about fifteen pounds.

Soon there were bags of cattle and hog feed in the backroom of the Lucas Cafe, and only a little later he had closed it down and was out on the road selling feed to farmers south of town. The work suited him because he had what folks in town called "the gift of gab".

For the rest of his life he would get up, eat a big breakfast, make his town visits and head into the country, sample case in hand. He would meander over to the farmhouse, taking care to get to know the dog. Then he would converse with the woman of the house for a leisurely time and proceed out to see the man on the tractor. He took his time, talked longer to farmers he liked more than those with the most money. On the way to the car he would ask the farmer if he needed anything and just to call if he did. Over the years he got more business and prospered.

Everybody knew Everett as an outgoing fella—whether he was trading cars, selling the minerals for the chickens and hogs, or just walking out of the Farmers and Miners Bank some sweet, warm, summer day. He might be still laughing about some joke that Jerry Baker, the banker, had told him, or about some story that he had told Jerry. Everyone knew how friendly Everett was in the ghost town—downtown. The way he had about him. Talk to anyone, Everett could. Rich or poor. It didn't matter. He had a pretty good chance of leaving people laughing, shaking their heads. "That Everett, he sure is a case," and they would say it in kindness.

When he got home tired and smiled out from the day's selling and gravel-road driving, he could get morose. Sometimes he would say to his family," I'm the only one out there making money for you. If I didn't hit those roads you all would starve." "Well," his kids would say, "that's your duty." "Nobody helps me out there," he would say truthfully, "and nobody knows what I go through." His family didn't know how to take it, so they tried to ignore it.

And sometimes he would sit in his Dodge pickup, sit there at the wheel for maybe a half hour, alone and in silence. Mae would call him for dinner and he would say he would come in when he was ready. He didn't tell his family what he was thinking. Just sit out there alone, somehow using the silence in the town to calm his soul or sharpen his sadness.

Maybe his sadness didn't show up when people might expect it. When his father, Ed, died at ninety-four, Everett sat in the car with his son and daughter, and they looked at his face trying to see grieving. He talked about normal things, didn't show too much of that pain and grief. There were those other times, usually as the sun would go down over the houses and sheds of the town, that he would sit and stare at his meaty hands on the steering wheel. Tired he was, and looking at the death of the town and his own demise; looking them in the eye. It was a meditation in sorrow that Everett would do, but the townsfolk or the farmers seldom saw it. He simply wouldn't allow it.

He had come back to Lucas to bail out of the industrial revolution, its grinding noise, and shuffling boredom. He knew that Lucas was in poverty and decay, but the place had a style about it that he could understand. Even if the people, lots of them at least, were a little nutty, life was on a human scale, a walking around and talking scale. He was at home with the Lucas folk. Sometimes when he would sigh a deep, full sigh, his children wanted to ask him what was the matter. Maybe it was nothing, they thought, and maybe they didn't want to know.

So Everett could get woebegone and he would say to his family, "Just wait. You'll have all this stuff here, all the things I have earned after I'm gone." That wasn't fair, Mae thought, but it disarmed her when he said it. But Everett didn't win all the contests in the family's emotional life. Often when Kay or Ronnie would ask for too much, he would throw up his arms and surrender to their demands without much of a fight. His love for his family mixed with frustration, but the love disarmed him from time to time. He would acquiesce.

Sometimes he would stand over the beds of his children at night. As he watched them sleeping it would be his moment of closeness to them, and sometimes his children felt him standing there and felt his love. It wasn't easy to express—his love. It came out in awkward, teasing ways like hugging his wife when she was particularly busy. He would never brag on his children to their faces. It was not the thing to do.

Once, when he was in his fifties, an old lover and her husband came to visit Everett. When Everett had gone with her before his marriage at thirty-three, he had been stocky and muscular. He was still muscular later in life but he had gotten heavy—almost two hundred pounds. He had lost most of his teeth. The visitors spent the afternoon talking and laughing with Everett. Everett's son thought, "What must she think of him now? She used to be crazy about him. That's what I heard. What now?" Her husband was extremely well-dressed and groomed. Everett's boy wondered if love is transformed into something else, or if it stays, or just rots like overripe fruit. Nobody would tell him that day.

In 1953, Everett's son entered his teen years. He was momentarily excited about being a teenager until he remembered that millions of other boys were teenagers. That took some of the wind out of his teenaged sail. Still, he thought, this is likely to be an adventure and I should record it for history.

He had gotten a dimestore diary, complete with lock and key. He decided to keep the diary when he was home with an earache. His first entry was on March 21, 1953. "Have hopes of getting a chameleon." No entries followed for the next week because he had lost the key. Then on March 30, after breaking the lock, he wrote, "Chameleon deal fell through. Grr!"

Since he was rightly convinced that he could never keep the diary away from his father's eyes, he decided to develop a code for his journal. He tried writing upside down and backwards, and he elaborated even more effective codes. But somehow he always hid the code translations where he could not find them. In the end, he knew he would simply have to write enigmatically, such as "April 17, 1953. You-know-who is moving to town. Watch out." It was his hope that he would always remember who "you-know-who" was and that he would always remember what to "watch out" for. Over the years he forgot.

Still he was right to worry about the prying, teasing eyes and, as it turned out, hands of his father, for later in the year he found entries in his diary with a different handwriting than his own. "May 1, 1953." "Horray, I think Toots Dixon likes me," and on May 16, 1953, "Gee, my dad works hard for my sister and me and I guess we don't appreciate all the lonely hours of work he puts in just to keep us all going. I'm going to be a lot nicer to my Dad from now on." Any handwriting expert could have testified that those entries had come from Everett. Nevertheless, maybe someone would read it who wasn't a handwriting expert. The only thing to do was to keep it out of the hands of strangers and gripe to his father. He did. "I don't know nothing about your silly book," Everett said, and he was grinning and looking away.

The boy should have been used to being teased and he was, sort of. But not totally. When he was five or six years old, his dad gave him a series of affectionate nicknames such as Ethelbert, Cuthbert, and Egbert or Eggie, for short. On turning seven, Dad began to call his boy Ratsy, Ratsy Roberts. Well, it did alliterate. Everyone laughed at the family gatherings when Everett called his boy "Ratsy". And the boy laughed, too. Still, it was an odd name and the boy hoped it wouldn't be permanent. His mother said, "Oh, Everett, that's an awful name. Stop being such a tease." "That's just a term of endearment," he would say, and everyone would smile again. It was all right.

They say the Welsh all love to tease and teasing is the way to prevent a person from getting the big head. In the spring of that year, Everett had developed another way to prevent his son from getting the big head.

It was the last day of the term at the Lucas School and there was a picnic on the school grounds, with the elm and maple trees budding out in vibrant greens. Since the Roberts family lived in the house just bordering the school yard, it was not terribly strange that Everett came down to see the kids and the teacher. It was slightly odd that he had stopped in to see Miss Marker earlier, for he was not wont to hang around the school that much.

The last day of school was the day that the kids got their report cards. The Roberts boy was a B- student, which was as high a grade point as he could receive and still be on good terms with his friends. Still, nothing to worry about. It was a little odd that Everett was around when Miss Marker handed out the report cards. All the kids were playing a highly animated, violent Lucas-version of tag, stopping only under orders from the teacher to pick up their report cards.

When Ronnie picked up his card, he looked at it vaguely and commenced the chasing of other kids again. But what did it say? "Student held back another year for unsatisfactory performance." What? And the grades were all changed to F's where there used to be B- minuses. He kept running and playing tag. Then he looked up at his Dad and he knew. His Dad said, "Let me see your report card, boy." And the boy said, "See it you, you don't have to see it; you doctored it up in the first place." Everett laughed and tried to play innocent but the teacher laughed (which she seldom did) and the kids laughed, and the jig was up. Later, Mae, the boy's mother, would say, "Everett, that was an awful thing to do. You're going to torment the life out of that boy." Everett just smiled.

All this teasing made the Roberts boy shy but it also instilled in him a deep need to tease other folk, too. And he was some sort of a "chip off the old Welsh block". A few years later, two events culminated in permanent innoculation against big-headedness in the Roberts boy, who was not sixteen-years-old, and terribly afflicted by the serious image of himself as another James Dean. (He had seen *Rebel Without A Cause* three times at the Chariton Theater.) When one begins to think of one's self as James Dean, one becomes serious. Being serious is one way to get the big head.

145

Everett did two things to innoculate Ronnie (or Ron as he preferred to be called in his teenage years) against the perils of big-headedness. One of the things he did was unintentional. Everett lacked only one thing to become a gentleman farmer—money. He made a decent-enough living, selling feeds to farmers. "Moorman Feeds—Buy only what you need but cannot raise." But Everett did have some land, about eight acres on the edge of town about a block from the schoolhouse.

The little acreage, or "the place" as Everett called it, had several rundown and rotting outbuildings on it. The man who had owned the place had been killed in a truck accident before he could fix up the place. From time to time Everett kept animals of various kinds on the place—chickens, runt pigs given him by farmers, a pony for his horse-loving little girl, Kay. The place was run down. All the sheds were in need of repair. The orchard needed weeding. But most importantly, the fences needed mending. Animals were known to escape from Everett's rundown acreage.

It was one late winter afternoon, with intermittent patches of snow, slush, mud and some greening grass in the hilly school yard. In the second-floor study hall, the Roberts boy was studiously looking over his appearance in the reflection of the glass in the classroom door. Low-slung Levis (beltless), a white shirt with the collar turned up like Elvis Presley in *Love Me Tender,* black loafers with white socks, hair slicked and coifed with Lucky Tiger Rose Hair Tonic. The boy was close to self love. He sat down, thinking vaguely lustful thoughts.

A scarce five minutes went by in his big-headed reverie when he heard someone laughing. He heard more laughing. He saw rows of students falling over themselves to get to the study hall windows. He leaped for the window with a strange, vague dread. Then he saw it. Humiliation. There in the school yard was his father, four-buckled-rubber boots flapping, shirt flapping, coat flapping, arms flapping, cussing and chasing seven confused, contrary pigs round and round in circles in the school yard. Everett would pivot after two or three going west and the rest would go east. The stick in his hand whipped nothing but air. And did he cuss! It was slight comfort that you could not hear him because all the kids saw him cussing the pigs across the school yard. Later Ronnie would learn the meaning of the word "ignominious". He certainly knew humiliation on the spot. It was a short chase really; no more than six or seven minutes. It sure did have a lifetime of teenage humiliation packed into it.

The other permanent innoculation against the boy's big head came in a rush one Saturday afternoon in the County Seat town, Chariton. Saturday afternoons were big shopping days in the County Seat and folks from Lucas and the surrounding town would come up to buy provisions for the coming week, much to the chagrin of the storeowners in Lucas.

The Roberts family would generally leave for town at one o'clock and come back at five. Mae would do the shopping, pay the bills and visit her parents, the Blues, who lived in town. Everett was glad to park on the Square (the northside, if possible) and look at the folks going to and fro on the side-walks. "I like watching the people," he would say. "People are interesting crea-tures." "Boring", his children would reply in near unison.

This particular Saturday, Everett was dressed down in his green work-pants, grey shirt, and shapeless, slouch hat. His son was working very hard at being the exact opposite of his father. He was the prince of fashion, teenage variety, in Southern Iowa. He spent many, many hours in front of a mirror looking heroic, sensitive, comical, anything but like his dad.

They had parked next to Spurgeon's Store, and the Roberts boy, nearly a man at sixteen, watched his reflection as it moved from store window to store window. Suddenly and with quick steps, the boy's father was following him as fast as his legs could go. Panic. The boy could not afford to be seen with his father in the first place. In the second, his father dressed so, you know, sort of trashy. All of these thoughts rolled through his head and somehow were read by his father. The Roberts boy started walking at a faster pace. So did his father, grinning at the lad's discomfiture. What to do? It would have been uncool to break into a run. And what if Dad ran along side?

The boy decided to cut his losses and call as little attention to himself as possible. There was dad, walking side-by-side with him. It could be worse, Ronnie thought. Suddenly it was, for walking toward the two Robertses was a young girl, attractive enough to be interesting. She would pass Ronnie and his dad in a few steps. Everett must have seen his big-headed boy flinch, for he was possessed at that moment of a teasing demon. Just as the girl passed by, Ronnie ducked his head. Everett yelled out of the side of his mouth in a hillbilly voice concocted just for the occasion, "Why, there's a good lookin' little filly for you, son!" Since one cannot wish oneself dead or melt into the convenient cracks in the sidewalk, Ronnie was forced to live and live it down. He was "got" in the argot of Lucas. Everett was having a good time. Lord, the man was a candidate for the Teasers' Hall of Fame. Teasing folks from getting the big head.

Ultimately, it is dangerous to tease someone over a long period of time because the "teased", with a minimum of talent, can eventually pick up the craft. Ronnie and Everett were getting Saturday-night haircuts from the Re-publican barber in town, Wayne Hooker. The Democrat, Mr. Cook, didn't oil the hair up so much but he kept less convenient hours. All the loafers sitting around, glancing at dogeared American Legion Magazines, were talking money and politics.

Like most other small-town folk and farmers, the fellows down at the barber shop would tease about money. The inexhaustible and longest running tease of all time had to do with the curious assumption that the other person has lots and lots of money and that they hide all traces of wealth 'so's nobody will know'. "Say, if I had your money I wouldn't worry about gettin' my brakes fixed. I'd just plunk down the cash for a new Caddy or Oldsmobile." That was the kind of tease just begging for a repartee.

147

Ronnie was getting a dose of Lucky Tiger Hair Tonic rubbed into his scalp in a none-too-gentle fashion and the smell of it mixed with the Lilac-scented talc in a way that startled the nostrils.

"Well, Ronnie, has your Dad got money buried over in that acreage? I heard he buried it in tin cans all over the place." "No," the Roberts boy would say, "he never shows it to me." "I show him too much," Everett would say, "the kid is breakin' me." Does your Dad keep pigs over there, Ronnie?" "Yes, I believe he's got about a dozen." "If you'd go and water them sometimes you'd know how many I've got," Everett offered.

"Well, does your Dad grow them little suckers pretty fast with the Moorman Feed he sells?" "Oh no, Dad doesn't use Moorman's. He says it's too expensive. He uses Kent Feeds." Laughter. Everett's face turns red. "Oh, somebody just gave me a half a bag of that stuff and I just wanted to use it up." More laughter. They laugh intermittently throughout the next fifteen minutes. When Everett drove his boy home, he said "You didn't need to tell them everything you know." "Well, it was the truth," the boy said. The story of Everett feeding pigs Kent instead of Moorman was still current in Lucas some thirty years after it happened. It still gets a laugh.

It was 1953 when Everett decided to run for mayor of Lucas. Mr. Cook, the Democrat barber, was urging him on. "You know you'd make a good one", and looking at Everett's boy, "you'd like your Dad to run, wouldn't you?" "Oh, not so's you'd notice." "Well, I can't believe you wouldn't want your pa to become mayor." "I don't care too much," the boy lied. The fact was that the mayor's race would call attention to the Robertses, which was what the boy dreaded. Since only Jim Spencer decided to run against Everett, and Jim was both senile and blustery at the same time, it was a sure thing that Everett would win. It couldn't be by a landslide; there weren't but a couple hundred voters left in town. No question Everett won.

"I *am* the mayor," Everett would thunder later, but only to his grandkids. The fact is, he took the nearly payless job pretty seriously. Not only were there city council meetings; there was road work to supervise; stray dogs to dispose of; stopsign violators to fine; and a dozen neighbors' complaints to listen to. Everett was up to the job. Working in the factories he took orders grudgingly. He had more freedom selling feeds. But in the mayor's chair he had some power. He was moderate and fair in the way he used it, and the folks in town thought he did an all right job.

Everett was on the cynical side when it came to authority. Many a local religious leader Everett castigated as "just in it for the money" or a "bunch of hypocrites". He wasn't cynical about Lucas, and he worked on it with the very limited money and power that he had.

Now the feed company was something else again. They held sales meetings designed to put pep in your step and make a smile your style. "Just a bunch of crap," Everett would say to anyone around him, including his boss.

He sold lots of feed so he could get away with it. The company divided their salespeople into competing groups. Everett was assigned to the Iowa Cyclones and got his picture in the company paper routinely for selling many tons of feed. "Stupidest damn thing I've ever heard of. Why don't they just leave me alone?" He wasn't a company man.

The company promoted Everett but he just didn't like it. He wouldn't get to see the farmers and b.s. with them if he was a district man.

At one salesmeeting at one of Southern Iowa's fanciest hotels, they began to sing songs like the Rotary Club. Then there was an inspirational talk about spreading the message to the farm folk. The chief motivator and moderator for the company gave away silver dollars to the top salespeople. Everett got quite a few dollars to clink around—enough to make his pockets bulge. He began to take some interest in the meeting. Then the company moderator-motivator began to tell a smutty joke to break up the inspirational-money-making ideas he had been spouting.

The joke had to do with a lady who had ten kids, one a year like clock-work. Then she stopped having them and told a friend it was because she had gotten a hearing aid. "How come?" "Well, my husband and I used to go to bed and he would say, "Do you want to go to sleep or what?" And she would say, "What?"

That's the damnedest, dumbest joke I've ever heard," Everett would say, and he would arch his right eyebrow up in distaste for the fourteenth time during the meeting.

Everett helped people in the town, checked on the old and feeble, did favors for folks, even loaned money to a couple of people who were desperate. He kept the roads up. All his relatives and several others thought he was the best mayor Lucas ever had.

Here and there he would make a mistake, but not many. He came into the Farmers and Miners Bank one morning and he was angry. Some fellow out south of town owed him one-hundred bucks and he had declared bank-ruptcy just to beat the rap. Gerald Baker, who ran the bank, said, "Well, Everett, I'm in the same boat as you. He owes me at least that much and he's a deadbeat and there's just no way either of us is going to get our money." "I'll bet you a case of pop I get my money, Jerry." "Well, that's a bet because you'll never get it," Jerry responded through the teller's window.

Several months later, Everett's morning town-rounds took him to the bank. "Say, did you ever get any money out of Old Mr. Watkins?" Jerry asked. Everett grinned. "No, I didn't but I tried pretty hard." Everett had called the debtor into his office (the mayor's office) and laid down his version of the law. "If you don't pay me that money, I'll have you here in Mayor's Court and I'll give you five years and a day for just breathing too hard in the city limits. The deadbeat wasn't all that intimidated. He consulted with a lawyer in Chariton, who sent Everett a threatening letter in return. "It didn't work," Everett grinned, and he owed Gerald Baker that case of pop until the mayor died.

If Everett was in a good mood he would sing. The better the mood the more funereal the song. If he was in a bouyant mood and things were going well, he would hum and sing "The Prisoner's Song" as done by Vernon Dalhart in the 1920's. "If I had the wings of an angel," he would burst out happily, "over these prison walls I would fly. I would fly to the arms of my poor darling and there I'd be willing to die."

The happiest moods of all would occasion "The Wreck of the Old 97", where Everett would shout so the neighbors could hear; "And they found him there with his hand on the throttle scalded to death by the steam." Those happy times were all too rare.

Two or three times a year he would dress up in his navy blue suit, put on a clip-on tie with a crisp, white shirt that Mae, his wife, had ironed, slick down his grey-white hair, and people would say, "Who is that good looking man? You don't look like yourself tonight. No, just kidding you Everett, you look real nice." "Yeah, I heard there was going to be Hollywood scouts here at the school play so I figured I'd be ready." Next day he would be in his baggy, grey-green outfit with his slouch hat with the grease spot on it. His eyebrows were white and growing up like John Lewis'.

It was in early spring of 1968 that he began to feel bad. He had not felt well for a long time. His energy was low and it was harder to get up in the mornings. He could still peal a laugh out of any Lucas folk but he didn't feel the laughter as he drove through the countryside in his beat-up, pre-driven, black Dodge truck. It was good for carrying a spare bag of minerals for the cattle or feed to a farmer who had forgotten to order the stuff when he had the chance.

One morning he stopped for coffee at the Ottawa Cafe, west of Lucas, and he had the folks there laughing, as he could do so well. He didn't dawdle long at the restaurant and he went out to his truck with a limp people noticed for the first time. His friends at the cafe watched out the window and they saw him try to climb into the cab of the truck. His leg wasn't working right. It didn't move correctly. He stood in the morning sun, then sat down for a moment. Folks from the cafe came out and asked if they could be of any help. No, he just needed a little rest. Sure enough, he finally got into the truck and was gone. People didn't think much about it then.

Everett did. He knew something was wrong with his body. He didn't approve much of doctors. "Just in it for the money," was what he thought and said. Something was wrong and it worried him. Mae noticed he had changed, became more silent and anguished. He was always saying he would leave her a rich widow. Now there was a different ring to his voice and a sudden emotion to it when he said to her, "You just don't know—you just don't know what's wrong with me."

It was a shock when the man who had wrestled the state champion of Iowa to a draw, the No. 1 salesman for the Iowa Cyclone Division of the

Moorman Feed Company, the teller of tall tales, the mayor of the town—re-elected again and again, sat on the couch with his family and said, "I don't think my life has amounted to much." That wasn't Everett and that began to worry his family. He didn't take his grandson, Nic, to the Dairy Queen to "live it up" anymore. Everett knew his time was coming. His strong arms and chest and back couldn't stop it. He didn't figure doctors could stop it either.

He got weaker. His vision blurred and he couldn't drive. They kept him in the county hospital for several days and he got worse. He had a major stroke and they rushed him to the Des Moines Methodist Hospital in a coma. His son drove straight through from Louisiana and his daughter from Wisconsin came. They got to the hospital after daybreak and came into the room expecting to see their father dead. But he had not died. In fact, he was regaining consciousness. Despite the fact that he looked horrible and couldn't see straight and was paralyzed on his left side, his exhausted children rejoiced.

Everett's body gained strength in the weeks that followed. He was feeling better. He got so he could crack jokes with the nurses. Sometimes he became disoriented. Once, on the phone, he told his niece that he had just been out south of town, selling feed. Then when lucidity returned, he was confused about why he had been confused.

"I should be getting better faster," he would say. "I am a strong man and this is not right." He was trying to walk again.

Everett said several times while in the Methodist Hospital that he knew he would get better if he could sit under his elm tree in the front yard of his Lucas house. He had sat there many, many days in the summer-green shade, in a lawn chair with his feet crossed, resting on the west side of the tree, itself. He may have thought about the healing powers of the tree, due to some old druidical inheritance from his family. More likely he enjoyed watching the tree grow at a slow enough pace for him to understand, enjoyed its gentle rustles, enjoyed its cooling, shaded air on the surface of his skin. He had worked under the tree, filling out his orderbooks for the company. He had seen neighbors roll around the corner of the gravel-dusted road, waving to him as he sat under the tree. Lucas was a peaceful place then, and under that particular elm could have been the most peaceful place in the town. Everett liked the peace. It made him content for awhile.

He didn't think the tree would heal him. It would make him feel better. Living in Lucas most of his life, he had learned to not expect too much. Sometimes the wanting to hold on to life would rush over him in surprise and he would moan. Sometimes he was stunned by his illness. Sometimes he saw his slide into death with the dispassionate eye of an observer.

Occasionally he would be hopeful. Not usually. He could choose the texture of his dying but he came to realize that he could not change it. With his vision half gone and his hand shaking, he wrote a post card to his grandchildren.

7-21-68

Dear Nick & Allen —
I am sitting in my room
so will write you a note
hope you have a good
time at camp
I would send you but I
some more
maybe someday I can
work again then I
can help you
grandmama has
gone to Centerville
W Blue going today
from grandpa & ...

A nineteen-year-old boy from a farm in Central Iowa was in Everett's room at the hospital. He had fallen off a silo and had damaged his brain. He could not talk. Everett would pull his wheelchair over to the boy's bed and say, "Come on now, you get out of that bed. You're just a lazy thing. I want you to tap dance and sing before the week is over." He got the boy to smile and he encouraged him when the boy began to walk and move about. Everett would say, "Do you want to hear some of that awful rock and roll?" The boy would nod a yes. "Then I'll turn it on." Everett would turn on KIOA and say, "I believe I'm beginning to like some of that damned stuff. Don't it make you want to dance up a storm?" The boy would grin or even laugh. Everett was at his bedside a lot.

152

After his stroke, Everett became what the doctors called "emotionally labile", which meant that he might cry if upset or that he might express fear. Everett had never done those things as an adult, not even at his parents' funerals. It was hard for his wife and children to see. Sometimes he couldn't eat his dinners and he might have ice cream to cool his throat. Still he would talk to his young roommate, encourage him to even entertain him if he could. The nineteen-year-old was getting stronger but after a time Everett was not.

The year before, Everett and other townsfolk had begun plans for the one-hundred-year anniversary for Lucas. It was in 1868 when the town got its official post office, and that seemed like a good time to date its beginning. The Lucas Centennial was planned for August of 1968. With Everett still in the hospital in Des Moines, the other townsfolk got together to make a real big shindig for the old town. Preparations for the celebration were going apace in Lucas' one-hundredth year summer.

People came to town from miles around to attend the centennial during the dog-days of that August in 1968. Lord, it was a big, happy crowd. There were rides for the kids, talent shows, drawings for prizes, music, stands selling Made-Rites and Pepsi. Political dignitaries were to be there. But more importantly, Duane Eliot, the local TV star, was to be there, doing his act with Floppy, his dog puppet, and selling autographed pictures for seventy-five cents a throw.

Everett slept in his small, white, shingled house on the hill. His sleep was too sound. He was groggy and weak when he awoke in the only bedroom with the air conditioner roaring like a World War II plane. Friends came up the hill to see him. Shy farmers and their wives came, and townsfolk who had not seen him since his stay in the Des Moines hospital. He would sometimes cry when his old friends came in. Some were flustered by this, others appeared not to be. People spoke either too loudly or too quietly to Everett.

On the afternoon of the second day of the centennial, his family asked Everett if he wanted to go down to the celebration. As mayor of Lucas, they thought he should make an appearance. The trick was to not let him get too tired. At two o'clock he was helped by his son into the Volkswagon Bug to go downtown. After being lifted from his wheelchair into the car, he held on to the dash and they proceeded down the rutted streets to the town's biggest doings of all.

They parked sixty yards from the platform where Duane and Floppy were putting the kids into hysterical laughter and squeals of untelevised joy. Everett couldn't see the proceedings clearly but, in little groups, the Lucas folk came over to see him, to shake his good hand, and to tell him they missed seeing him around. "Yeah, I wish I was back here, don't know if I ever will make it," Everett would say and cover his face with his good hand. One of Everett's cousins came by and told him that the celebration would not have been a success without him and the town wouldn't have the new fire station without him. Everett said, "Yeah, I helped some, didn't I. But I don't know. I don't know what to do next," and he burst into tears.

This made his cousin nearly weep and the announcer on the big Lucas Centennial stage was saying something about "Let's give Mayor Everett a big hand" over the loudspeakers. Everett was too weak and tired to hear and his eyes were glazed. His son took him back up the bumpy gravel road to his home, loaded him into his wheelchair, and put him to bed. Everett's wife, Mae, hoped he hadn't overdone it. He fell into a deep sleep for the next ten hours.

The next morning was a hot, sultry Sunday. The left side of Everett's body, his face, and shoulder and arm, was spasming. As his wife and children massaged his arm and neck and face, they knew that he was having another stroke and that oxygen was being denied his brain. They knew that it takes the brain cells time to die after a cerebral accident—a curious medical term they had read about. Everett fell back asleep. The next day, the ambulance took him back to the hospital in Des Moines. He had lost his appetite and there was little the hospital could do for him. They brought him back to the Lucas County Hospital to die. He seemed to be in a coma then and had not spoken in weeks when the nurse in charge came into the room. She said that the sheets seemed a little wet and that Everett had had a little accident. "I did not," Everett said in a voice so loud and strong that it startled her. Everett would talk no more. He was staying alive only because his heart was so strong, the doctors said.

Mae sat with him and fed him over the next few months. One of his sisters came in to pray for his soul. "You love Jesus, don't you, Everett?" she said to him. He didn't respond. Another sister sat with him and held his hand.

He died that first week of November in 1968. His wife called her son in Louisiana to tell him his dad was dead. When he received the call, her son was watching with glazed eyes, Richard Nixon's victory speech. When the phone call came, Richard Nixon was promising a presidency we could all look up to. "Yes", Everett's son thought, "this day is all of a piece and the world will get no worse than this." "I will survive and the world will never be this bad again." That, of course, was more of a wish than a promise.

John Is Gone

John L. Lewis did not have happy years toward the end of his life. His health was failing during the 1960's, as he entered his eighth decade. His beautiful home in Alexandria, Virginia, was stuffed full of French antiques and memorabilia. People who knew him best in that period of his life all testify that he was lonely in spite of the wealth he had accumulated.

He was becoming too fragile to make his visits to the long-time friends in Lucas. His living children, one a surgeon and one a union organizer, did not see the old man much toward the end. John L. did visit his old friend, Dan Tobin, late in life. Dan was seventy-nine when John L. came to see him in Indianapolis. Dan had been president of the Teamsters Union when John was doing his organizing. After the two old men had passed pleasantries to each other, John L., looking more fragile and vulnerable than anyone had seen him, said, "Dan, I came to see you and have a chat because I guess I am lonely, very lonely. It is not so good to be alone with only a chauffeur in a home with eleven rooms. It becomes very lonely, especially at night."

John L.'s old friend looked back at him and suggested that John needed to become more mellow—less harsh in his dealings with people. Of course, it was too late for John to change and there was no reason to do so late in life. He was to spend those last years, a lonely man, who in the minds of many was nothing more than a trouble-maker for a popular president. John's hair had turned snow-white but his famous bushed-up eyebrows were as dark and shaggy as when he was a young bull of a man, fighting for labor.

When John retired as president of the United Mine Workers Union he left the reins of the union to the worst sort of men, such as Tony Boyle. Tony was later convicted of the murders of the Jock Yablonsky family. Yablonsky was trying to reform the union to make it democratic and to get it out of the hands of organized crime. His successors would succeed in this effort but Jock and his family paid the price for reform with their blood. John L. was not a good judge of the men he had chosen to replace him, and his disdain for democratic union politics made him the pawn in an ugly game.

Moreover, John was unable to protect his miners from the mechanization which destroyed more than half of the jobs miners held in the 1940's.

Those with a dislike for the old man may have taken Shakespeare's point that "the evil that men do lives after them; the good is oft interred with their bones." The convenient truth in that statement hides other truths about John L. Lewis. Regardless of his tactics and regardless of the ultimate failure of his political imagination, John did something no one else in his time did quite so well. He spoke for the working poor and the industrial slaves of his time. His strength and the sarcastic invective against the uncaring defenders of wealth were music to the ears of the numberless working poor in the America of the 1930's. No one else spoke with more power or got more for working folk than John L. Lewis. Because of that his followers were eager to forgive all his missteps and sins. He told off the big boys and he got away with it. On the other hand, he was no blameless hero, no force of purity and self-righteous justice. It could be that the world has too many heroes, anyway. Like another labor leader of John L.'s time said, "If I could lead you out of the wilderness, someone else could come in and lead you right back in."

Eleven years after his death in 1969, the Lucas folk decided they would celebrate John L.'s one-hundredth birthday. It was difficult to put the celebration together. The town was old and most of the people were old as well. Most of the young folks had never heard of John L. Lewis. Betty Spoon, the secretary of the John L. Lewis Memorial Association, said that people in town gave lip service to the celebration but just wouldn't support it financially.

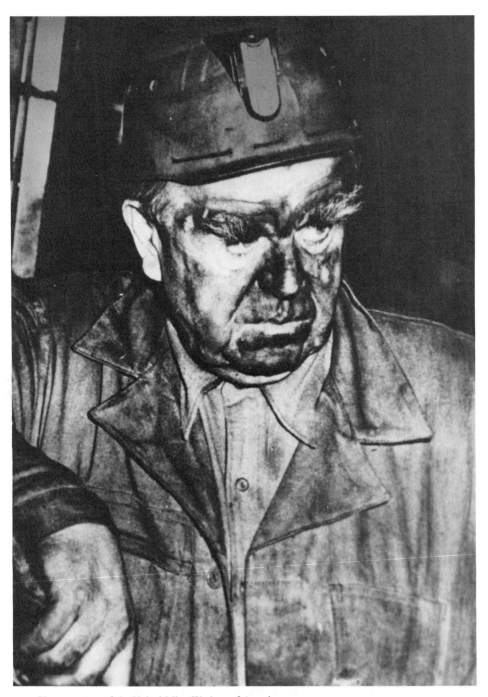

Photo courtesy of the United Mine Workers of America.

The *Des Moines Register* for February 12, 1980, had fun with the old town's difficulties. Their front page byline read, "Lucas drive to honor John L. Lewis caves in." That sounded like poetical justice, all right. John L. was gone and his town was going, too. That was the message of the piece and who could dispute it?

John L.'s town seems played out and John is gone. Yet that is not the end of the story. John had one message for the people he supported, the nobodies of the world. That word was "organize"! That was the message he preached to miners, farmers, blacks, steel workers and other people with hard work and insecure futures. Organize!

In January of 1985, about two hundred farmers and United Auto Workers stood in the arctic cold on a Lucas farm. A young farmer's machinery had been repossessed by the Production Credit Association, and there was to be an auction sale. Someone in the crowd yelled at the auctioneer, "You don't have to profit off the misery of others. You don't have to do the dirty work of the lenders." The auctioneer relented and called the credit association. They gave him the go-ahead to postpone the sale for several weeks to give the farmer a chance to refinance his equipment. Although the odds were still against the farmer, he now had a chance.

John L. did not say that organizing is a guarantee of success. People may organize badly or too late. The odds are likely to be against the little person, anyway. To organize is to give yourself a chance. If you had an old bulldog like John L. helping you, you had a fighting chance. John L.'s ghost might have enjoyed seeing the auto workers getting together with the farmers. He might have felt a little vindicated about what he believed.

Everyone agrees that John L.'s vision of justice for the working people in America was flawed, even tragically so. Still, he had a vision and that made him a rare person, indeed. In the land of the blind, the one-eyed man is king, so they say. The ghost of that jowled, old Welshman from Lucas looks down at America with a glaring eye and a rumbling voice. He says "organize!"

What Is Left of Us

I was angry at Lucas when my family and I stood on the frozen November cemetery hill south of the town. My Dad, Everett Roberts, was being buried in the Goshen Cemetery and an early snow mixed with the late afternoon sky. Damned old rotten place, I was thinking, nothing but death about it. I was anxious to go back to my home in Louisiana. My anger half covered my grief and horror at my dad's death but everything fit the dismal scene—barren trees, grey on grey sky, dying town, straw-colored weeds, and the early death of a man devoted to a ghost town. Phyllis, my cousin, said again and again she would never come back to Lucas. I understood that. There was nothing but pain and sorrow in the place. She would never come back. The cold wind and random snow flakes froze our tears and our faces.

I came back to the town over the next several years to visit my mother in Lucas. She was alone in the small house Everett had fixed up for her but she was not happy in the town. It was hard to get groceries, hard to get things fixed when they broke down. She was lonely. Besides, Lucas was her husband's town much more than hers. She had her church and her neighbors, but it was his town. She moved from her house of thirty years with little regret. In Chariton, the county seat, she would be less isolated, less disconnected from the world. Neither she nor my sister nor I felt too much attachment to the house in Lucas. It was not a shack but it was not a nice house, either.

Everett had put quite a bit of money and effort into the house but it was never much of a house. He had put lots of effort into Lucas as well.

I would come back to Lucas in the summer or fall to visit my friends and kin. All the grownup kids from my high school class have left town. Still there are people to see and places to review and unfinished feelings to resolve. When I come into town nowadays I find the road just south of the highway closed. It used to flood out half the time, anyway.

The road is gone now for the most part but it reminds me of why the Southern Iowa ghost town is implanted so firmly in my head. The road goes south and whenever I am in a different part of the country or a different part of the world, trying to figure out my directions, I imagine "south" as the image of that dirt road. North is the street going up from where the fire station used to be. East and west are visions of Highway 34. I imagine the rays of the sun on a particular day of the year beaming down on Lucas, and I can find my way around the countryside without a map. Home is a place of intersecting

lines—a place from which all other places are measured. Many Americans have not lived long enough in one place to learn these measurements. A childhood in Lucas gave me that.

Although I continue to do it, it really is too drastic to call Lucas a ghost town. In fact, the place has a factory, Lucas Industries, where several hundred women do electronic assembly work for near-minimum wage. The plant is a large, windowless steel shed and looking at it depresses me much more than looking at the decaying wooden buildings in the town.

There are some substantial buildings left in town. The Masonic Hall still looks good; the Rogers Hardware is still going; and the Harness Shop, while unoccupied, is still sturdy. The old false-front store next to the Harness Shop is being torn down for lumber, and one sun-splashed summer day I looked at the powder-blue sky through its vacant roof. The blue walls matched the sky and the roof was lined with fullsome green tree tops. That was a moment of splendor in the process of Lucas going back to nature.

One of Roy Palfreyman's old wooden storefront buildings was held together by a large cable stretching around the diameter of the building. It had looked as though the building's walls would fall in four directions when they tore it down, finally. Mr. Hooker's barbershop looks slightly shabby, with its green-shingled siding and white false front. Inside the shop one light cord hangs down from the ceiling, with a bare 100 watt bulb at the end. It always produced enough light to cut and nick the backs of the necks of the Lucas men and boys.

Across the street from the barbershop, Robinson's Store and Movie Theater stand in ruined shambles. Goldenrod is growing up precisely where they used to sell penny candy to the kids. The Lucas Tap is still going great guns. They have made the front windows smaller to prevent more breakage. Recently they took a Pac Man game out of the place to prevent it from being broken. Ghost towns have their lively moments still.

Whenever I go back to Lucas I go to the Farmers and Miners Bank to see Gerald Baker, who has run the bank for many years. By 1986 Gerald, and his family before him, will have done business in the bank for a total of 100 years. That is called stability.

Gerald Baker combines a progressive political attitude with a deep-seated conservatism with regard to Lucas traditions. His pa was like that as well. In fact, he ran for office in Lucas during the Teddy Roosevelt era as a Progressive. In his mid-eighties, Gerald goes to work every day in the bank. He works hard as he has done his entire life. The bank is a treasure house of artifacts from the history of Lucas.

Gerald shows me the land grant given his grandfather to take possession of land in Lucas. It is signed by Franklin Pierce in 1856. Gerald shows me photos and publications from the boom-town days. He tells me stories I had never heard about my family and his family. He is as interested in the happenings of today as yesterday. As for tomorrow, he is stoical.

Gerald Baker's bank is the only one left in Iowa with a private charter. When the only other private bank in the state failed in 1983, the national news media swarmed around him. "Was there a panic at the Lucas Bank?" they asked him. "If I have a customer who's nervous, I want him to come and get his money. I've got it. It could pay off all my depositors today," he said. And it was true.

The news reporters asked Gerald Baker if he would sell his bank to the big operators in Des Moines after he got too old to run it. He just said that he would shut the old bank down. Leave it be. "I'm proud of this bank," he said, "I don't want a scallywag to get ahold of it." Sometimes it seems that in a person's life, or in the life of a town, nothing is left save honor. Gerald Baker is hanging on. It is the honorable thing to do. Gerald has an easy laugh but he is a stubborn man.

When I walk out of the sloping, marble floor of the Lucas bank, I feel a kinship with this man who has known me since childhood and my family before I was born. I feel this because I admire Gerald Baker's attitude toward the world and because he still cares about the small fragment of the world that is Lucas and was Lucas.

The truth is (and we Lucas natives must admit it), from an economic or political point of view, towns like Lucas are, as some Southern Iowans would say, "worthless as teats on a boar." If the towns like Lucas disappeared from the landscape of American life, most economists and politicians would not worry about it for more than thirty seconds.

Many people view small-town life as superfluous, unneeded—just hangers-on hanging on. Of course, the same thing is said about family farms, coal mines and so on. Moreover, our entire Midwestern America is referred to as being part of the "frost belt" or even the "rust belt". If the economy is bad here, we should junk the area and all move to Houston or Phoenix. Some people do that. Some are more stubborn. And, of course, some people resent being considered unimportant in the first place. Scientists tell us that if we are stupid enough to blow ourselves up, the news of that destruction couldn't reach another galaxy for several million years. As it turns out, we are all expendable and we are all unimportant, except to each other. That is a lesson to be learned in a dying town such as Lucas.

So, while Americans are fascinated by the lifestyles of the rich and famous, they live the lives of—what is the proper word—nobodies, the little people, the ordinary, the unremarkable people. Once in a great while a voice like that of John L. Lewis speaks for the ordinary people, but the usual thing is that the ordinary people get spoken to by experts, millionaires, political hucksters, and the rest.

Growing up in a town of no importance teaches us once again (for it is so easy to forget) that we speak to each other in face-to-face ways to give life meaning. Sometimes we are cruel to each other, sometimes boring, and sometimes terminally silly. The important thing is that we are something together and very little alone.

People bored of small-town life may indeed need to leave it or they may need to look at it in a slightly different way. Iowa's small towns are hardly full of broad-stroked physical beauty or television mini-series glamour. They must be observed in a different way than the Grand Canyon or the French Riviera. To see the fascinating varigations of humanity and complex coloration of subtle relationships between people, a sort of mental microscope is needed. Look closely at the lives of ordinary people. Look long and lovingly at their sins, their sometimes heroism, or their frequent absurdities. What people call the human condition is all there with more complexity than the nuclear physics.

To love a person or a place is to learn it. To learn it takes time. It requires staying awhile. To love a small unimportant fragment of humanity is to become human. Any good citizen of a ghost town knows that to be true.

My own microscopic view of Lucas commenced while I was a small boy in the place loved without condition by a big affectionate family. On the other hand, I was constantly beat hell out of by the bigger bullies in town. Lucas provided me with a combination of love and terror that shapes my identification with underdogs today. Lucas taught me about death and sex, though not at the same time, thankfully. Lucas taught me about dreams and broken dreams, and how people go on living with no dreams at all.

With all that stuff going through my mind, it is no surprise that I still dream about the place once in a while. A few weeks ago I dreamed they had dammed the Whitebreast Creek and somehow got all the mud out of it. In my dream I was watching the rowboats cruising around on it. It was some sort of sun-drenched, late spring day, and I was walking above the creek looking for relics of the Whitebreast Mines. I remember feeling lazy and happy in my dream. In another dream, I saw the town transformed, rebuilt, repainted. I asked people in my dream, who had put new false fronts on the stores and who had painted the houses in muted pastel colors? Someone told me it was some rich yuppies from Des Moines and didn't Lucas look better. I was mad as hell about strangers fixing up my town. It just wasn't right.

Really, the only way communities like Lucas survive is if the children in the town fulfill the uncompleted dreams of their parents by continuing their lives in the place. Naturally, most families don't work like that. My father had a dream that I would work with him, selling feeds to farmers. There would be a sign on the feed store saying, *Roberts and Son* in bold letters. I was too bookish, too much unsettled, too much in need of the rest of the world to stay for him. Albert Baker has three generations of his family in town but he is an exception. The restlessness of generations and the economy tugs and pushes people from Lucas.

So Lucas is going slowly back to nature and that is not altogether sad. In fact, the people who still live in the town, about two hundred of them, know how to take things with a laugh when they are not in pain or burdened with worry. I think they laugh better than most folks do in more affluent parts of the countryside. That is because they know how silly it is to have the big head and sort of, kind of, just pretending to be something you are not. In that spirit of laughter, I wrote a letter to my old, dying friend, Lucas. It goes like this.

Dear Lucas,

My Grandma Kate told me there always was a Lucas and that there always would be a Lucas. Of course, she also believed that cats would suck the air out of newborn babies and that you only plant potatoes by the right phases of the moon.

The fact is, Lucas, you and I know different. You have died quite a few times, maybe as many as some Hindu holy men.

You died when they shut the mines down again and again. You died when the windmills around the countryside stopped squeaking and when the rails weren't kept up on the C.B. & Q. line. And you died some more when people parked junk cars in their yards, and when young people left you to find work in Des Moines.

Part of you died years ago when young men were crushed by falling slate in your mines; other parts when the houses got abandoned and torn down for lumber.

What I mean to say, Lucas, is that you are played out, worn down, pruned back too deeply to ever grow again. You are passing into the indifferent beauty of Miss Southern Iowa's parent—Mother Nature.

In a way, Lucas, all your stories seem like the fevered dreams of an old man. I know you are more than that. The realistic thing about you is that you are home. You gave us a sensuous, particular home. We want to be at home everywhere but we cannot. We come back, in our minds, to you.

Lucas, it seems that all the dreams of your dead were like bubbles. When they touched each other they would burst. We still know how to laugh in town when our dreams fizzle and when you go back to nature.

We don't want to fall into your past like leaves off a dying elm tree. Your past was wonderful and terrible, but it is as clean as bleached bones now.

Don't hurry back to unplotted streets and unmarked hills. Take your time.

Final Word

Meridel Le Sueur is a novelist, philosopher, and poet. She has written a number of works about the struggles of working people, especially women, during the great depression. Among them are SALUTE TO SPRING; THE GIRL; and NORTH STAR COUNTRY. She was born in Murray, Iowa only twenty-five miles from the town of Lucas. She was eighty-seven years old when she wrote this letter. She has great passion for issues of human justice and the survival of our planet. She does not care much for capital letters as her letter shows. She has given me the idea that I would like to live a long time, but only if I can be like her.

Ron Roberts

september 13, 1987

dear ron roberts

your book is amazing . . . i am living long enough to see everything revealed . . . becoming more visible . . . the illusion fading and from the horizon the appearance of just reality . . . the oppressed being seen and articulate . . . the portraits of the inhabitants of lucas are wonderful and the portrait of the young boy more real than huck.

strange i spent a week in lucas and got the roots of novel i am writing now at the cemetary at lucas . . . its a new kind of novel and could be even larger . . . its like a blueprint but it is a beginning of telling the lives of a colonized people. i have been looking at murray and i believe the tore down the white puritan house where i was born. i gave a lecture their two weeks ago and picketed with the priest the new munition factory you can see from murray . . .

but i cant understand why you are so placid about this brutal story you tell. it is now the time of the public hearing of the revealment of the rascals indictment of the cruelist exploitation . . . the colonialization of iowa must be revealed . . . i was part of it. we all were part of it. now it is owned by absentee land lords corporations murderers of the land and and people. yes this must be said plainly and shown plainly.

it is hard to see this clearly and state it clearly sometimes. i think i have helped conceal it by lyricism or pity or even sorrow . . . it is not enough. it is literally no choice, either reveal it or be entirely destroyed and our civilization. it is simple.

lewis had that passion. he said the destruction and death of the miners would go around the earth two by two. you say he wept. there is great condemnation in his speeches and life.

it is good to show the strength and beauty of these people, to keep the ruins alive . . . this is what will save the world . . . the only thing. the rising of the oppressed people of the world who have nothing to lose but their chains as marx said years ago before the bomb.

it is time to tell it all . . . you have a wonderful tender revelation of these people who were paid a dollar and a half a day for their labor. it is wonderful now the revealment of a generation like yours telling it with vision and compassion. you do indict the whole exploitation by the way you show them the love you have for them. but pity is not enough now. i do thank you for your tender and compassionate depiction of the death of the town and these people.

i heard about the negro settlement [in Lucas]. dorothy [Driftmeir] showed me the remains of their segregated village full of bottles caps and they couldn't be buried there . . . like the jews in shenandoah had to be buried across the river in nebraska with a rabbi from omaha . . . when can we meet and talk about it . . . i am very moved by you and the book. we must have more more. . . .

love

meridel